ANN L. ROE

PORTRAITS

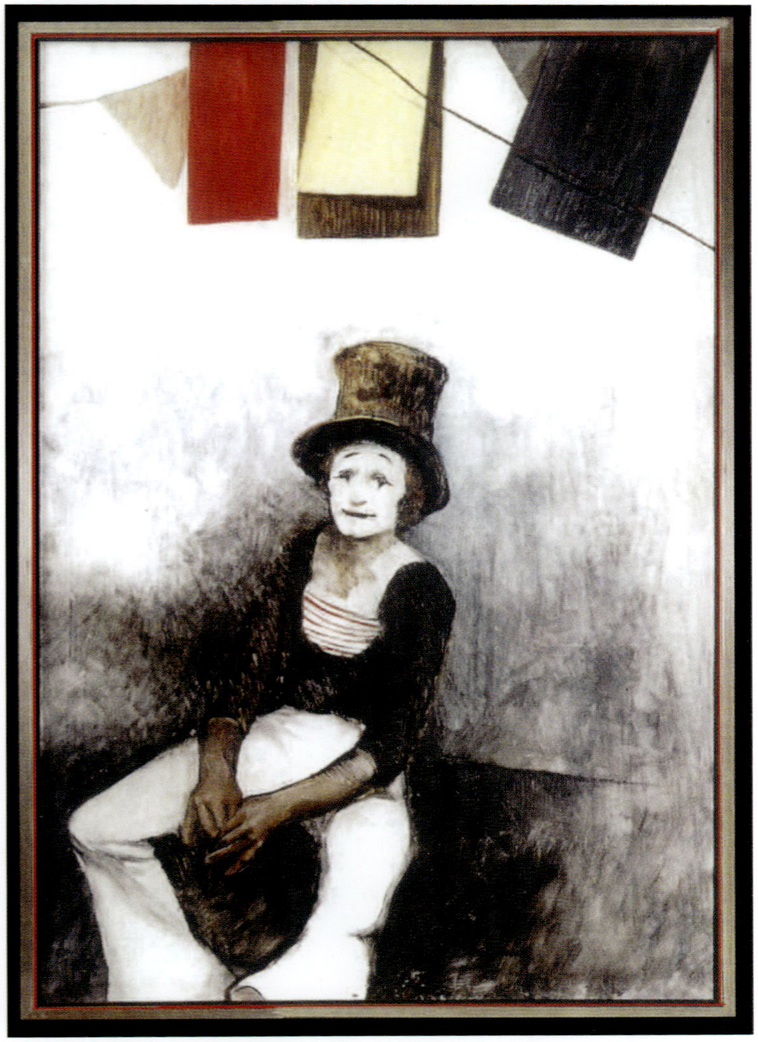

My Life Through Pictures

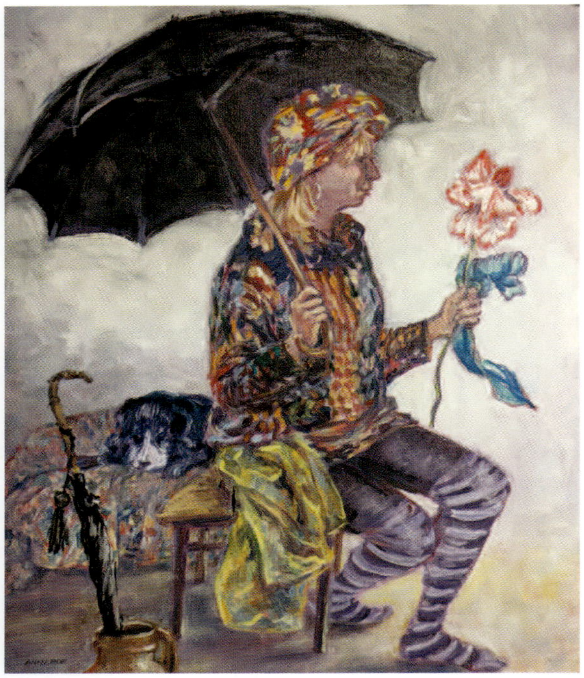

Maggie Luff – a delightful if idiosyncratic portrait of a close friend.

First published in Great Britain in 2025

British Library Cataloguing-in-Publication Data.
A CIP record for this title is available from the British Library.

ISBN 978 0 85717 046 0

HALSWOOD
Halsgrove House, Ryelands Business Park, Bagley Road, Wellington, Somerset TA21 9PZ Tel: 01823 653777
Fax: 01823 216796
email: sales@halsgrove.com
Halswood Distribution is part of the Halsgrove group of companies.
Information on all Halsgrove titles is available at: www.halsgrove.com.

FSC www.fsc.org MIX Paper | Supporting responsible forestry FSC® C014540

FOR MY FAMILY

"You know life... its rather like opening a tin of sardines, we are all of us looking for the key."

Alan Bennett, writer, actor, diarist. From Beyond the Fringe 1962.

The jacket and title page illustration is a painting of Marcel Marceau, the French mime artist. I have always been fascinated by unusual and clever people and Marcel Marceau was certainly one of those. I had read a book about him and his work as a mime artist and as a teacher of his craft and was inspired to paint this picture of him. The painting now resides in Melbourne, Australia, bought impulsively by a paediatrician. I'd drawn his children that morning and he'd noticed the painting whilst we were all having lunch together. He bought it off the wall and so it began a new life in Australia.

Foreword

I first met Ann Jones twenty years ago. I only wish it had been earlier. Ann's sheer exuberance for life, which illuminates her drawings and paintings, is wonderfully infectious. One always leaves her company feeling a whole lot better about life.

We first met in Exeter at the South West Academy's annual Open Exhibition where Ann was exhibiting two portraits under her nom d'artiste Ann L. Roe. Ann signed her early works using her maiden name, A. L. Roe (and continues to do so), as female artists were still struggling to be taken seriously at that time. And serious is what Ann is when it comes to her art.

Take a look at the examples from Ann's sketchbooks included here and one can see that, even from her earliest student days, the capacity to draw well was fundamental to the progression of a career in art. Later, as Head of Art at a Devon grammar school, one just knows that, while her lessons would be full of fun, Ann's students would leave education with a firm understanding that having an appreciation of art was fundamental to their future wellbeing as adults. Many former pupils remain in touch. Her own family clearly learned that lesson too; children and grandchildren making art in various forms as a matter of course.

Ann's love of people would almost inevitably lead her towards portraiture. It is not the easiest of genres for the professional artist to pursue for there is the obvious requirement to satisfy two parties in successfully completing a portrait – the artist and the sitter. And if the latter isn't happy then the portrait remains unsold. Happily Ann's patrons invariably, and understandably, love her work.

The drawings and paintings included in this book are just a fraction of a lifetime's artistic achievement. Working with her to put this book together has been a great privilege and pleasure.

Simon Butler
2025

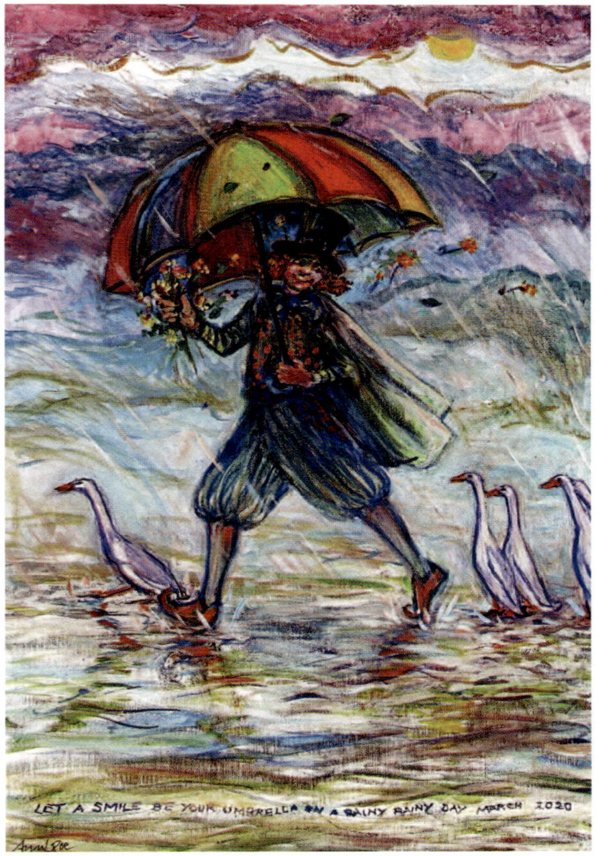

"Let a Smile be Your Umbrella on a Rainy, Rainy Day." The words to this old musical hall song appeared on The Chelsea Arts Club newsletter during the Covid lockdown in 2021 and inspired this happy picture. The Indian Runner ducks were in Terry Boswell's garden when I visited her (Terry's portrait appears on page 51).

Acknowledgements

For the huge number of commissioned works from a wide variety of friends and acquaintances who have sat for me, I thank you all so very much for the pleasure it has given me to paint your portraits. In the blink of an eye a child becomes a young person and now many of my sitters are adults, some even at an age considering retirement. How the years have flown by!

Thanks also to all the folk from Gemini Digital Colour who, along with Mike Roberts, finalised the photographing of my paintings with great care. A big thank you too to Dominic Lee at Gemini for the excellent cards and other promotional material they have produced for me. My excellent framer, Philip Bate, whose artistic flair has enhanced the appearance of many paintings is also due my thanks.

Grateful thanks to all those who have provided photographs of their portraits for use in this book, without which it could not have been so profusely illustrated. Other individuals who must be included are Owen Saer, himself author of many books on the Welsh language and who provided useful ideas on the structure of this book in collaboration with Lolo, and Hazel Webb who transcribed my words for the text of this book requiring many visits to me at home. Thank you Hazel! In retrieving paintings, sketchbooks and other material from my studio Robert Collier provided vital help.

Without the encouragement and support of my family and close friends this book would not have been possible. Your enthusiasm and practical help has meant so much. A special mention must go to Xanthe, for the time she spent on meticulously proof reading my writing, and to her family who must have wondered whether she would ever come home!

Last but not least thanks to my collaborator and editor Simon Butler whose professionalism has been an inspiration. Our work over the two years it has taken to complete the book has been a formidable task, but an enjoyable one, as Simon told me at the outset that it must be. I can't thank you enough for your delightful charm and enthusiasm.

* * *

There have been so many wonderful artists, past and present, who have been a delight and great influence on my life: First my Canadian grandmother, whose paintings surrounded me as a young child. Frederick ("Freddie") T W Cook who lived in Polperro and painted "grockles", the harbour and underwater scenes. Madame Louise D'Aussy Pintaud with whom I painted alongside in her studio in France. Gustav Klimt whose exotic, colourful paintings I remember seeing in London in the early days of public knowledge of his work. Augustus John's portraits including one of Dylan Thomas. Dame Laura Knight who captured travellers and circus performers so extremely well and an excellent mother and child portrait which was exhibited at the Royal Academy. Drawings by Stuart Tresilian, my lovely art tutor at art college, his ability to capture animals was excellent. Zdzislaw ("Zeich") Ruskowski, a wonderful polish artist who used unorthodox colours for his landscapes and portraits. Philip Sutton's totally original way with colour and his spontaneous flair for painting everything around him. Stanley Spencer's portraits and particularly, two drawings of children that left a lasting impression when I saw them hanging on the wall of a friend's house. Alan Cotton's excellent knife paintings and sketchbooks. Graham Sutherland's portraits including the one of Winston Churchill, which tragically, was later destroyed by Churchill's family as Churchill disliked the portrait. Michael Beech's enchanting and creative 2D and 3D work. Thank you for all the admiration and joy you have given me over the years.

Contents

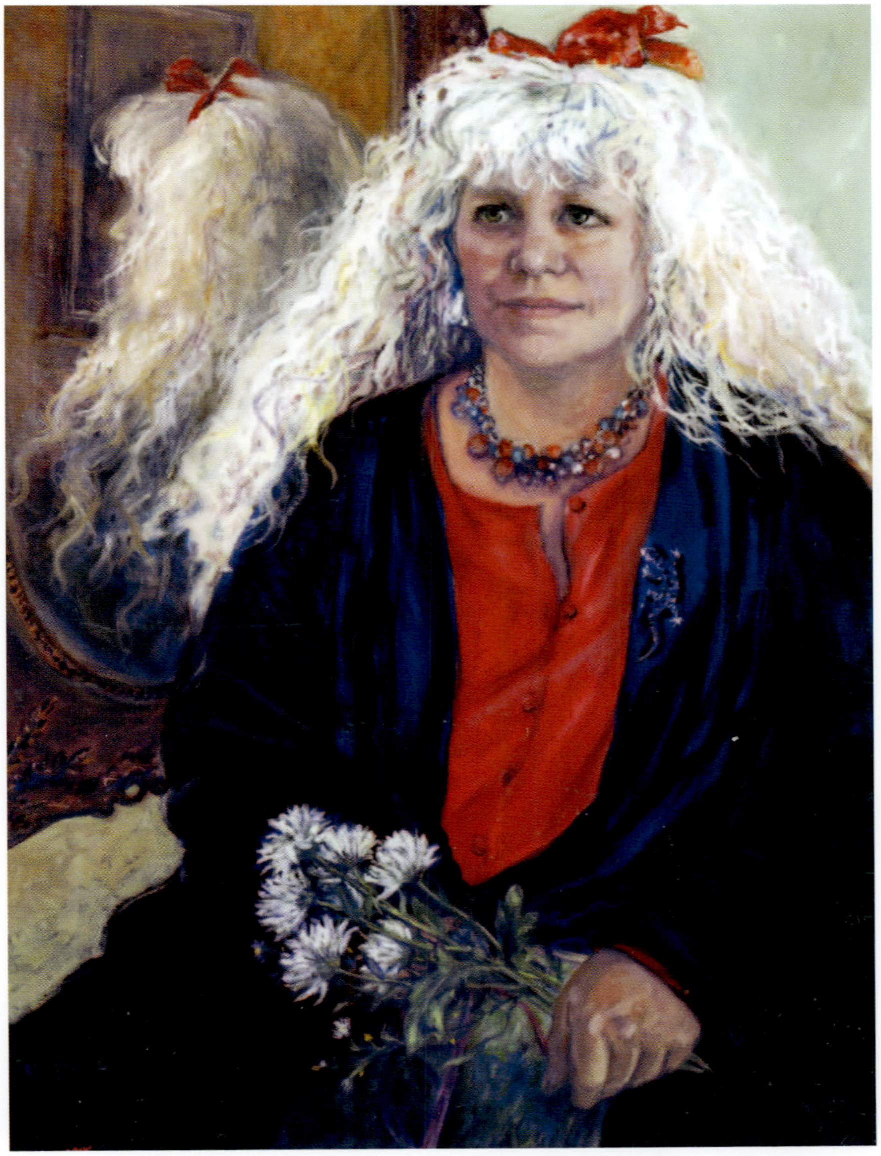

Xanthe Mosley. An superb artist whose work appears in the RD&E hospital in Exeter.

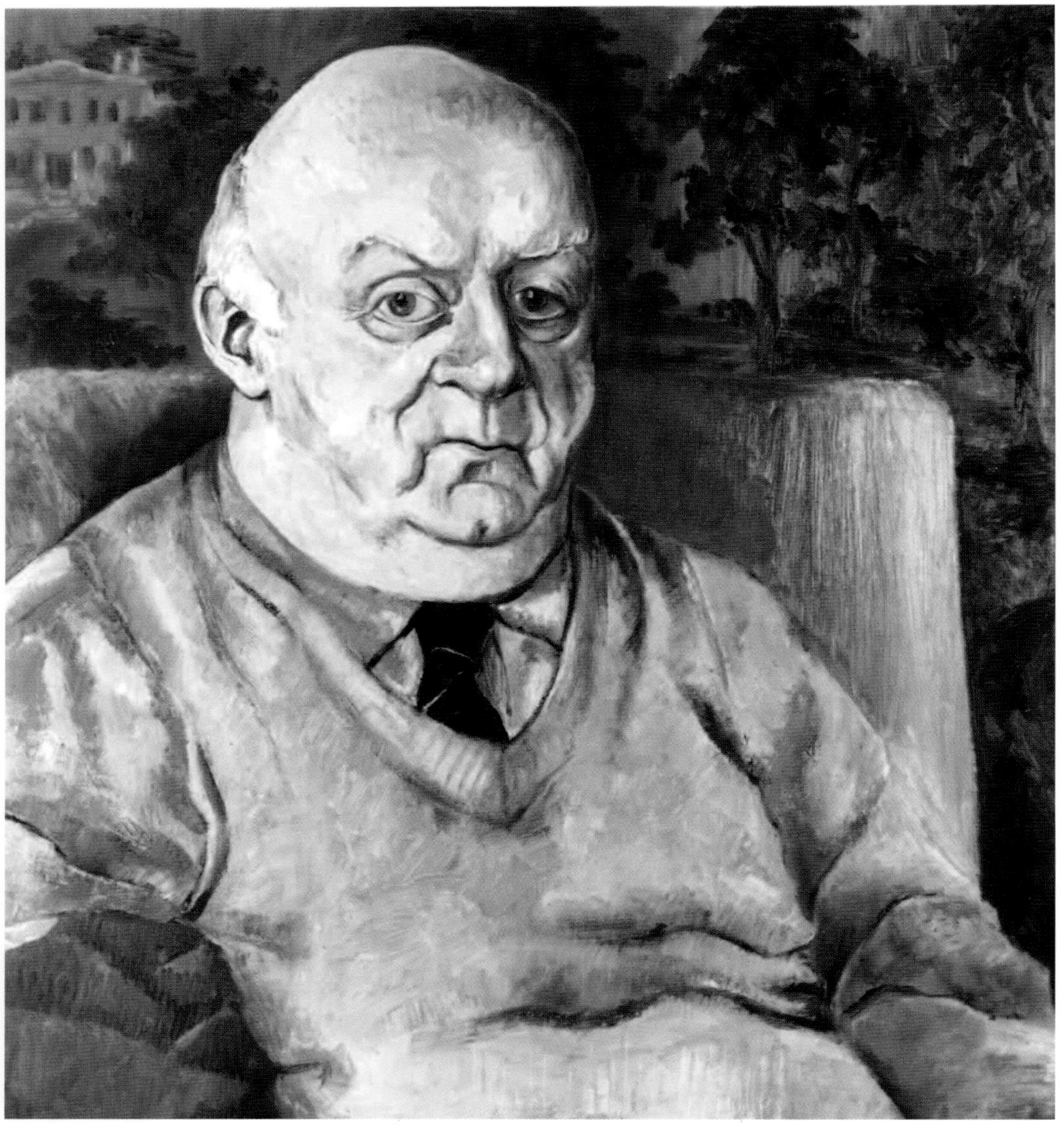

This is one of my earliest portraits (sadly no colour photograph exists). It is a portrait of Commander Reynolds who sat for me in his music room while I stayed with him in his beautiful old house in Cornwall approached by a long narrow lane. His wife made a pudding each day, which I had never eaten before or since. It was quite popular in Cornwall I believe, it was called junket!

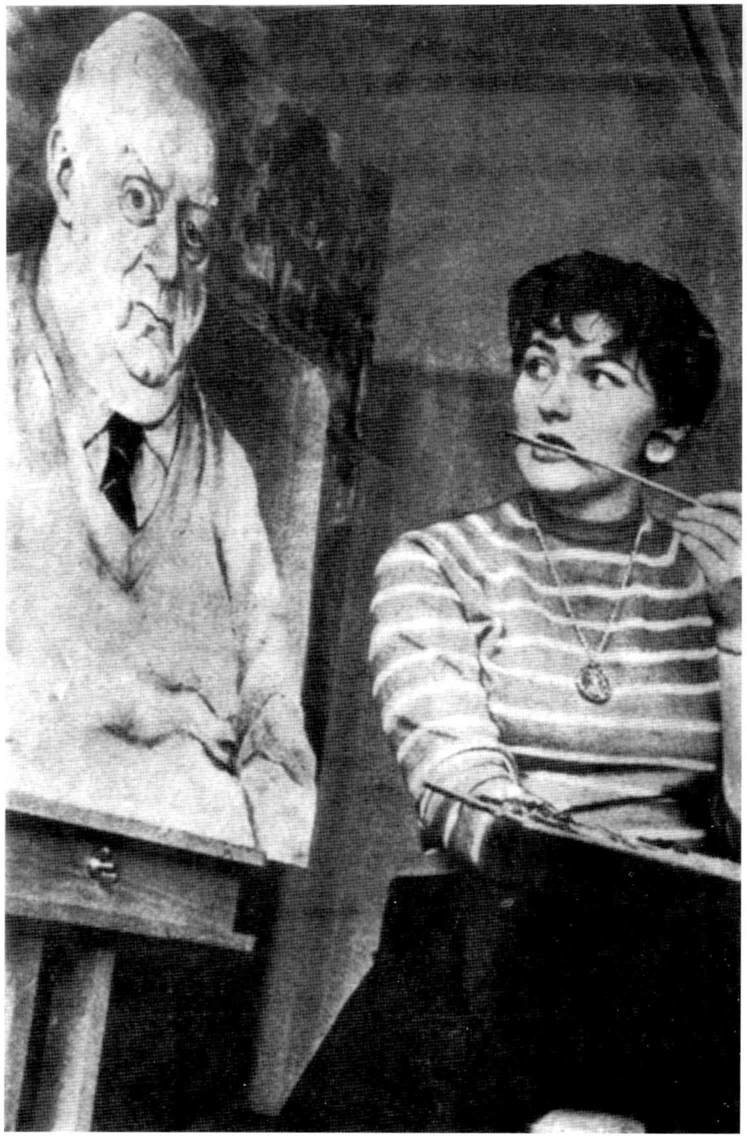

Shortly after I painted Commander Reynolds' portrait, a journalist heard about it and I was photographed alongside the painting. The article was published later when I was away and so my father stood in for me, rather exaggerating my standing as an artist. 'Do not believe all you read in a newspaper' – I cannot remember who said that, but it was true on that occasion!

Beginnings

At the onset of the Second World War I was just a small child. Our home was requisitioned by the government, so we went to live with my grandparents. My father had joined the army and spent much of the war abroad.

Schooling for me was a memorable happening as I went to a number of boarding schools in Reigate, Harrogate, Somerset, Suffolk and finally West Heath in Sevenoaks. I left school at 15 when my lovely grandfather died. He had always paid for my education and had always been a great influence on my upbringing. I can remember his soft hands washing my back in the bath when I was very small while singing old music hall songs to me. He wrote for a London newspaper on the subject of music hall shows.

I remember Grandpa Sims once made a shadow puppet show out of an old wooden clotheshorse and lit by candles. Together we performed Cinderella using puppets that he made with moving limbs, with the ugliest of ugly sisters! He also made a doll's house for me and I remember sitting in winter evenings up against his legs beside a spluttering gas fire as he read Charles Dickens stories to me. When I was away at boarding school he wrote to me weekly in copperplate script and told me everything that was happening at home, all in rhyming couplets.

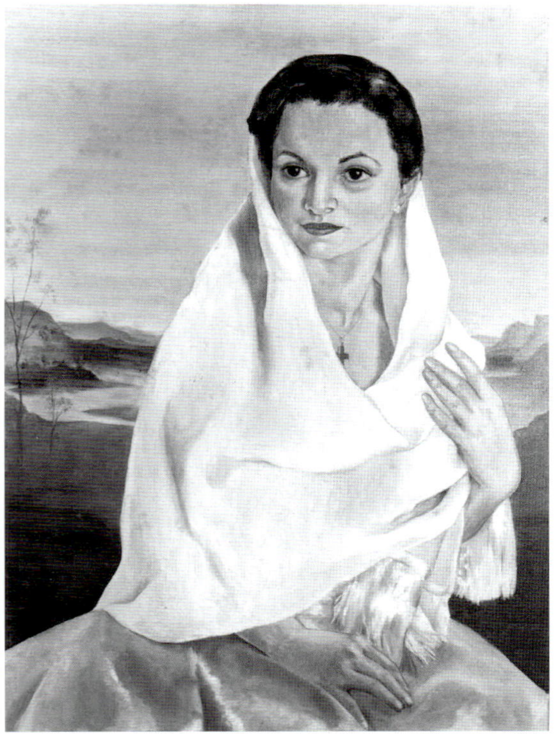

My portrait of Liz Goring with whom I attended school in Southwold and in Sevenoaks. Liz and I attended the Greenwich Ball together when we were 17 and she found my dance partner (who kept stepping on my toes!). Her parents ran the famous Goring Hotel in Belgravia where I often stayed in their private quarters.

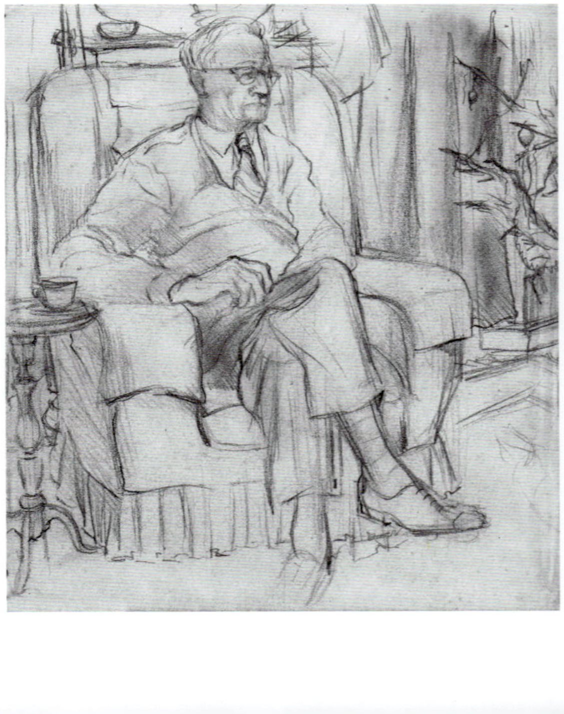

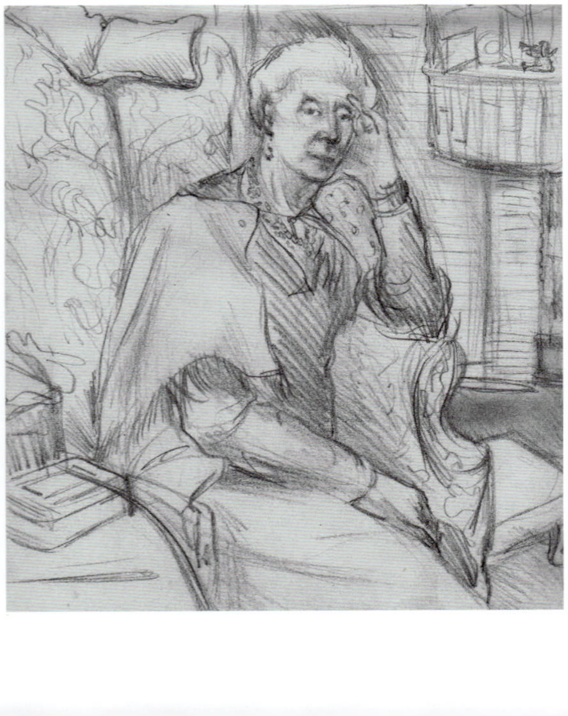

Drawings from an early sketchbook of my grandfather, Dr Richard Ely Roe, and grandmother, Gertrude.

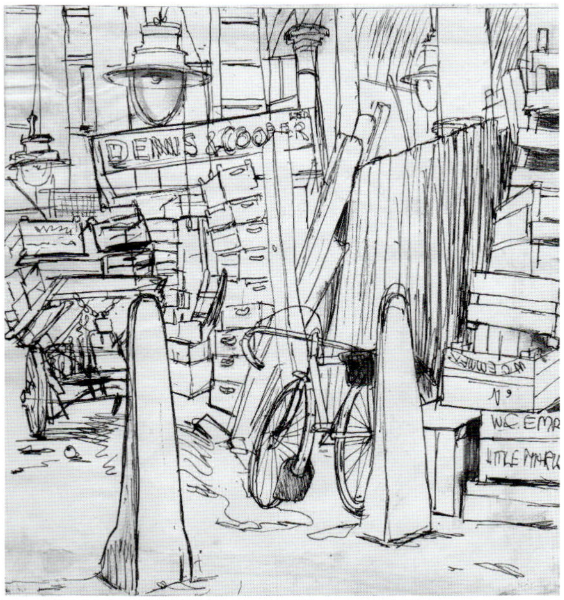

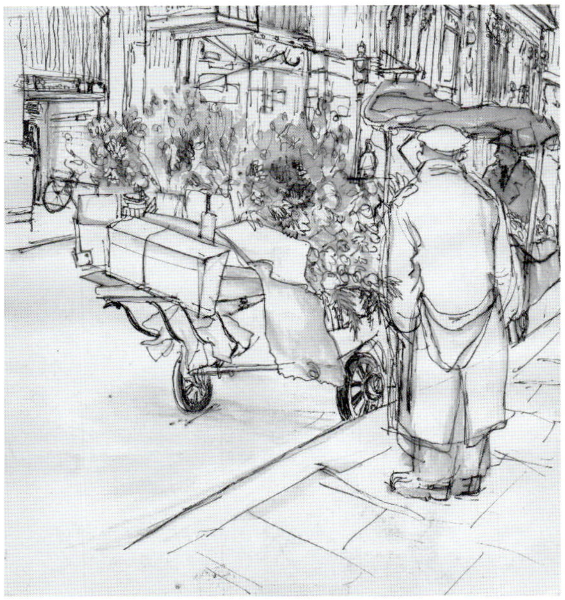

Drawings from an early sketchbook of Borough Market from where my grandfather ran his business J.O. Sims Ltd.

My grandfather had built up a successful fruit business, travelling to Nova Scotia in Canada from where he imported apples. The J.O.Sims business is still being run by a member of our family very successfully. While in Canada my grandfather met a Canadian artist who was to become his wife, my grandmother. They had three children, a girl (my mother) and two sons. Our home was full of my grandmother's paintings, some painted directly on to the walls. My cousins have some of her paintings. Sadly the large one I have of her has been damaged during our many house moves.

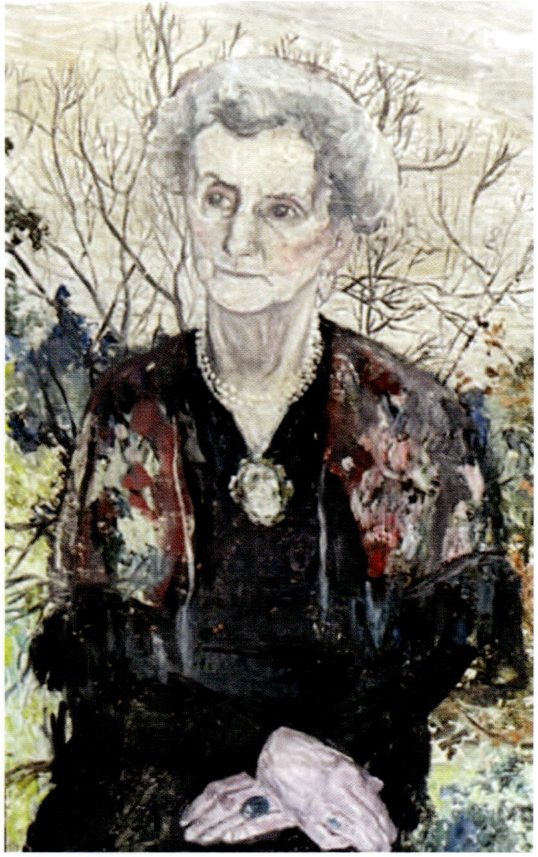

Granny Roe, a lovely lady. This portrait of her I painted when I was 16.

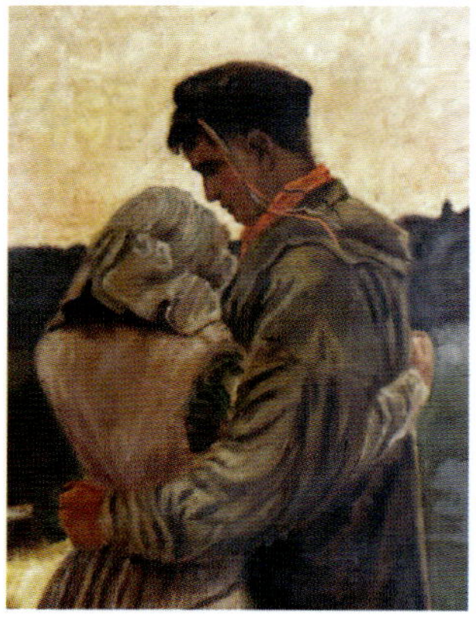

Detail of a painting by my Canadian grandmother which she had based on an early Victorian painting.

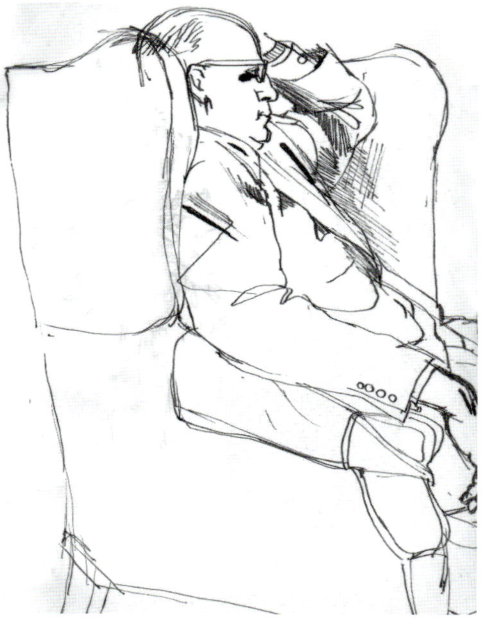

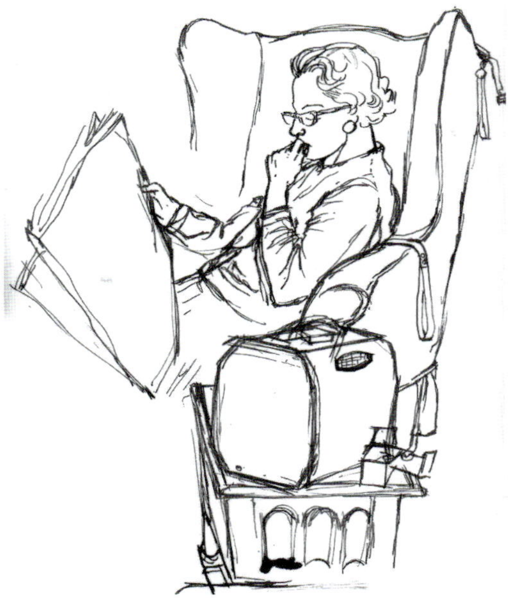

Sketches of my mother and father Haughton Roe and Olive Roe (née Sims).

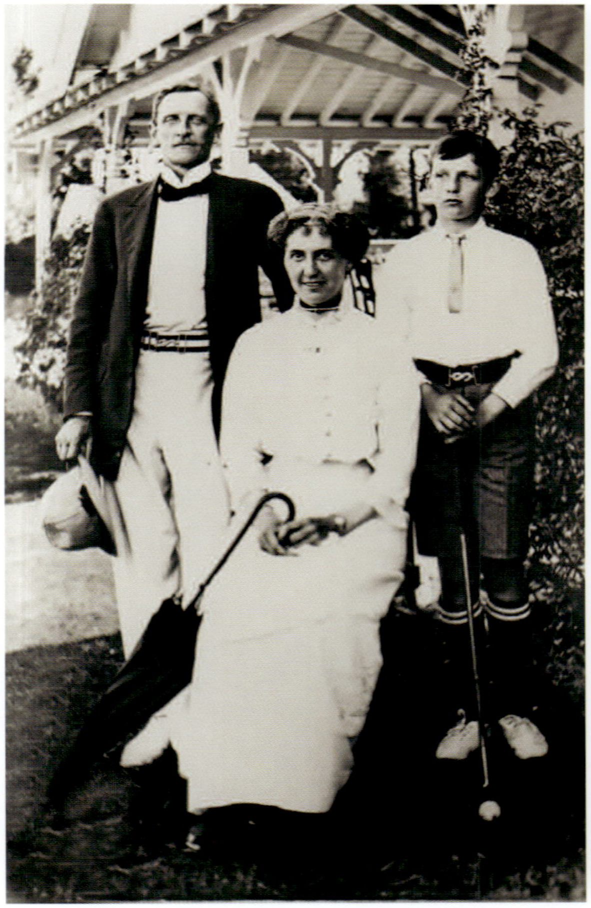

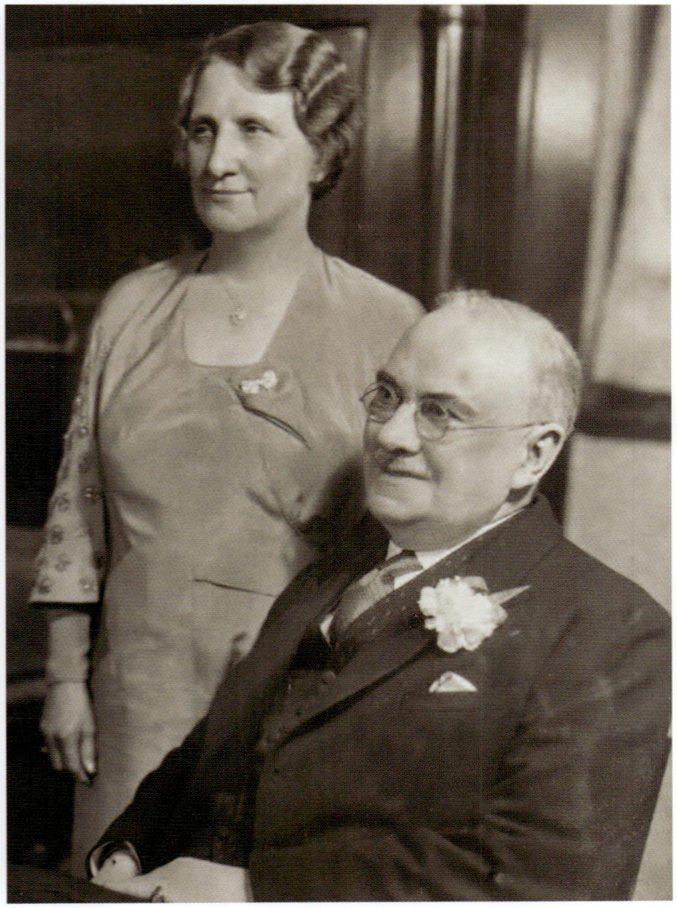

Left: My father as a boy in India standing with his parents, my grandparents, Dr Richard Ely and Gerturde Roe. Right: My paternal grandparents Clara Louise and Joseph Oliver Sims.

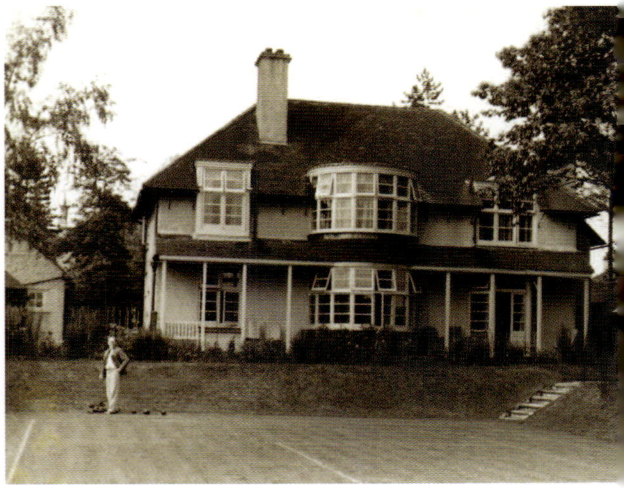

'Green Garth' the Sims' family home in Purley with my father on the lawn at the back of the house in the late 1940s.

My father's family were in the medical profession, his father was a doctor, Richard Ely Roe and his wife's (my paternal grandmother) father was also a doctor. Somewhere in the family archives on my father's side there was a relative who was Horatio Nelson's right-hand man, Vice Admiral Cuthbert Collingwood. This family surname continued through my father's cousin who lived near us in Purley and was our family doctor, also called Cuthbert Collingwood.

I spent 21 years in my grandfather's home. My Canadian grandmother died when I was about 3 or 4 years old. In the photo opposite I believe the figure about to play bowls is my father on his return from the war where he had been a Major in the Royal Corps of Signals in North Africa. Our house was close to Croydon Airport, a target for the Germans during the Blitz, so I was sent away to a variety of different schools to avoid the bombing. A bomb did fall on our lawn but did not explode. It was disarmed by an army bomb disposal team. I was away at that time so missed all the drama.

My sister, Viv, arrived after the war and is eleven years younger than I am, so her life differed greatly from mine.

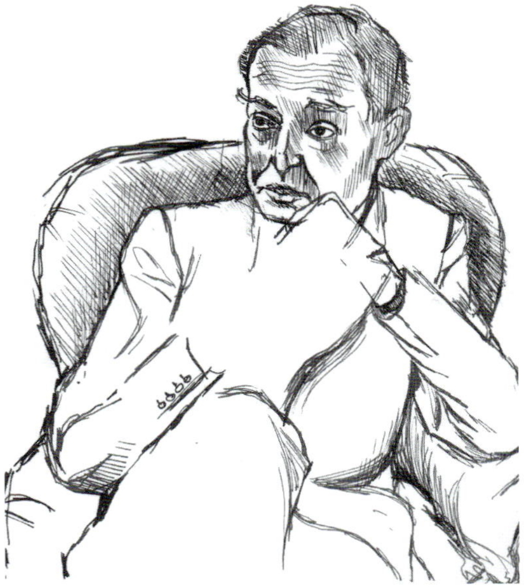

My stepfather, Wing Commander Kenneth Evelyn Parker.

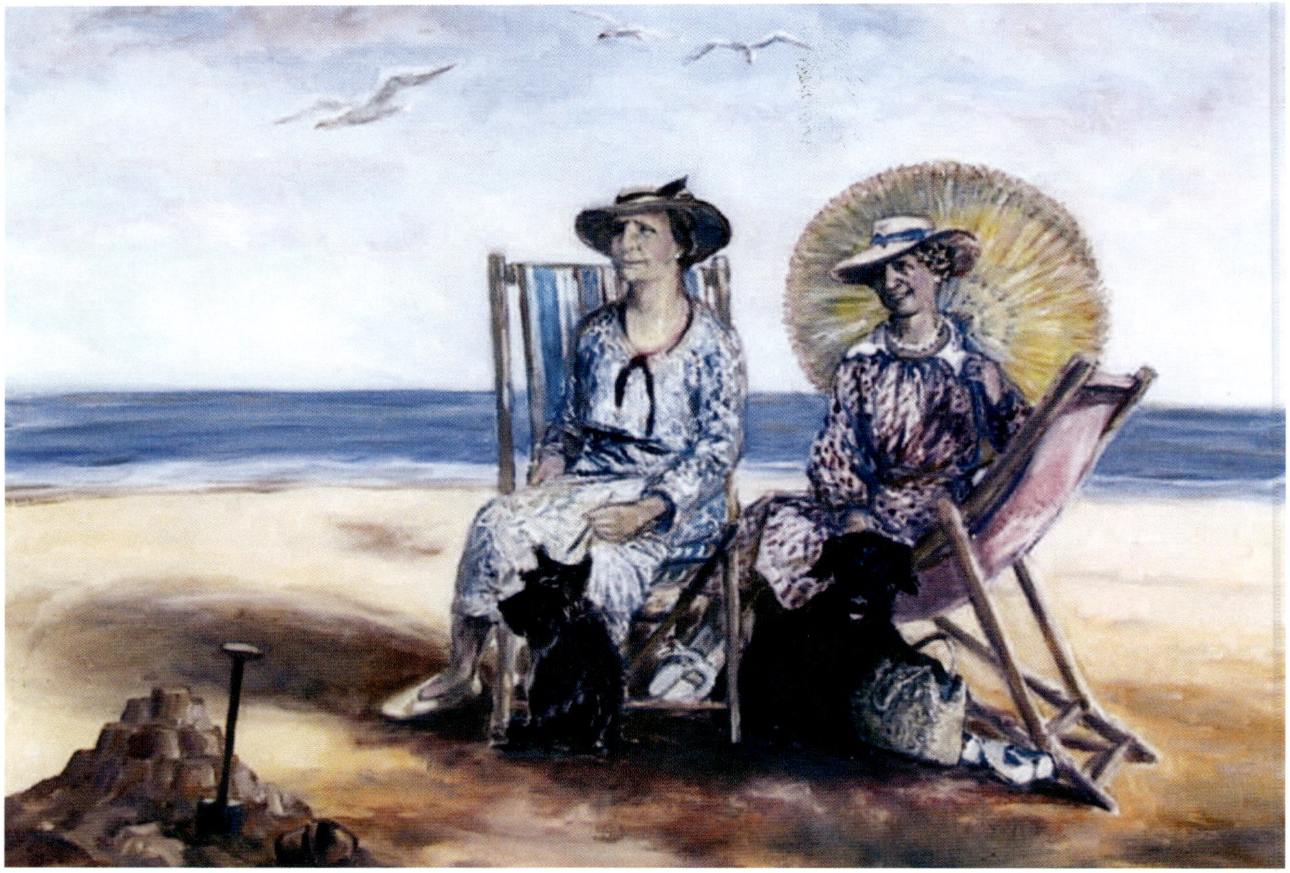

A painting of my grandmothers on the beach at Birchington-on-Sea in Kent, along with the family dogs. On the left is Granny Sims with Granny Roe on the right.

Sample images from my project 'Take A Card' based on the history of playing cards – part of my coursework at Brighton Art College. The final work comprised 42 pages illustrated with playing cards from throughout the world, each with a descriptive text which I had researched at the V&A and the British Museum.

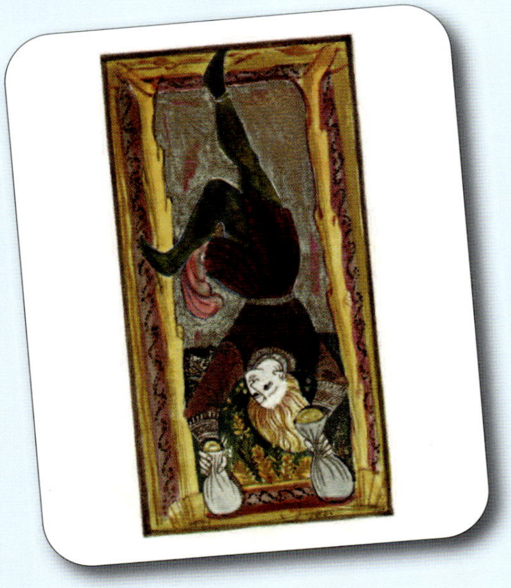

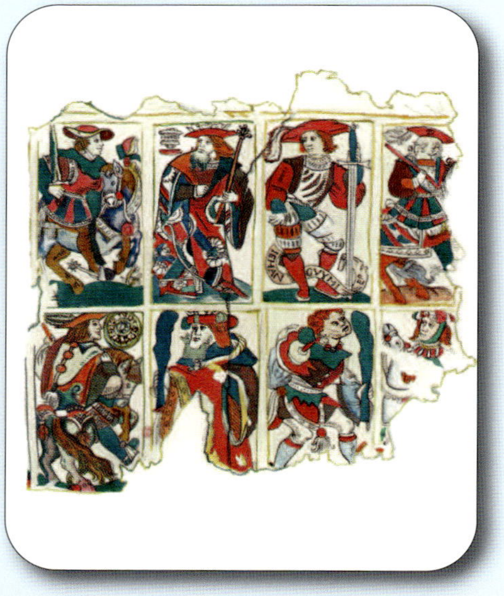

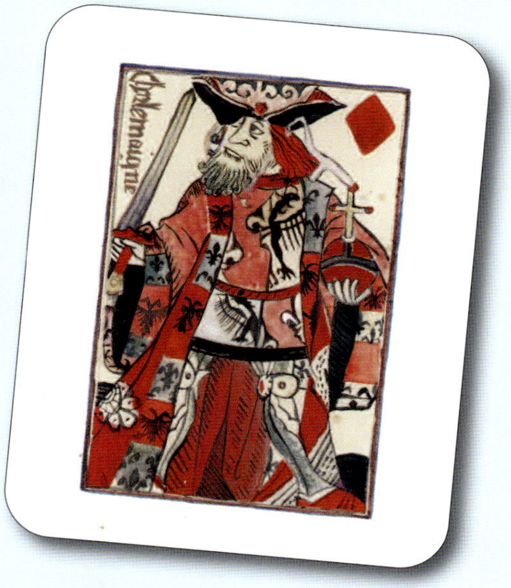

After I left school, I went and stayed with a French family. Madame Louise d'Aussy Pintaud was an artist of some repute in France exhibiting her work both close to where she lived in Ciboure, near St Jean de Luz, and also in Paris. Later the French named a square in honour of her work. France was a great adventure for me and it is where I bought my first oil paints and canvases. Monsieur and Madame Pintaud were the kindest and most charming couple and I was able to paint alongside Madame Pintaud daily in her gloriously huge studio. They had two dogs, an old one who stayed mostly in the kitchen where the odd bits of food were on hand. The second dog was a dachshund called Ali whom I adored, and who went everywhere with me in and around the town.

Outside my bedroom window lay the little harbour and one day I spied an elderly gentleman with paints and an easel, painting the harbour boats. I remember running downstairs to see how he was getting on. I cannot remember his painting, but he turned out to be the Earl of Glasgow. I became friends with the Earl and his wife and English friends of theirs. We went for walks together and the Earl wanted to present me at court in Scotland as a debutante! This did not happen but I *was* later presented at court at Buckingham Palace.

On my return to England I continued to paint and was accepted at the Regent Street Polytechnic School of Art, where I spent three years before going on to the Brighton College of Art to take my teaching qualification. During my student days and pre-Poly, I painted anything and anyone who would sit for me including my school friend Elizabeth Ann Goring, my grandmother, our gardener and my little sister. I also helped complete a mural along with John Spencer Churchill on a pub's courtyard wall in Kensington.

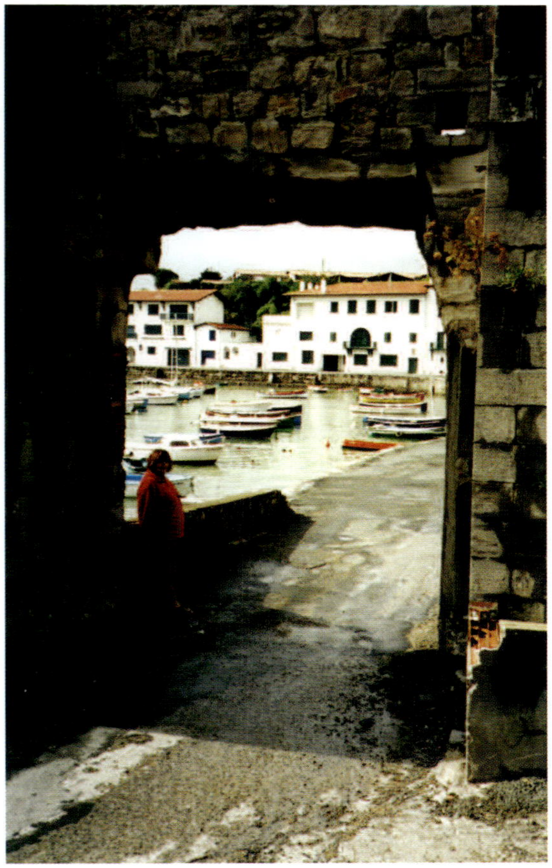

Visiting the harbour at Ciboure in later years where I had spent such a seminal period in my career as an artist.

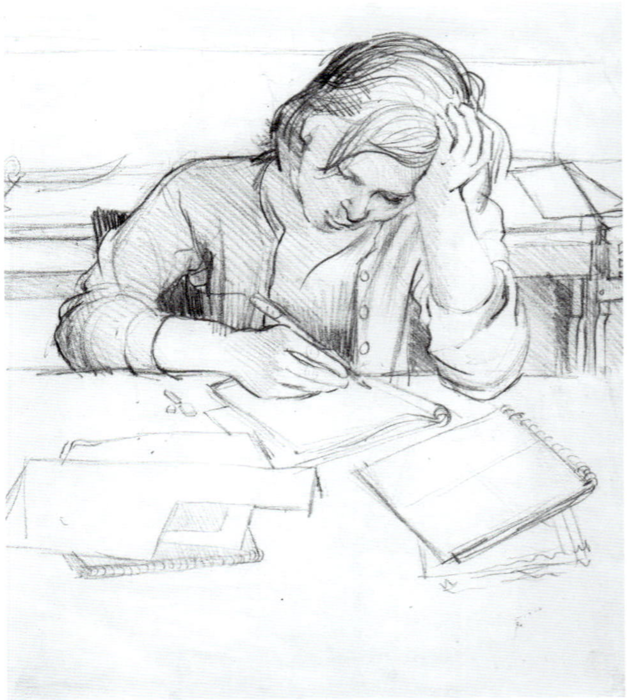

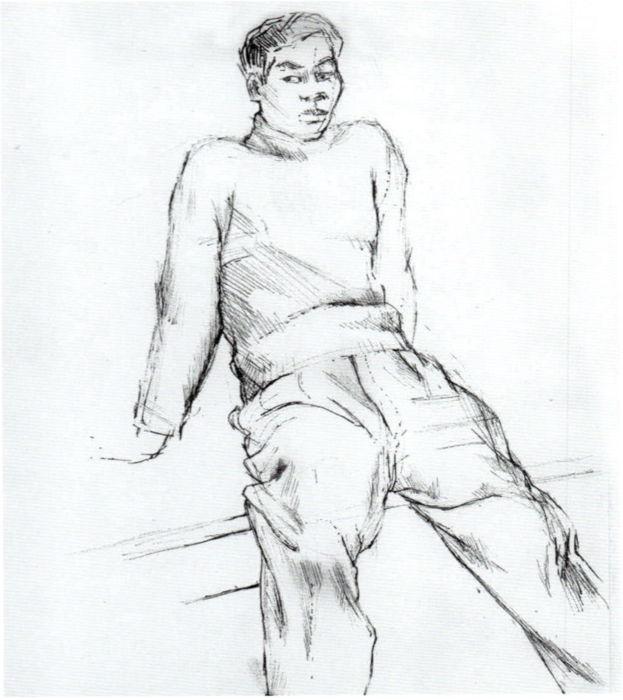

From my early sketchbooks.

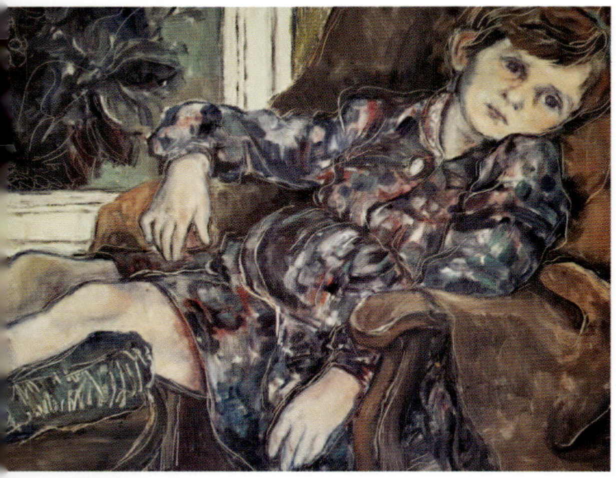

A portrait of my sister, Viv, painted when she was feeling poorly.

My tutor at the Poly was Stuart Tresilian who was always referred to as Tris. A memorable and kindly teacher, his ability to draw animals was brilliant and quick. He famously illustrated a number of Rudyard Kipling's books. We often visited London Zoo with our sketchbooks where I recall Tris's wonderfully rapid and masterful drawings. The V & A was another place we often visited. Borrowing stools, we moved freely among the wonderfully varied exhibits, drawing and painting anything which fascinated us.

After the Poly came my year at Brighton Art College where I returned to work on my book about the history of playing cards, researching the subject at the V & A and at the British Museum at weekends. This was a formal part of my course at Brighton.

London was an exciting place to be at that time. Mary Quant had a shop in King's Road with her chic clothes, and I worked for a short while nearby at the Chelsea Pottery. While I was there, a party was held where the Chelsea set descended for an exceedingly bohemian event. I remember a smartly dressed man in a pin striped suit attempting to create something out of sloppy clay on an electric pottery wheel. By the end of the evening he was covered in clay which had been flung out in all directions.

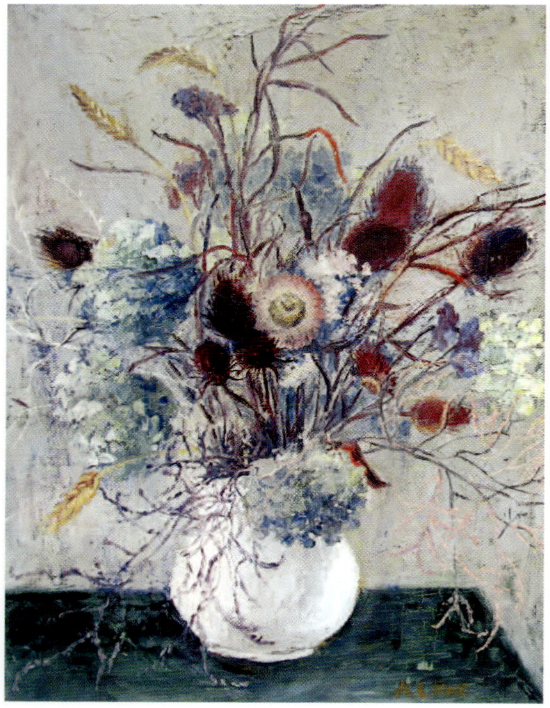

An early flower painting which I exhibited on the London Embankment, a favourite spot for students selling their work.

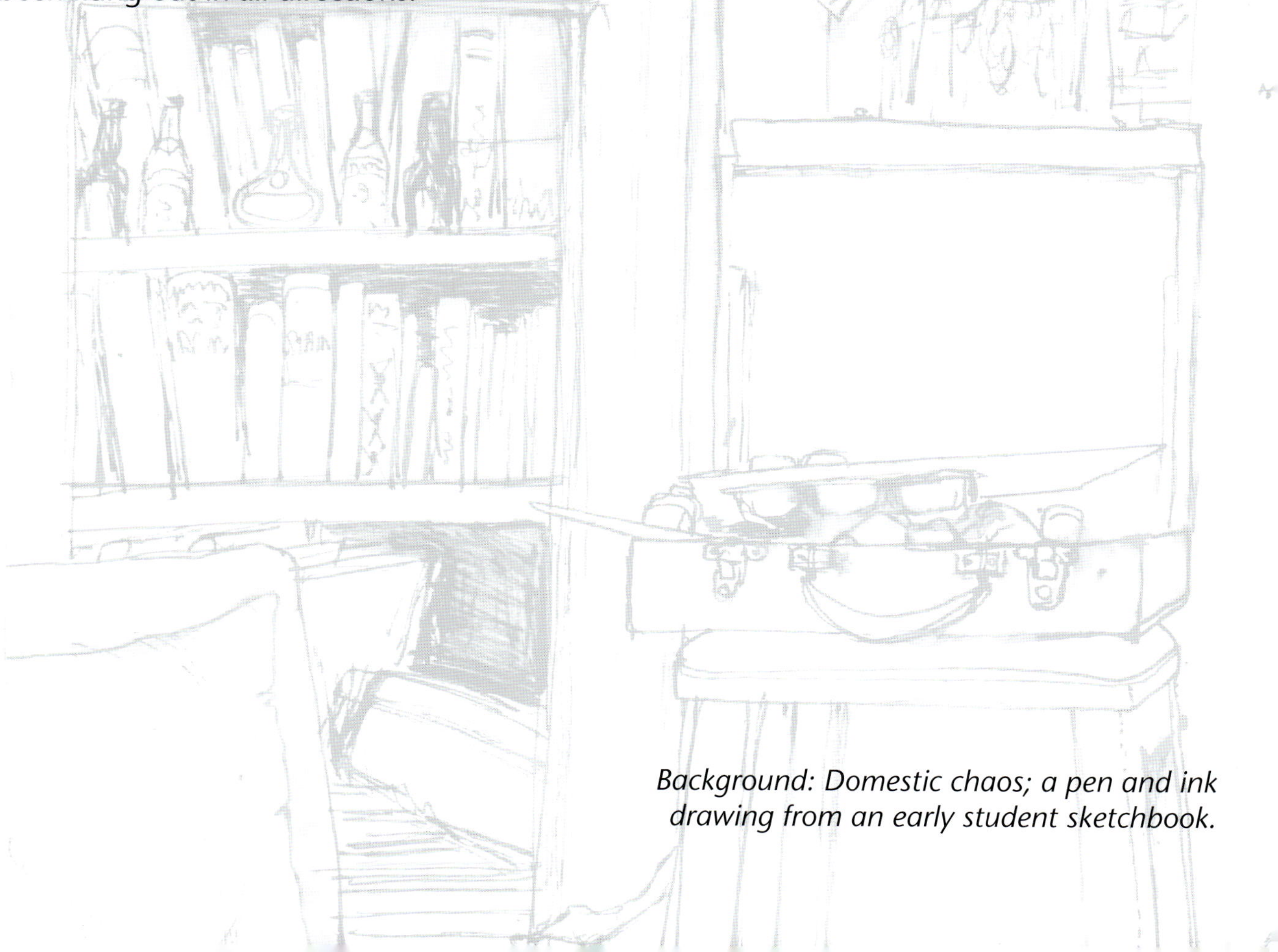

Background: Domestic chaos; a pen and ink drawing from an early student sketchbook.

Somewhere amongst the party crowd there was a massive pot of bouillabaisse soup and great quantities of wine. In a corner there was an artist sketching quietly. He eventually finished the drawing of a woman which he offered to her but she took one look at this unassuming man, and said she did not want it. If she had only known! The artist was Pietro Annigoni who had recently finished his famous portrait of Queen Elizabeth II.

At around this time I was asked to contribute illustrations for some sports pages for the *New Junior Encyclopaedia Britannica* for which I produced 120 drawings. My first commissioned portrait was of Jill Tweedie whose parents were friends of my parents. Jill's mother was Turkish and her father Scottish. He had been offered a knighthood but refused it as he did not want it to change his life in any way. Jill was very beautiful with dark eyes, raven hair and a statuesque figure; a real head turner wherever she went. I often saw her cycling past our house with the inevitable guy cycling behind trying to catch up with her!

Jill's life story really got going when she went to Canada, where she met and married a handsome Hungarian, Count Bela Cziraky, who had previously been captured with many other young Hungarians by the invading Russians and sent by cattle truck to Siberia. There they would have remained had it not been for some political agreement enabling a small number of these young men to be released and returned home. A random choice had been made and Cziraky found himself on another cattle truck back to Hungary. Leaving his parents and family members behind he took off for Canada where he eventually got a job working for the German car firm, Volkswagen. The Count spoke many languages and also taught dancing to many an adoring Canadian lady!

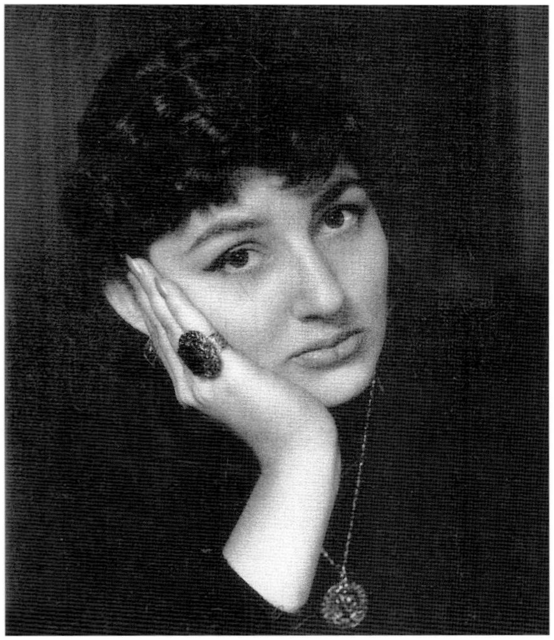

While at college I was photographed by a professional photographer in Bond Street.

My mother and I went to see them in Canada, firstly in Ottawa, where on a bitterly cold day we witnessed a service being held in a square for the Hungarians overrun by the Russian invasion. There was a fundraiser for relief parcels that were being sent to Hungary.

We met Jill and Bela on another occasion in Montreal, where they were then living. They took us to a series of nightclubs and finally we ended up in a large, dark attic room lit by candles. The place was filled with people, many were exiled 'White' Russians. There were moments of silence in the room while someone stood up and sang or spoke. It was quite extraordinary and very moving. Near the nightclub I saw a little lady crawling up a flight of steps to a church and on every step she was praying and praying.

I never saw Jill or Bela again. They had three children, sadly one died of cot death, and then the marriage collapsed. Jill came to London, where she met a Dutch film-maker and had another child. This relationship did not last, as then she met the journalist and author Alan Brien. Jill wrote several books and was friendly with Germain Greer (of 'burn your bra' fame). She won the *Guardian's* Writer of the Year Award for her articles about living with illness in the last period of her life, following her Motor Neurone Disease diagnosis. Jill died in 1993 aged 57. I often wonder what happened to my rather stilted portrait of her which I had completed in 1953 when I was quite young.

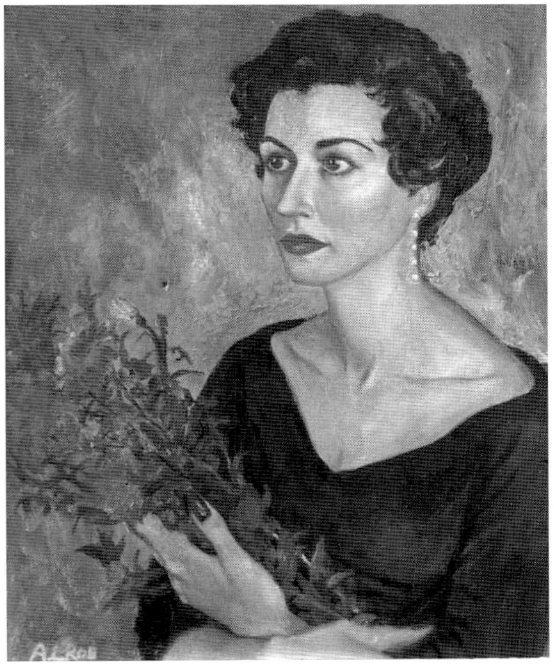

My portrait of Jill Tweedie (the original in colour).

From my early sketchbooks

"When I was young I exhibited under A. L. Roe – not giving my gender. Women artists were very differently thought of in those days. Certainly not to be taken seriously..."

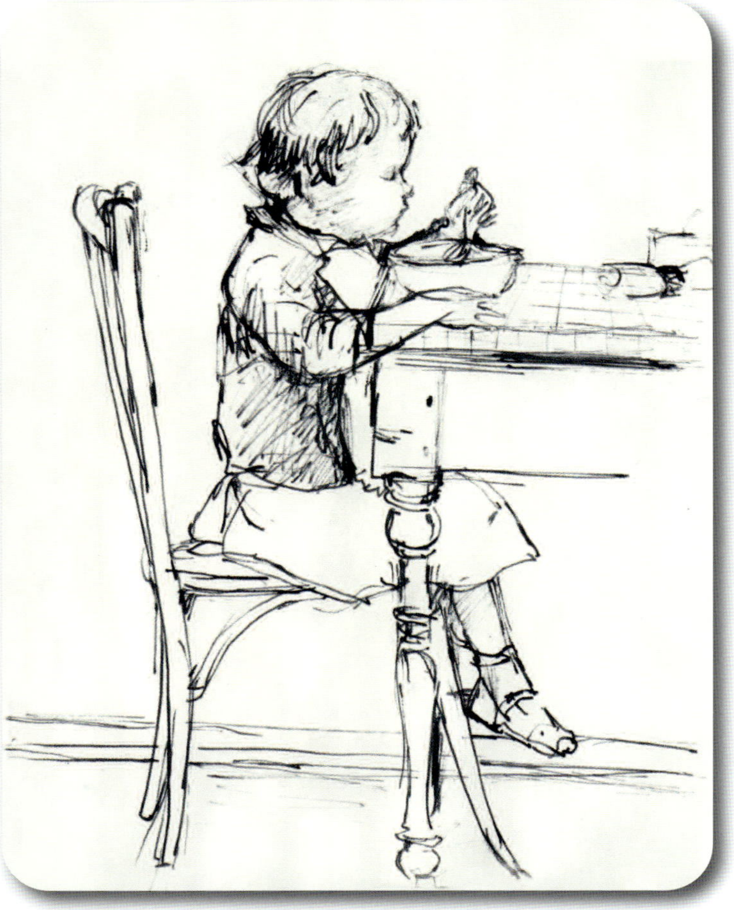

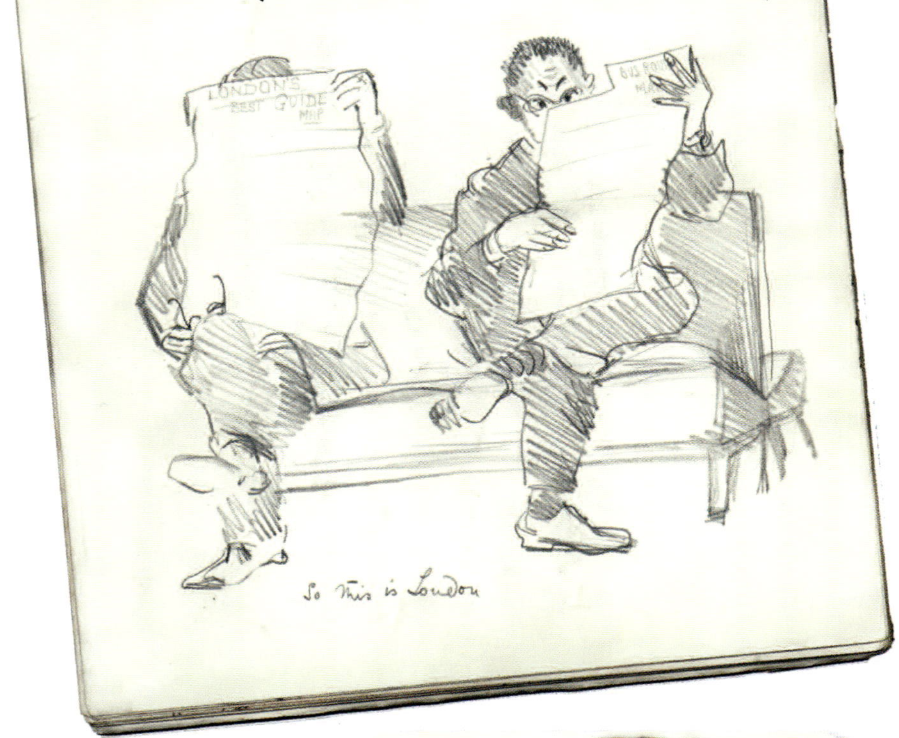

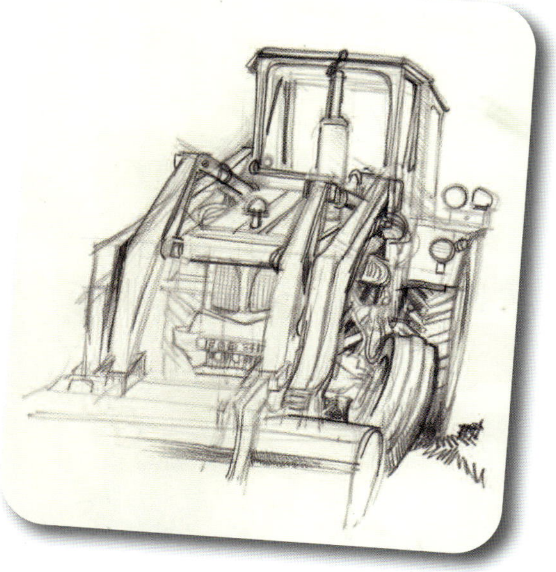

From my art college sketchbooks. Above left: Isabella, the daughter of an Italian friend, eating pasta using only a fork for the first time. A big moment!

Above right: "So this is London!"

Right: Leonora Box at art college. Her family made some of the early Ealing Comedies. Leonora lived in a caravan in her parents' garden.

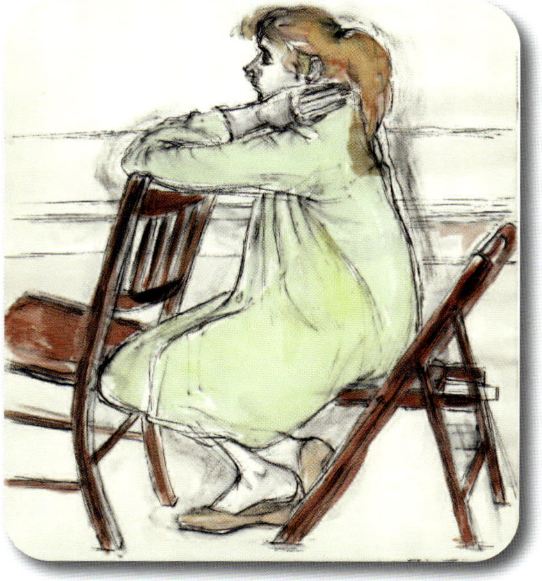

From my early sketchbooks

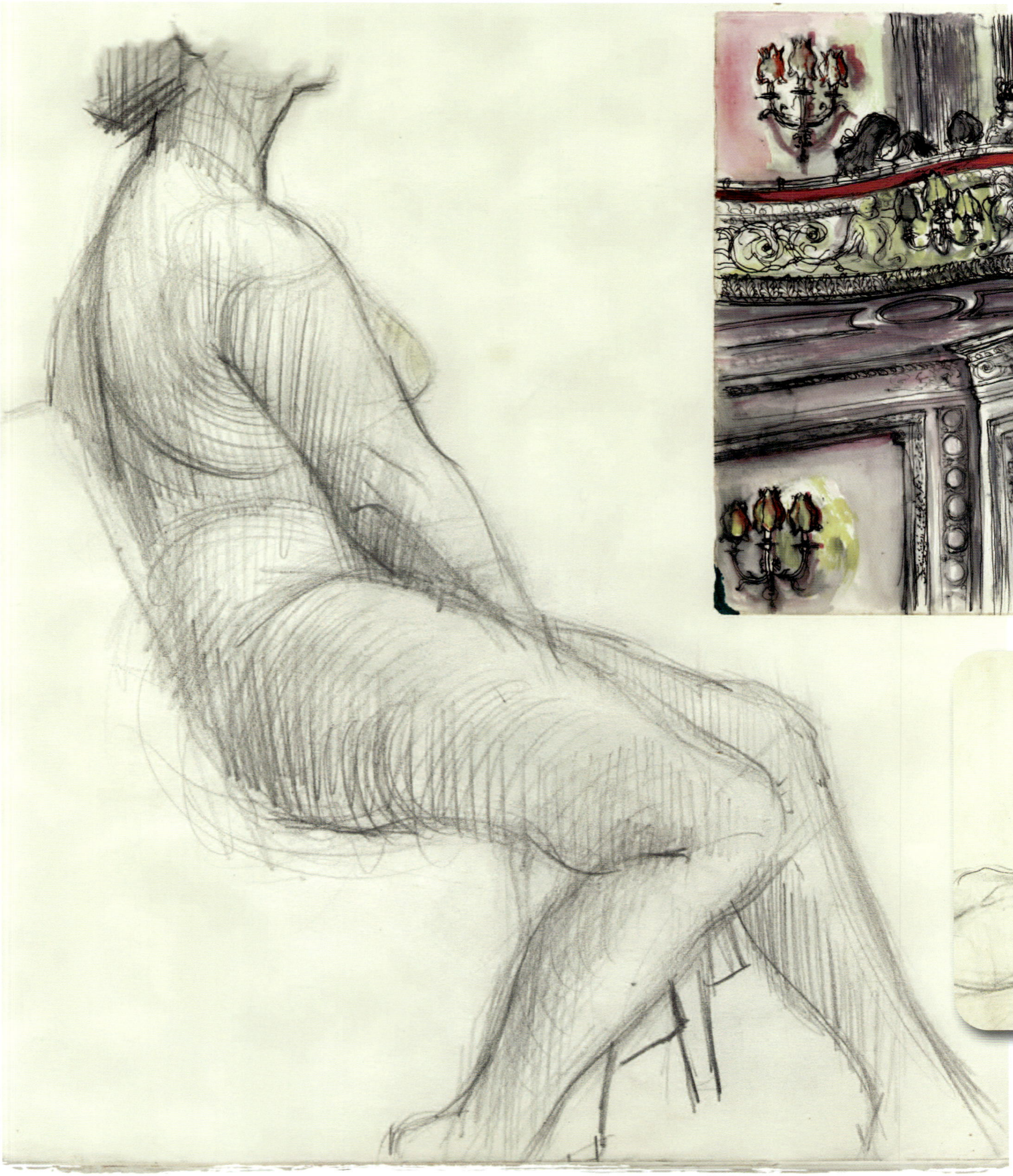

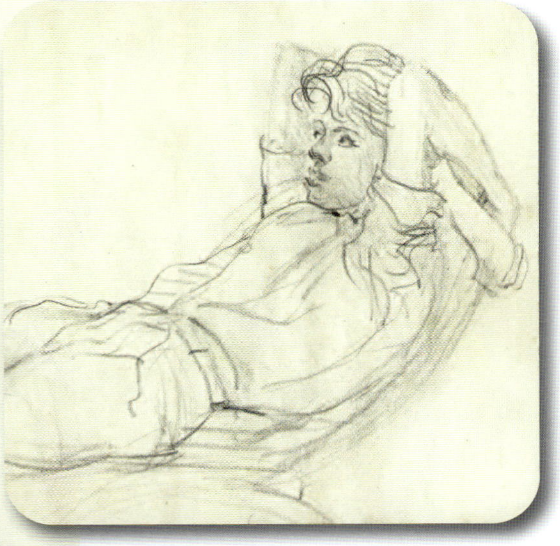

From my art college sketchbooks.

My Family
A Life in Art

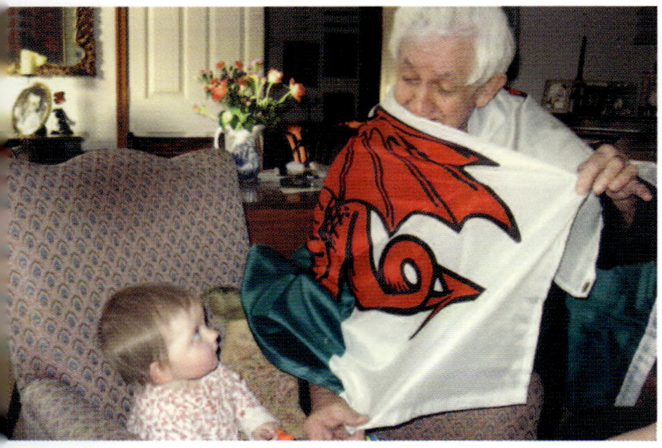

That 'charismatic Welshman', Alan with Alys our eldest granddaughter. Below: My young sister Viv in a Dutch costume which my mother had brought back from the Netherlands.

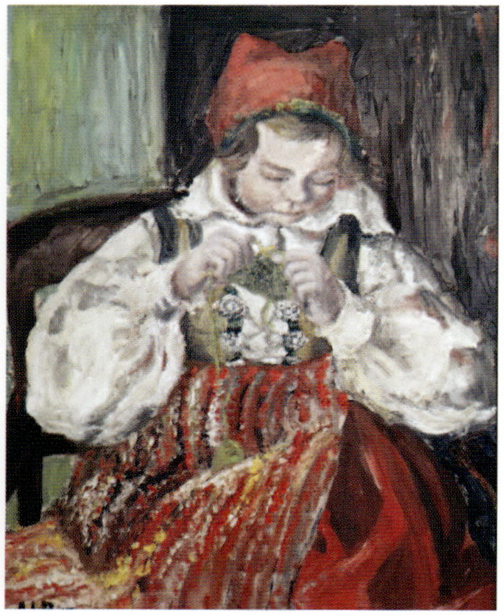

Art and music runs through my family's veins and pops up in the work of my cousins, my own children and grandchildren. I have painted, drawn and made things out of anything and everything all of my life. In my childhood days we often held musical evenings around the piano with me playing my violin and everyone singing. My mother's brother, Wilfred, married a Welsh lady, Kathleen Llewelyn, who played the piano by ear. Two of her granddaughters are in the musical theatre industry.

My sister, Vivian, was eleven years younger than me and sadly I missed much of her growing up. I was at boarding school and then, later, we were separated when our parents split up.

My painting career was restricted for a time due to family events and, having found a teaching job, we eventually moved to live in Devon, with my two lovely children and our little dog called Popoff. Then suddenly, there was this handsome, charismatic Welshman entering our lives and Alan was to become my soul mate for the rest of my life. We had two more children, so life was very busy.

I taught in many schools and enjoyed working with primary school children which had the added advantage of being able to take my young son with me. On one occasion, to my horror, I saw him dropping powdered coloured paint into the school fish tank, watching with fascination as the colours dissolved in the water. Luckily, the fish were all rescued.

I taught for one year in a girls' convent school and in a local school for about five years. Here we made shadow puppets and a stage was built so we could take the puppet show out to local venues. For this we involved the music department along with the many children and puppeteers.

My lovely, clever, funny family are game for anything magical. When Alan introduced me to his delightful family I again found them full of music and art. Although I never really got to grips with the Welsh language I feel sure that had we lived in Wales I would have learnt to speak it. I painted a portrait of Megan, Alan's cousin Judith's daughter, who sat with their dog. The portrait now hangs in their Cardiff home.

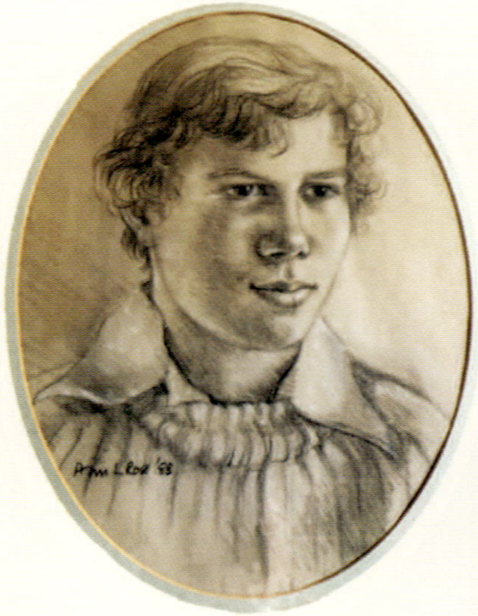

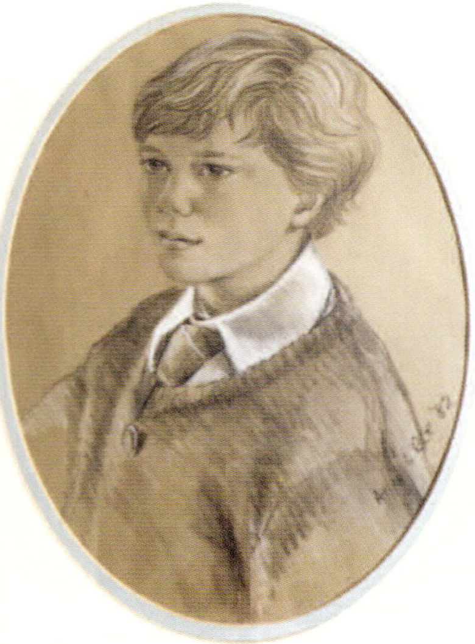

EARLY PORTRAITS OF CHILDREN

I've always enjoyed painting children. Many, whose portraits appear in this book, are now themselves adults with children of their own. A number remain friends to this day.

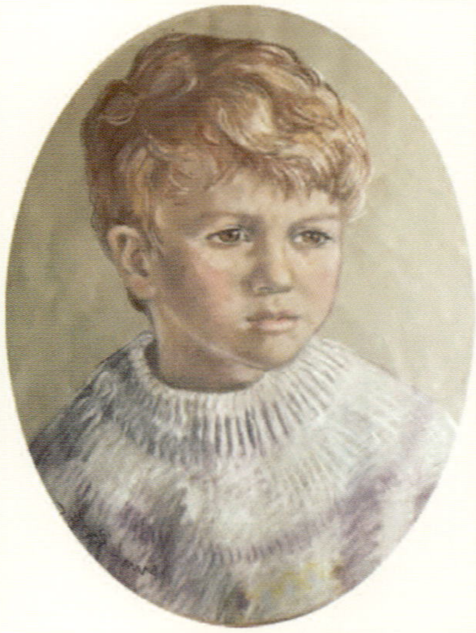

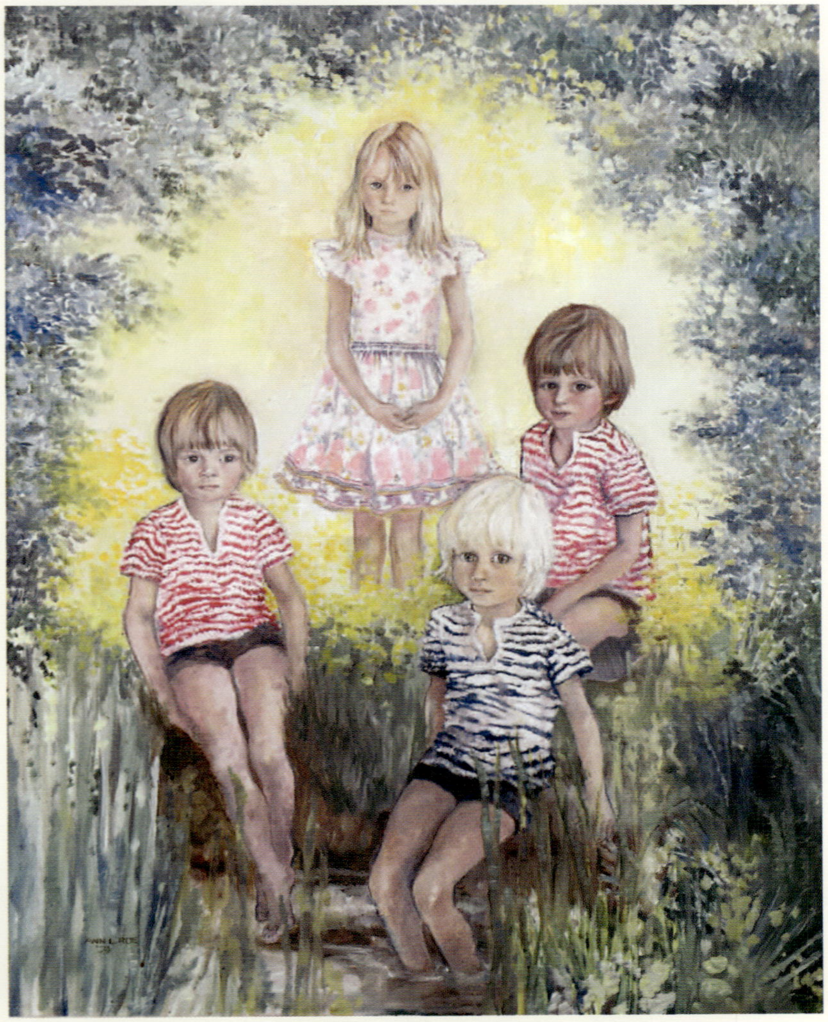

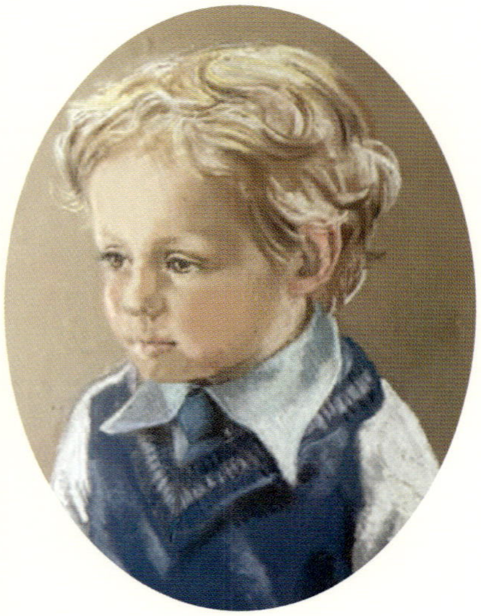

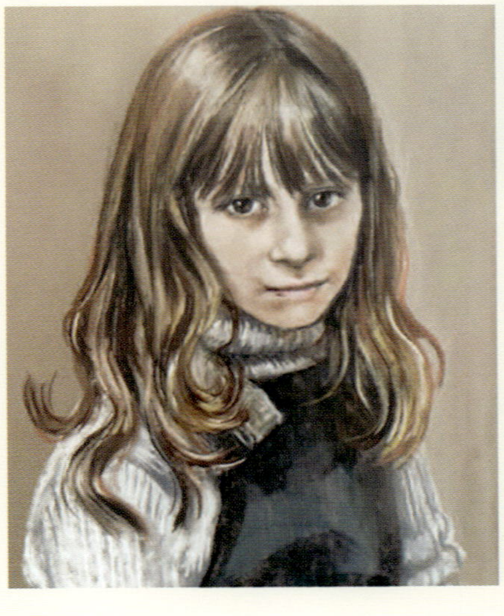

Centre picture: The Pady Children. The two vignettes at the top are l-r: Andrew Ransford and Caroline Ransford. The remaining four small paintings are members of the Rendell family from Colyton; Alan and David (left and right centre) and Mandy (right). Karen Rendell (left), now Karen Eyre, has been a close friend of my daughter Xanthe ever since primary school. Karen's grandfather used to frame my paintings.

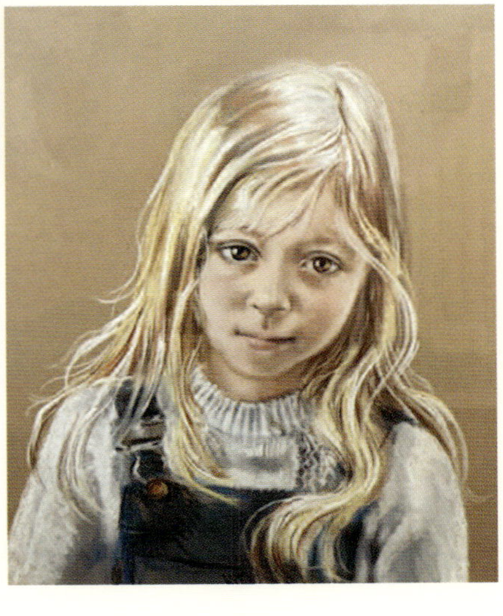

FAMILY PORTRAITS

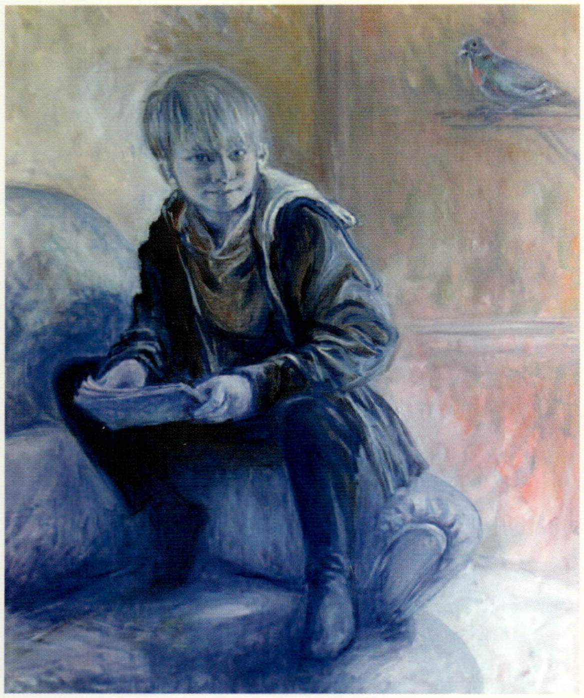

Jacob, my grandson, painted with a visiting pigeon.

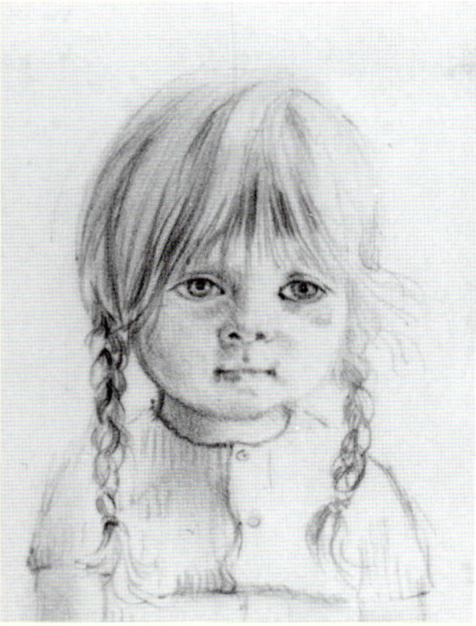

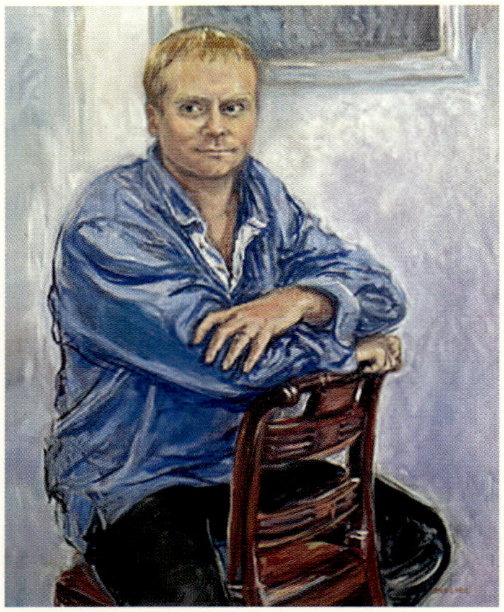

Centre left: A sketch of my daughter Xanthe, aged three. Right: Chris Breens.

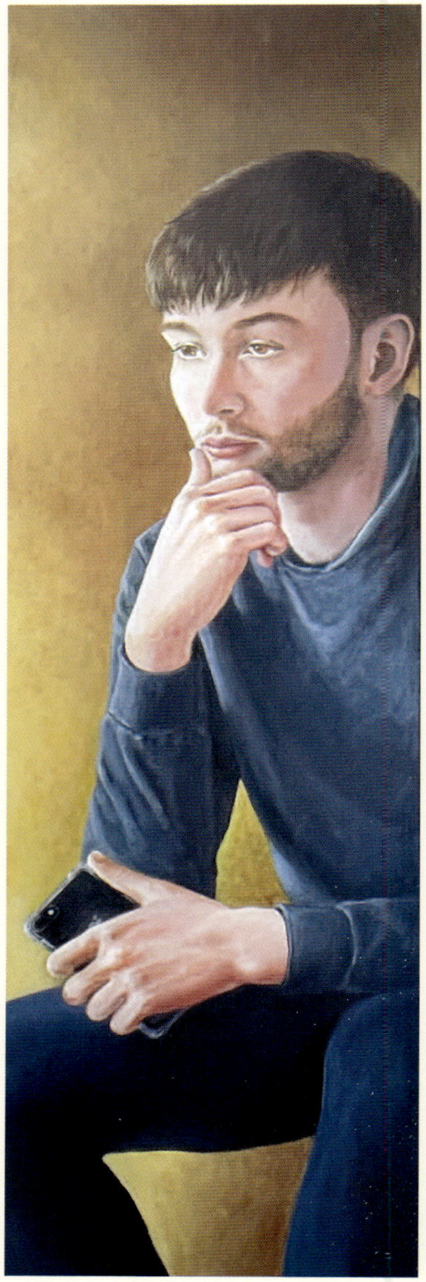

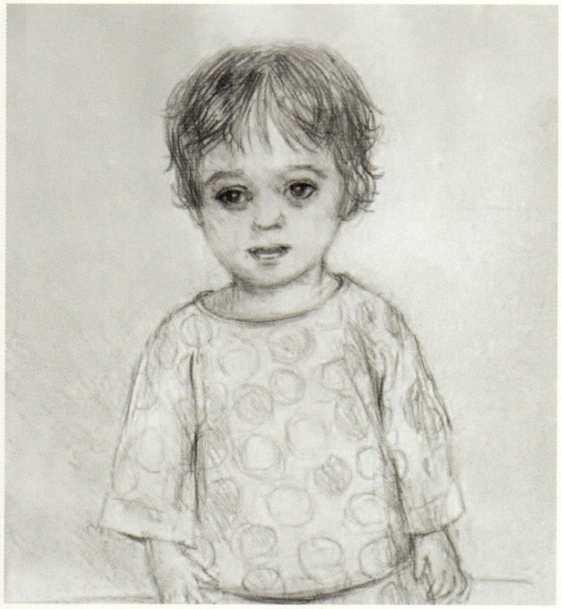

'Ready for Bed', my granddaughter Sofia from my sketchbook in 2011.

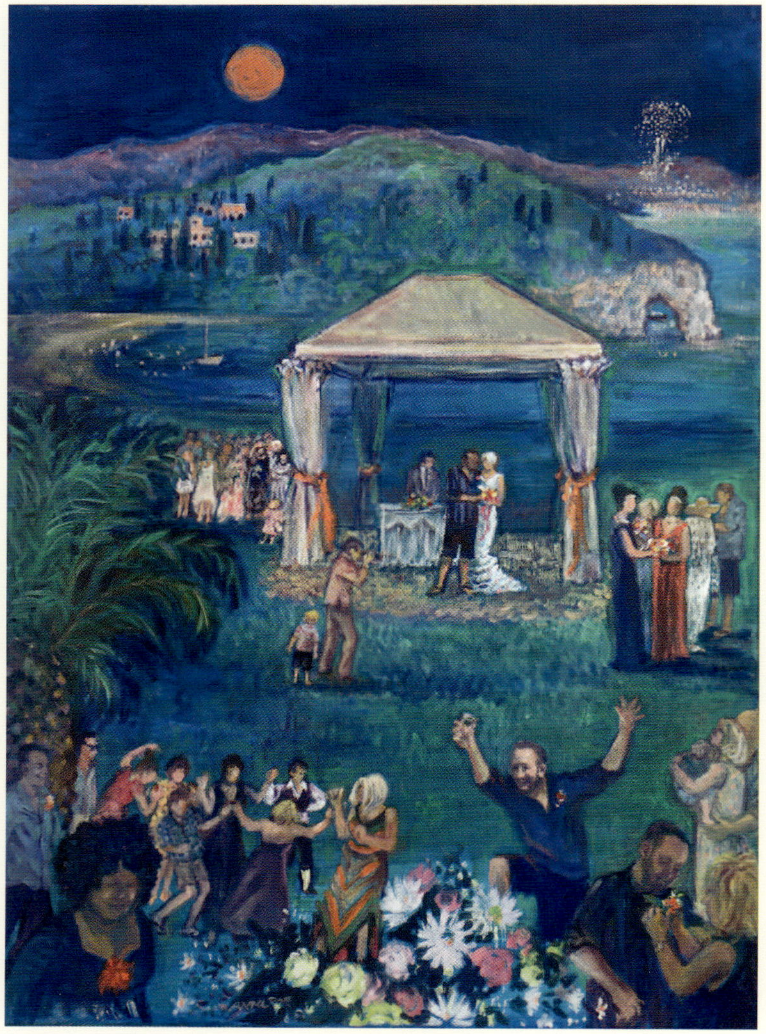

Above: Lolo's painting of her son Ben. Left: A happy painting of Joss and Alex's wedding in Greece.

FAMILY PHOTOS

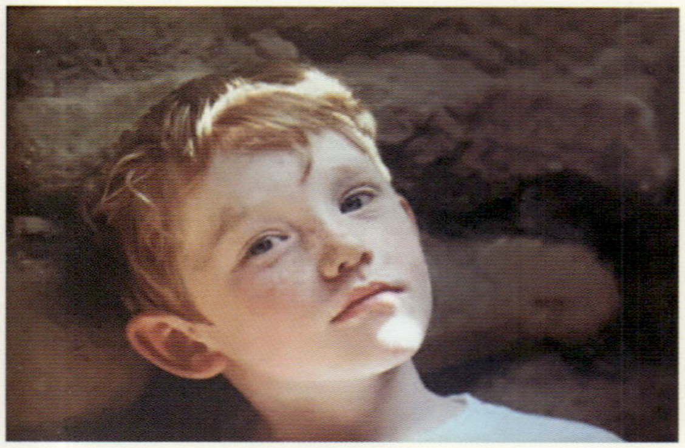

Adrian's son, our grandson, Luke.

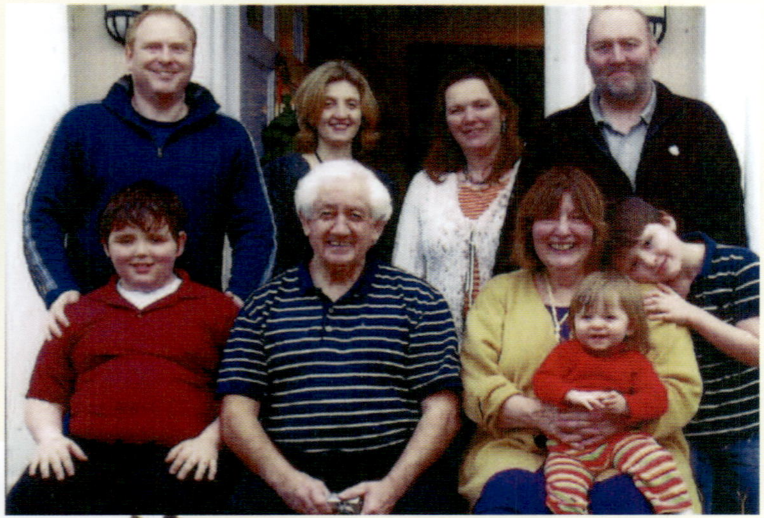

Above back row: Chris, Xanthe, Lolo and Andy. Front row: Tom, Alan, Ann with Alys and Ben.

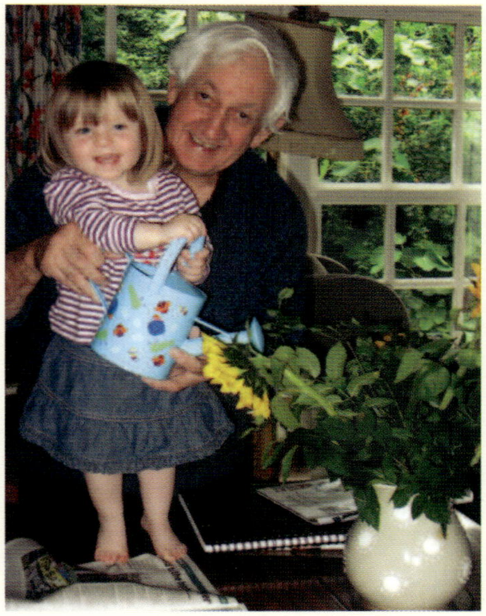

Alan and Alys.

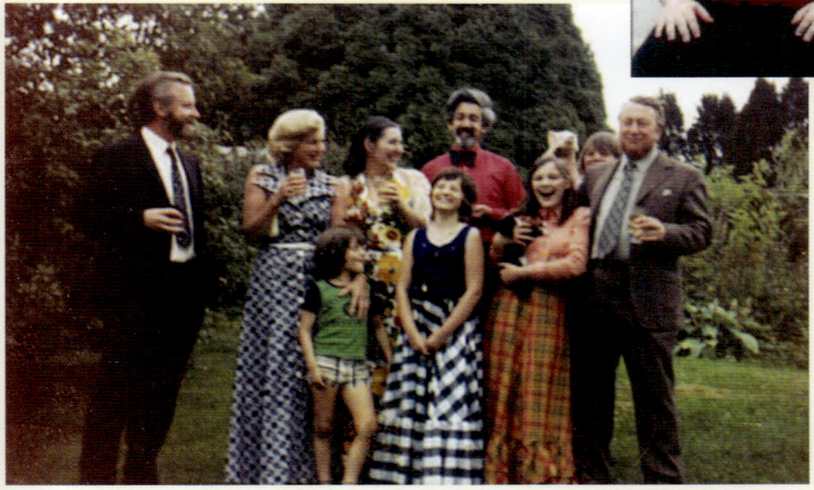

Alan and Ann and Adrian with pet piglet (Willy Grint) Lolo with her cat, Alwyn, Brigette (an Austrian friend) David Shaw (our vet) with his wife Doris and a musician friend Alan Thomas.

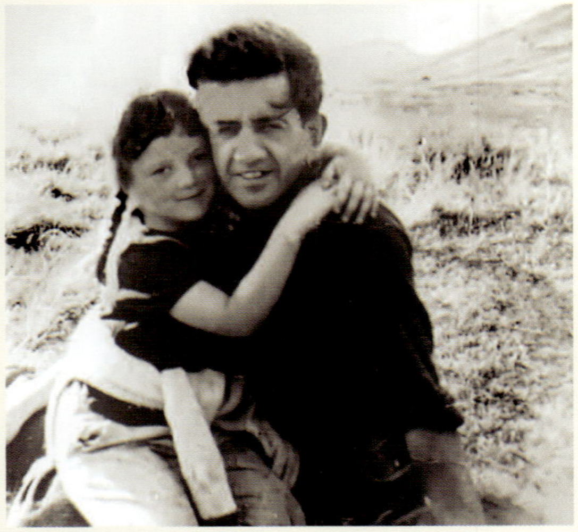

Alan and Lolo.

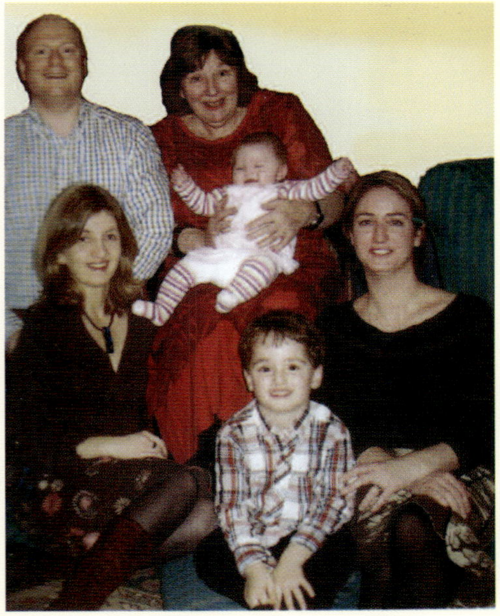

Above back row: Chris and Ann with Alys. Front row: Xanthe, Oliver and Jo.

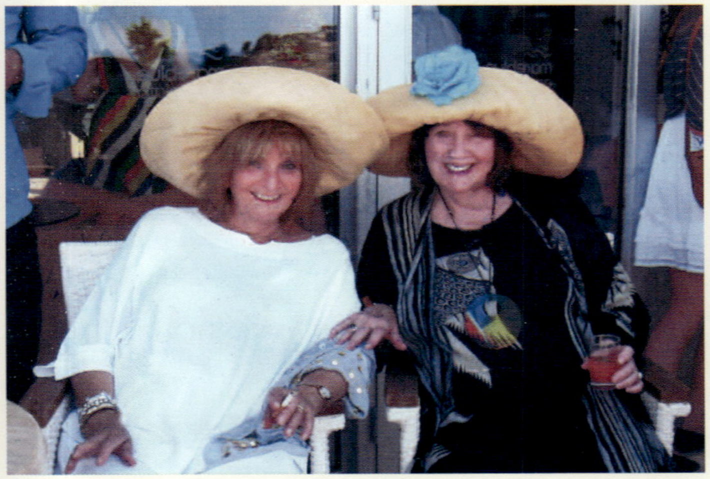

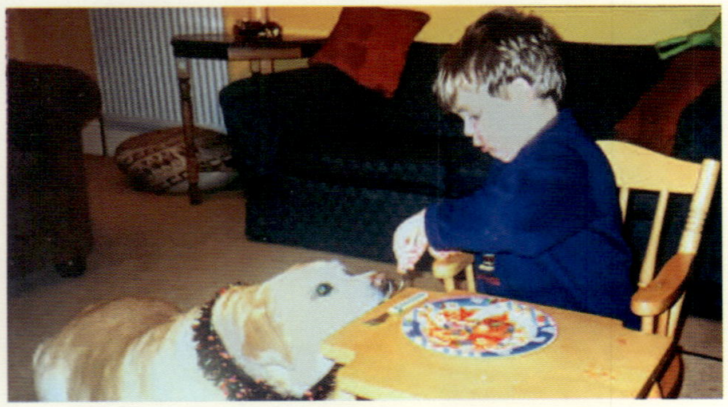

Far left: My sister Viv and I.

Left: My grandson Tom feeding Daisy the labrador.

A FAMILY LEGACY IN ART

All of our children have artistic leanings. Our eldest daughter Lolo went to Art College in Exeter and took a degree in Graphic Design. Lolo has always helped me in my creative work. When Alan Cotton invited me to paint a 3D otter in his charity work for the Dartmoor National Park, Lolo helped me to produce some 3D additions to my painted otters. I eventually painted three otters, two were auctioned, one of which was sold for £7000. The other one was sold separately to a Dartmoor café owner. Lolo has made a series of jewellery pieces based on 'A Midsummer Night's Dream', a creative necklace, plus a pottery whale with a fisherman in his boat balanced on its tail!

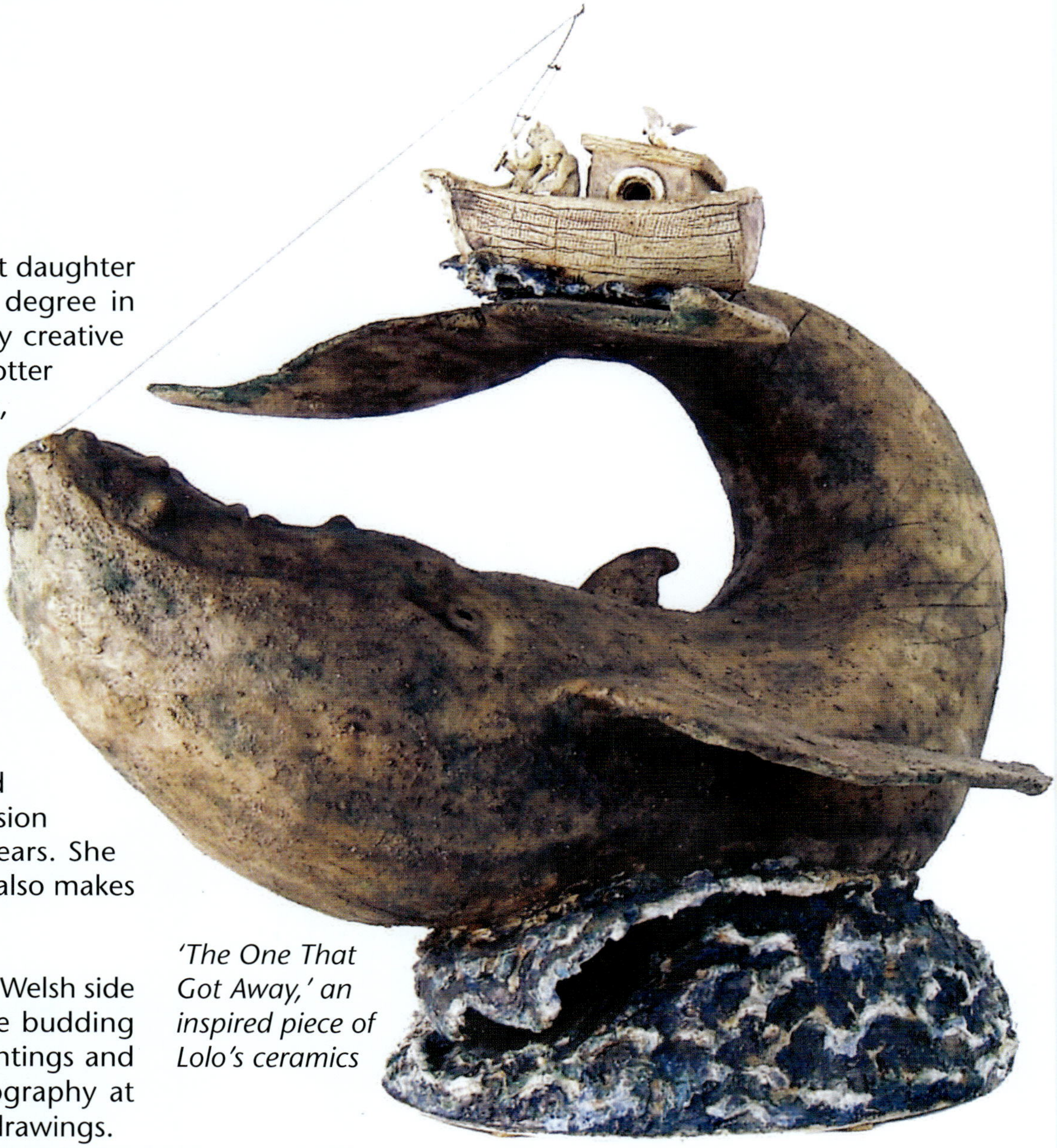

'The One That Got Away,' an inspired piece of Lolo's ceramics

Daughter Xanthe studied textiles at A-Level and after a four-year degree in Drama, Film and Television she went on to work in TV production for ten years. She paints furniture, using unusual paint colours, and also makes jewellery.

We have artistic traditions across the family, on the Welsh side as well as the English side. My grandchildren are budding artists. Sophia fills her bedroom with creative paintings and writing, Alys is studying Art Graphics and Photography at A level and Jacob produces original, detailed line drawings.

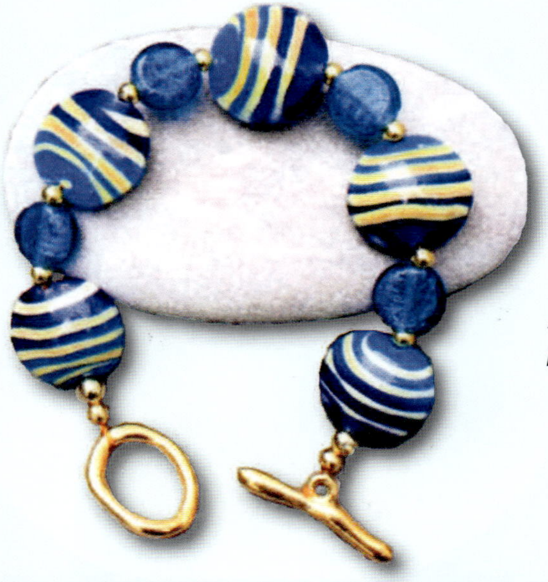

A jewellery bracelet by Xanthe

My sister has taken several courses on painting in recent years and enjoys it a great deal. Dafydd Saer, Alan's cousin is a clever watercolourist and uses his sketchbooks continually. In the past of course there was Granny Sims the Canadian artist. So, all our family have had an upbringing with art and music playing a significant part. On the Sims side of the family, it is now music and the musical theatre that occupies their lives, with Sonia recently gaining a CBE for her theatre work in London and New York. Her sister Maria is also well known in the theatre world winning a selection of Olivier Awards. It is a pity that we cannot visit to see their productions and concerts in London very often because we live here in beautiful Devon, and it's too far to visit London as often as we'd like.

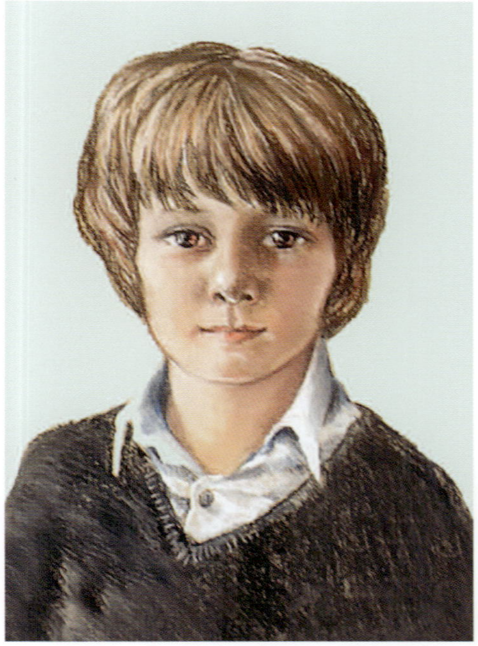

Amry, my youngest son.

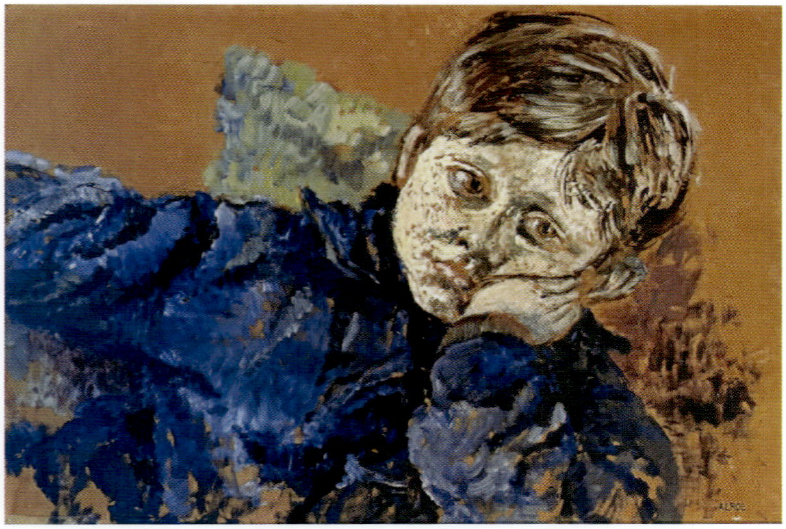

Adrian, my eldest son, when aged four.

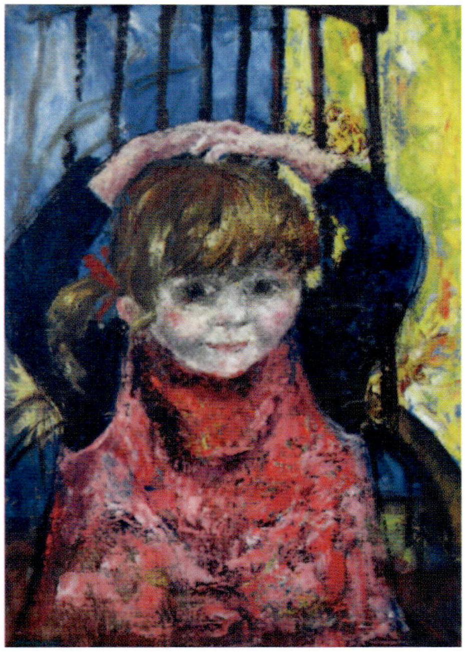

Lolo when aged three.

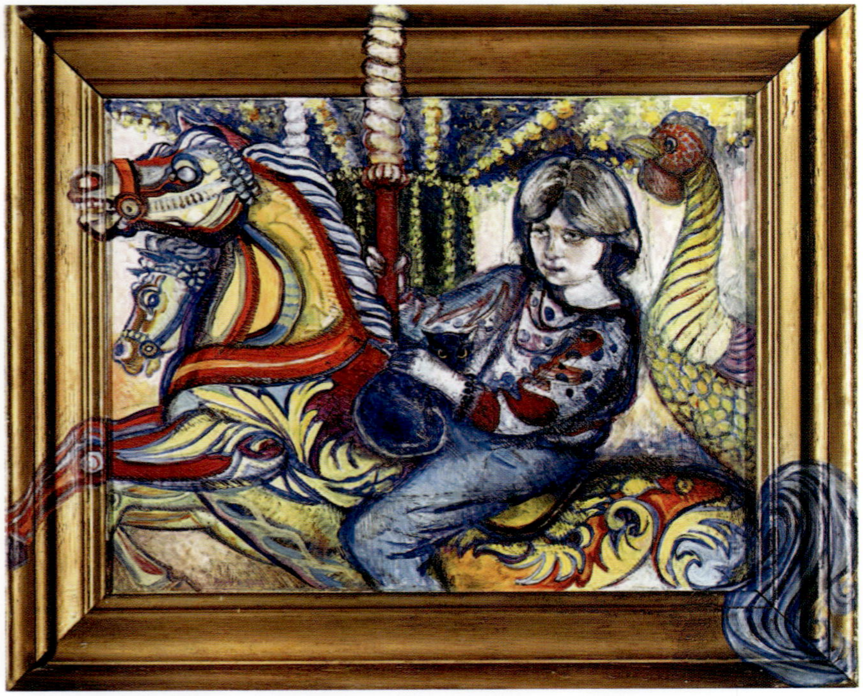

Xanthe and Kerry cat riding the merry-go-round.

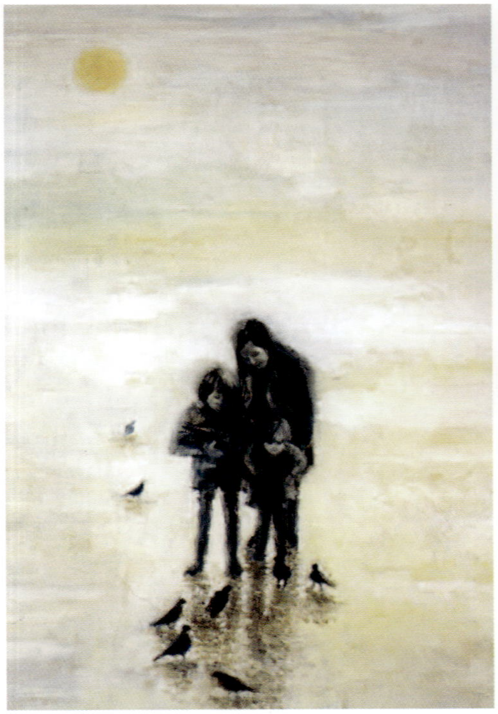

My painting of Lolo, Amry and Xanthe feeding birds.

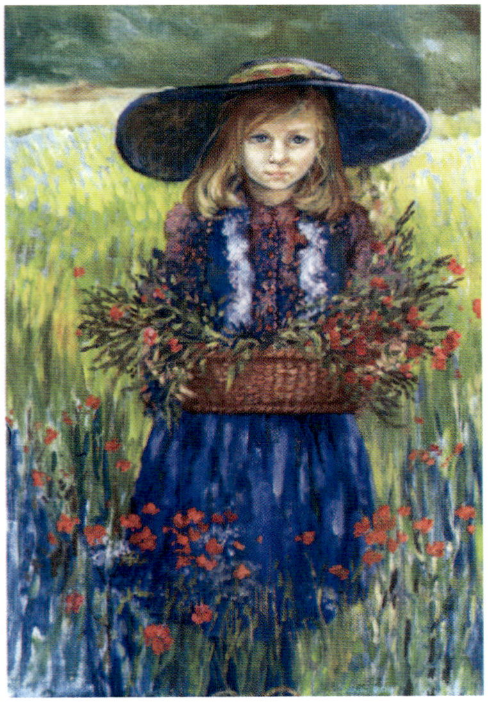

My daughter Xanthe wearing my debutante's hat!

EARLY PORTRAITS OF CHILDREN

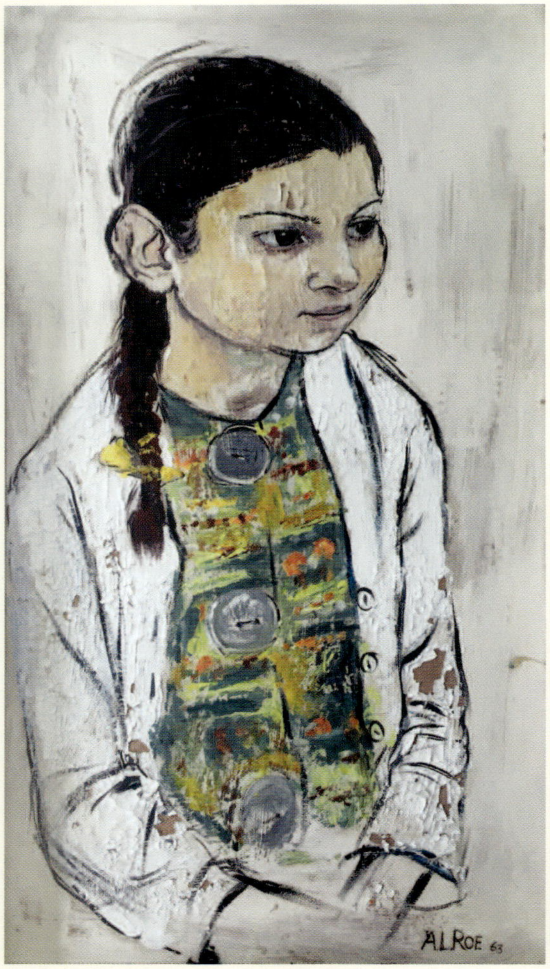

A favourite early Devon portrait from 1963. This is Morfydd Manley, a charming girl who later married a boy in her class at school. Her father had come to Devon on his honeymoon from Wales, fell in love with the county, and never left. I occasionally come across Morfydd in the area and it's always a pleasure to see her.

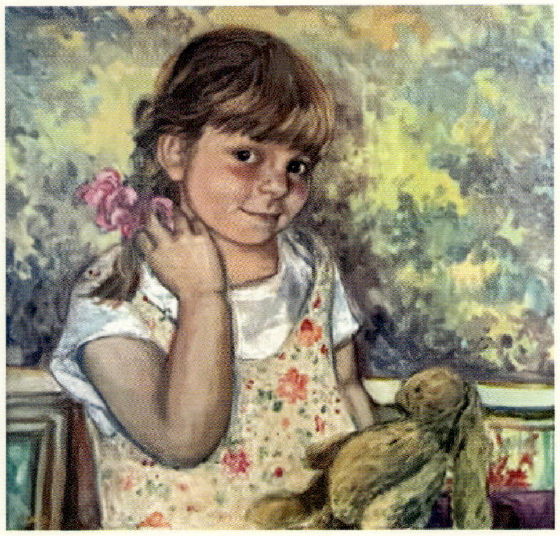

Alys, my eldest granddaughter.

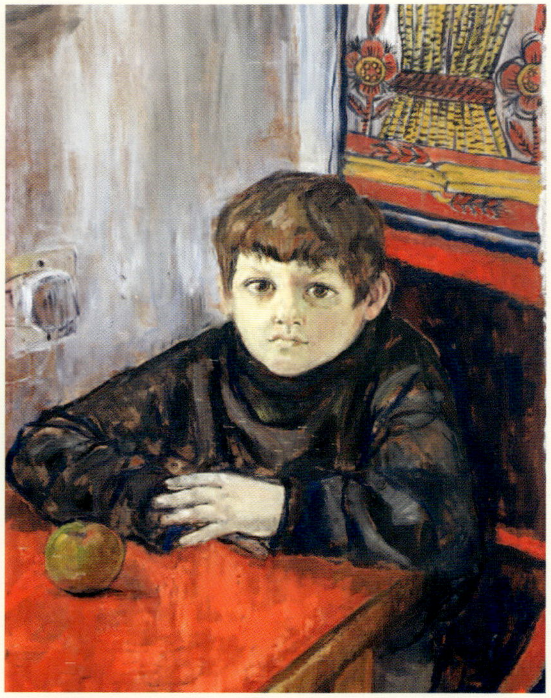

Dean was seven or eight years old in this painting and a similar age to my son Adrian. He was a willing sitter and with his quiet and calm expression he posed several times for me. This large painting of him sitting at the kitchen table is my favourite.

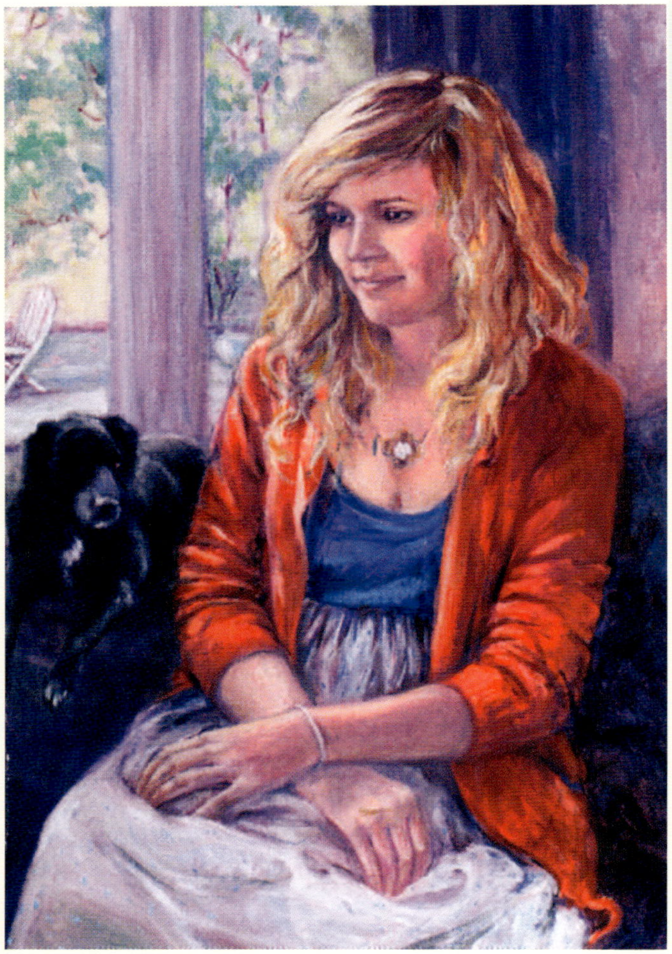

Megan, Alan's cousin's daughter.

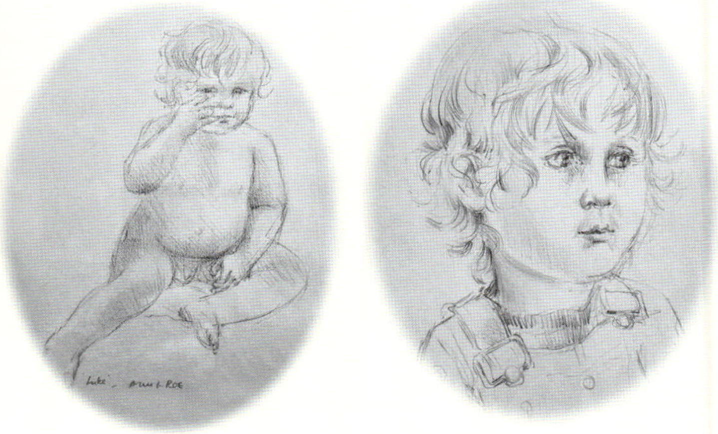

My nephews Luke Mackenzie (left) and Joss Mackenzie, 1977.

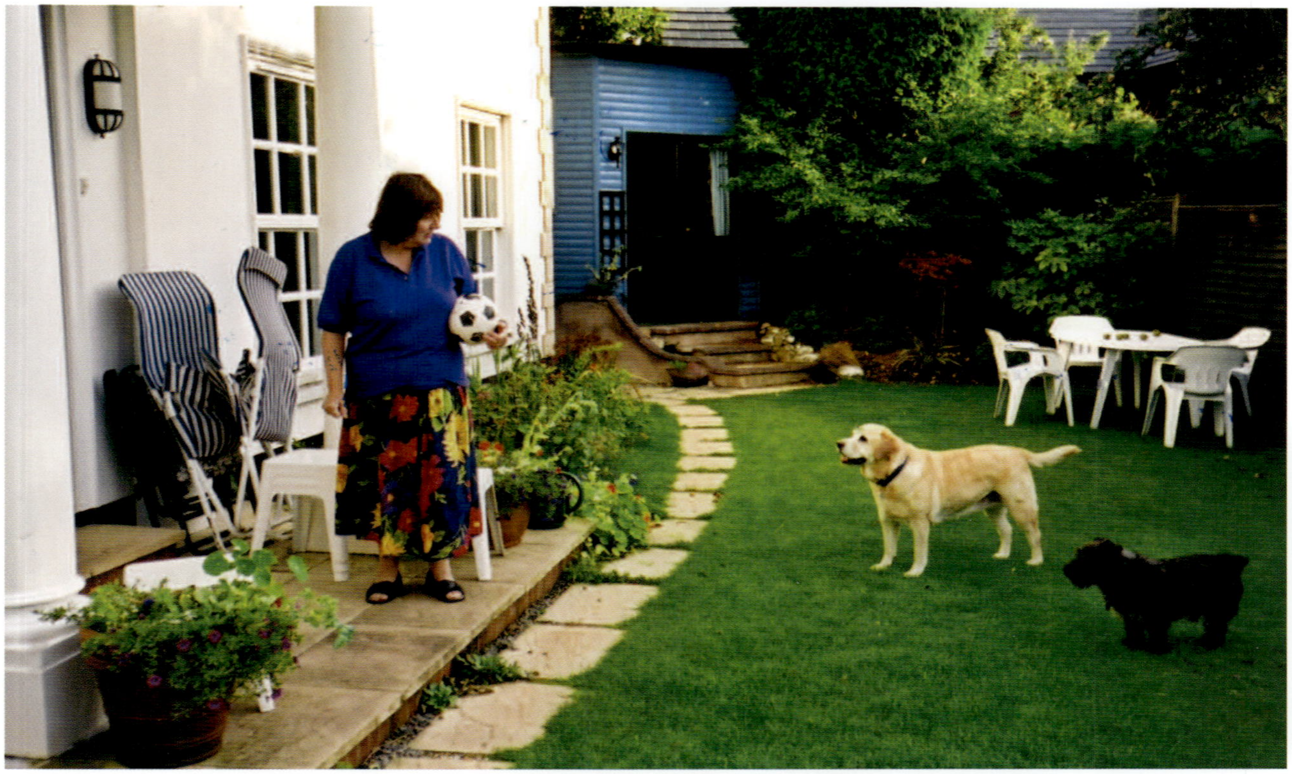

Playing with our dogs Daisy and Bowie in the garden at Rupack House, the home Alan and I built after moving from Oroolong House. My studio is seen in the background.

Alan and I did many things together, travelling, teaching, entertaining, singing (mainly Alan) and performing amazing magical happenings with Simon (Alan's magical protégé). More on this aspect of our lives follows towards the end of this book.

But perhaps one of our most exciting and ambitious projects was building our new home and a studio in the kitchen garden of our old house.

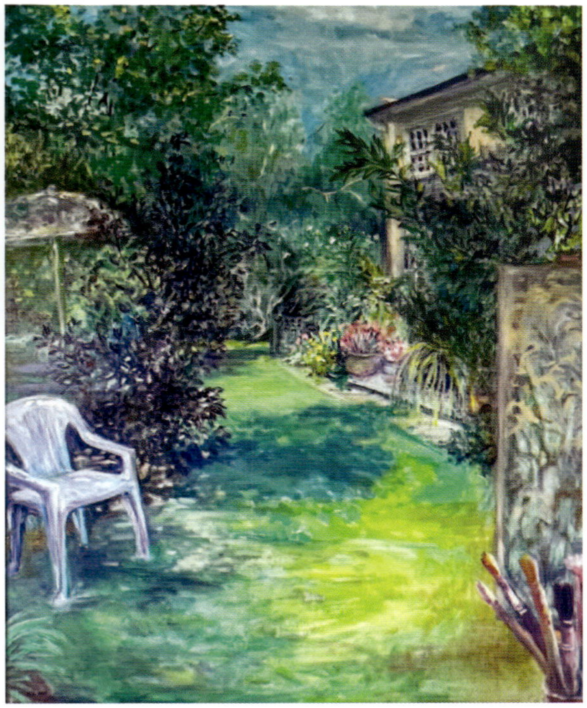

The garden at Rupack House.

* * *

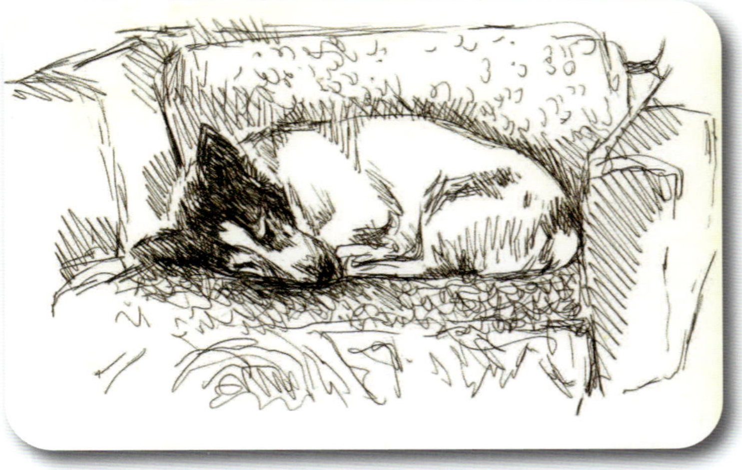

As a family we have always loved animals, we have housed some wonderful rescue dogs. My son Adrian also rescued a piglet who grew and grew and was totally house trained. A cat also arrived which Lolo adopted.

Then there were birds and rabbits (often used for Alan's magic performances), including a large white rabbit called Hoppy who loved eating wallpaper – and Alan's duffel coat!

Left: Jester, our little rescue dog. He had a memorable, feisty personality.

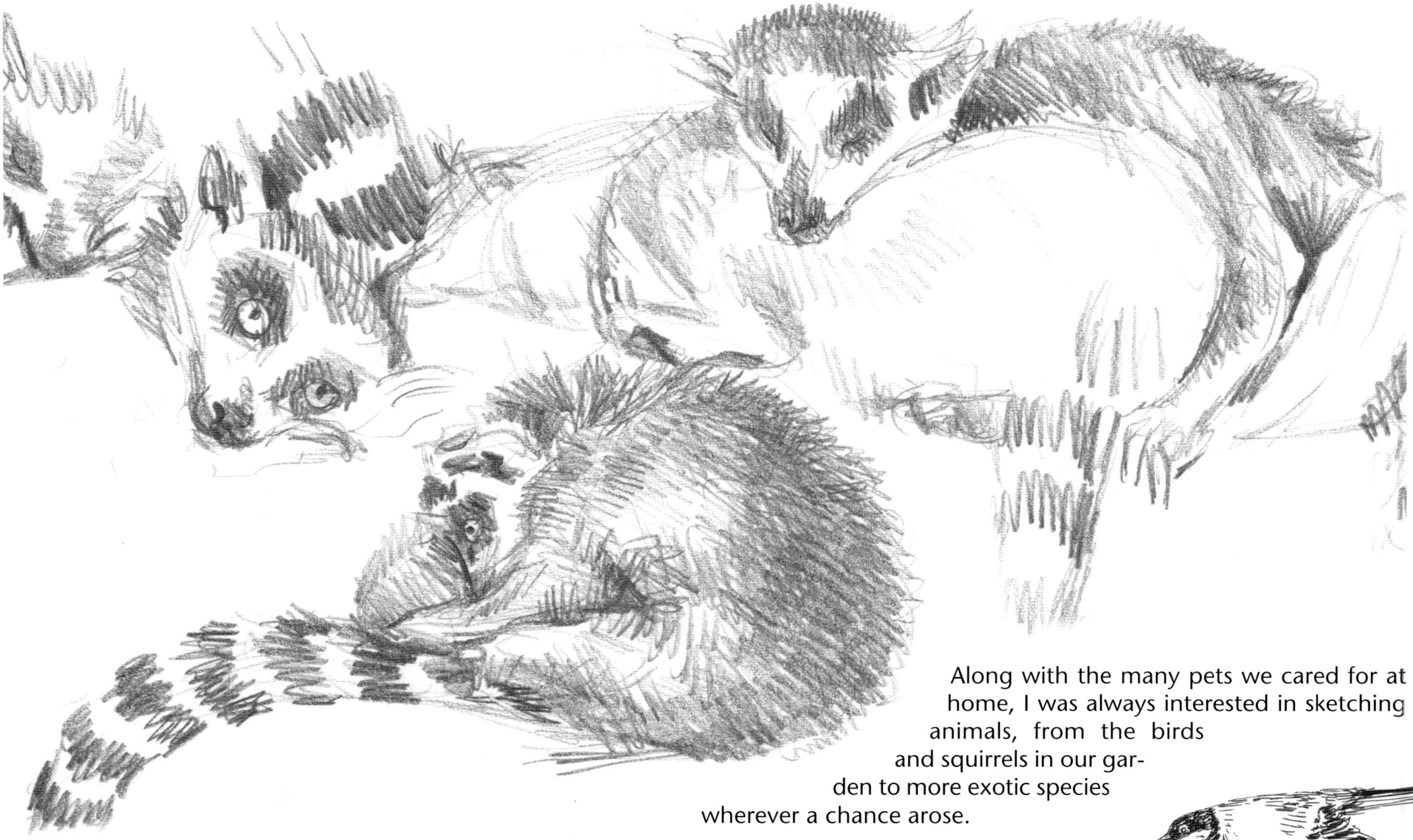

Along with the many pets we cared for at home, I was always interested in sketching animals, from the birds and squirrels in our garden to more exotic species wherever a chance arose.

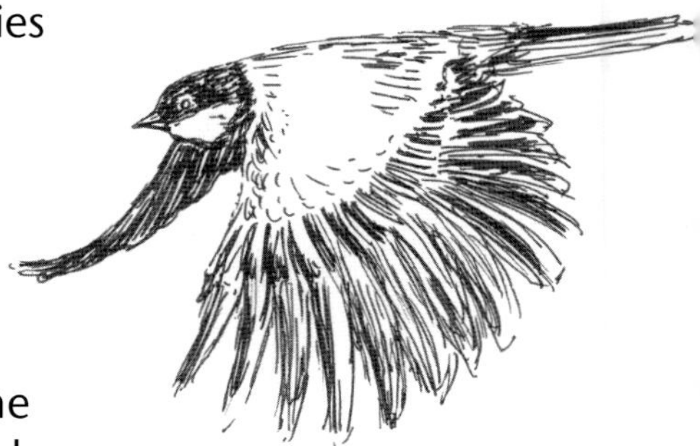

Sketchbook studies of Lemurs.

Opposite: From our garden – a Great Tit in flight.

In the early 1970s I was able to apply my talents, and those of my students in the Colyton Grammar School Art Department, to produce *The Elefriendly Recipe Book*. The project's aim was to raise awareness of the cruel trade in ivory which was endangering African Elephants. Philip Cox the papier mâché artist/sculptor and his wife came and spent days with us to make a wonderful life-sized elephant. Dougie Board, a local builder, prepared the wooden frame on which the papier maché was built up and I found bristles from a broom which made super eyelashes. Four of my A level 6th formers produced the recipe book, contacting well-known people to contribute recipes and photos of themselves. Miranda Whitten was a superb guiding light and much of the layout and the writing of the book was under her tutelage. David Shepherd had written a moving tribute at the start of the book and Andy Jones of Wheatons in Exeter designed the book for us.

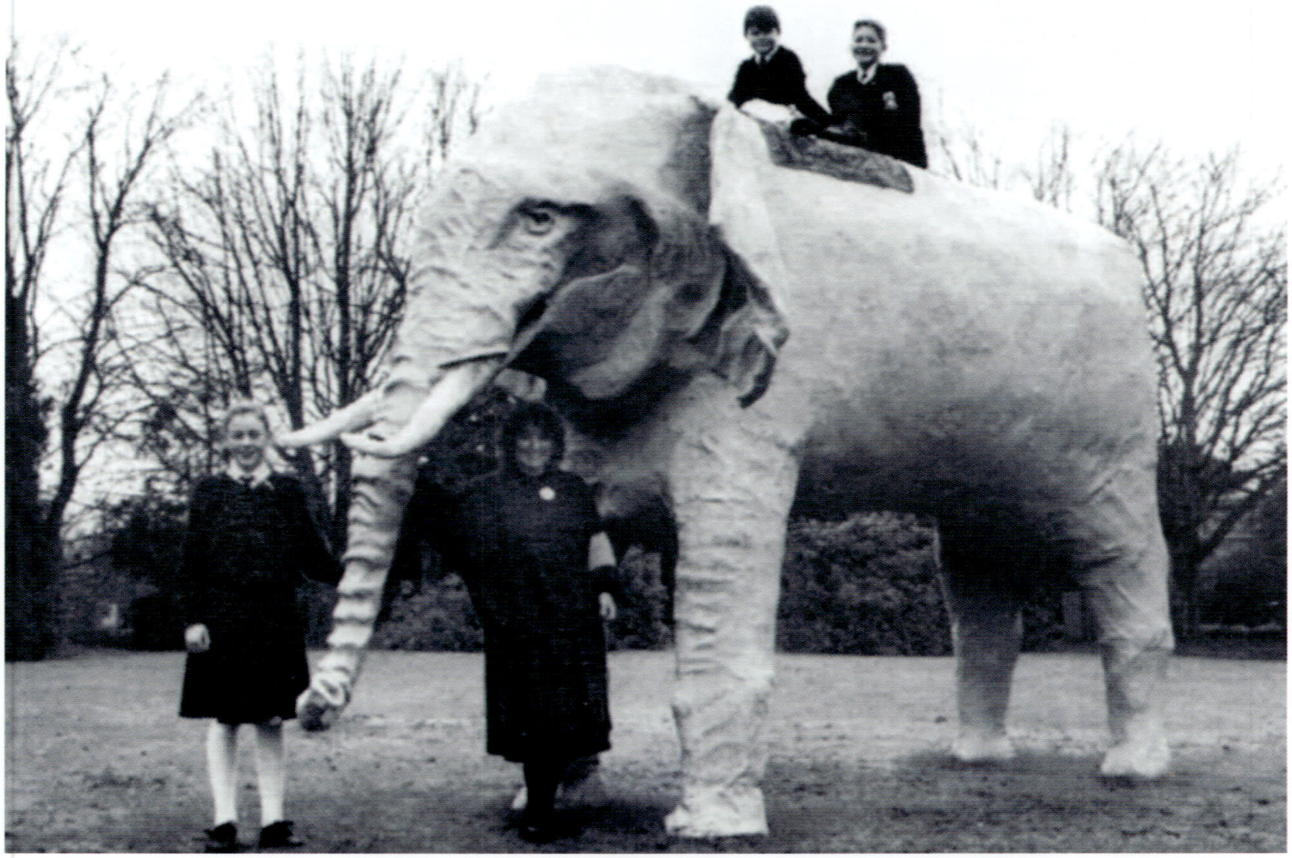

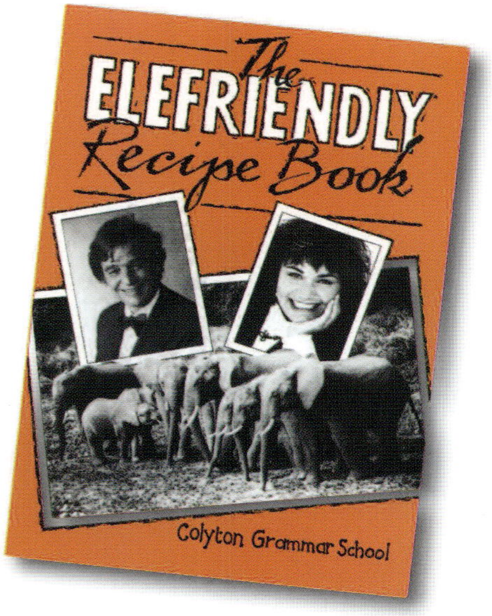

I'm joined by students of Colyton Grammar School to celebrate the publication of The Elefriendly Recipe Book *which was full of recipes provided by celebrities. The huge papier mâché elephant was designed by Philip Cox.*

The West Country Treasure Diary was a book that we produced in 1993 by students of Colyton Grammar School in support of The Devon Wildlife Trust. It was coordinated by Emma Silvester and Louise Webb plus a team of A level art students. The diary gave clues to be solved which would lead to a treasure prize. Les Baker wrote the amazing clues and Pippa Burton made the silver treasure – a decorated box housing a beautiful miniature book, sitting on a luxurious velvet cushion produced by Jean Ransford.

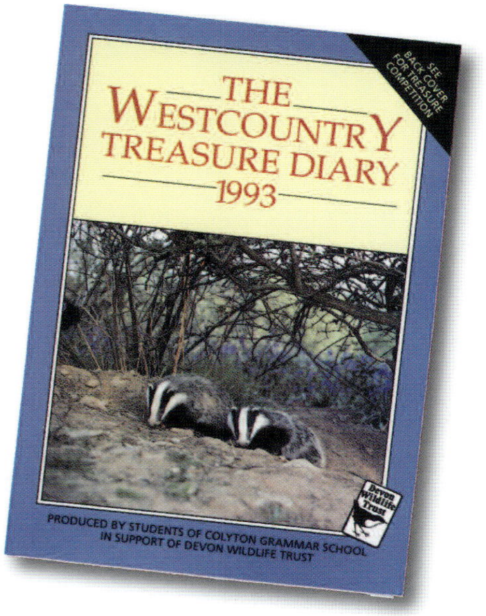

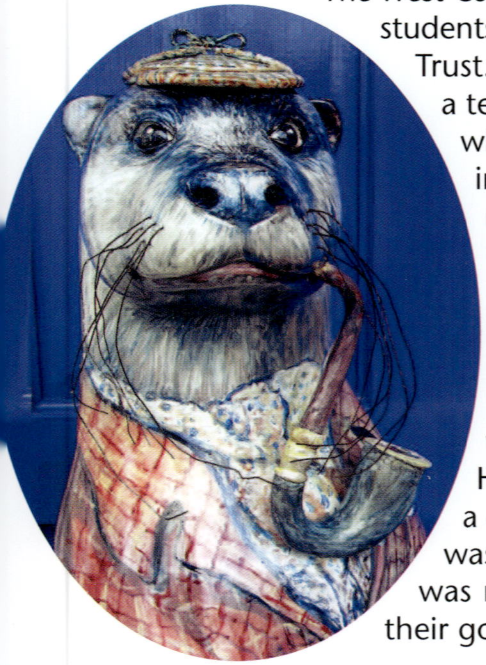

The photo on the left is one of the three otters I painted for which daughter Lolo had made the 3D additions. This one depicted the Sherlock Holmes Hound of the Baskervilles story, which was set on Dartmoor. It was auctioned at Bearnes Hampton and Littlewood in Exeter and sold to the owners of a cafe in Moretonhampstead. This particular fund-raising event was motivated by the artist, Alan Cotton. Thousands of pounds was raised for the Dartmoor National Park Authority to continue their good work in conserving and protecting the moor.

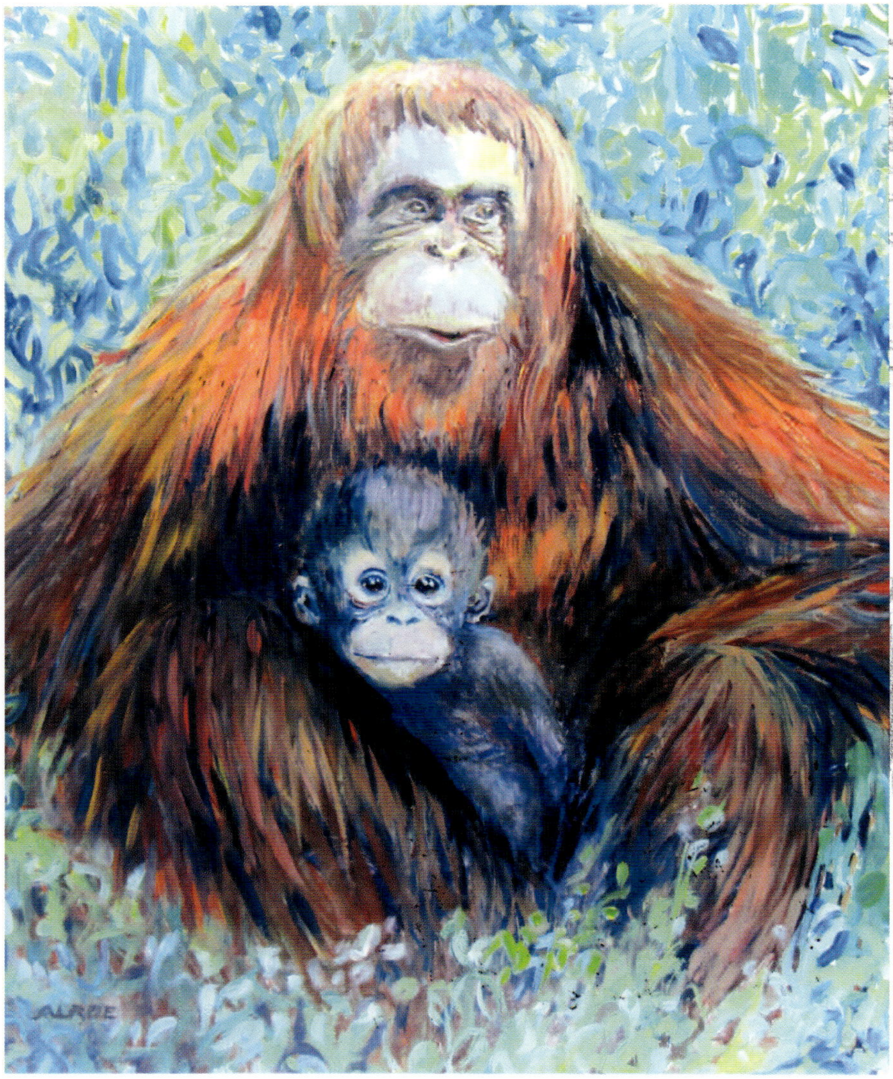

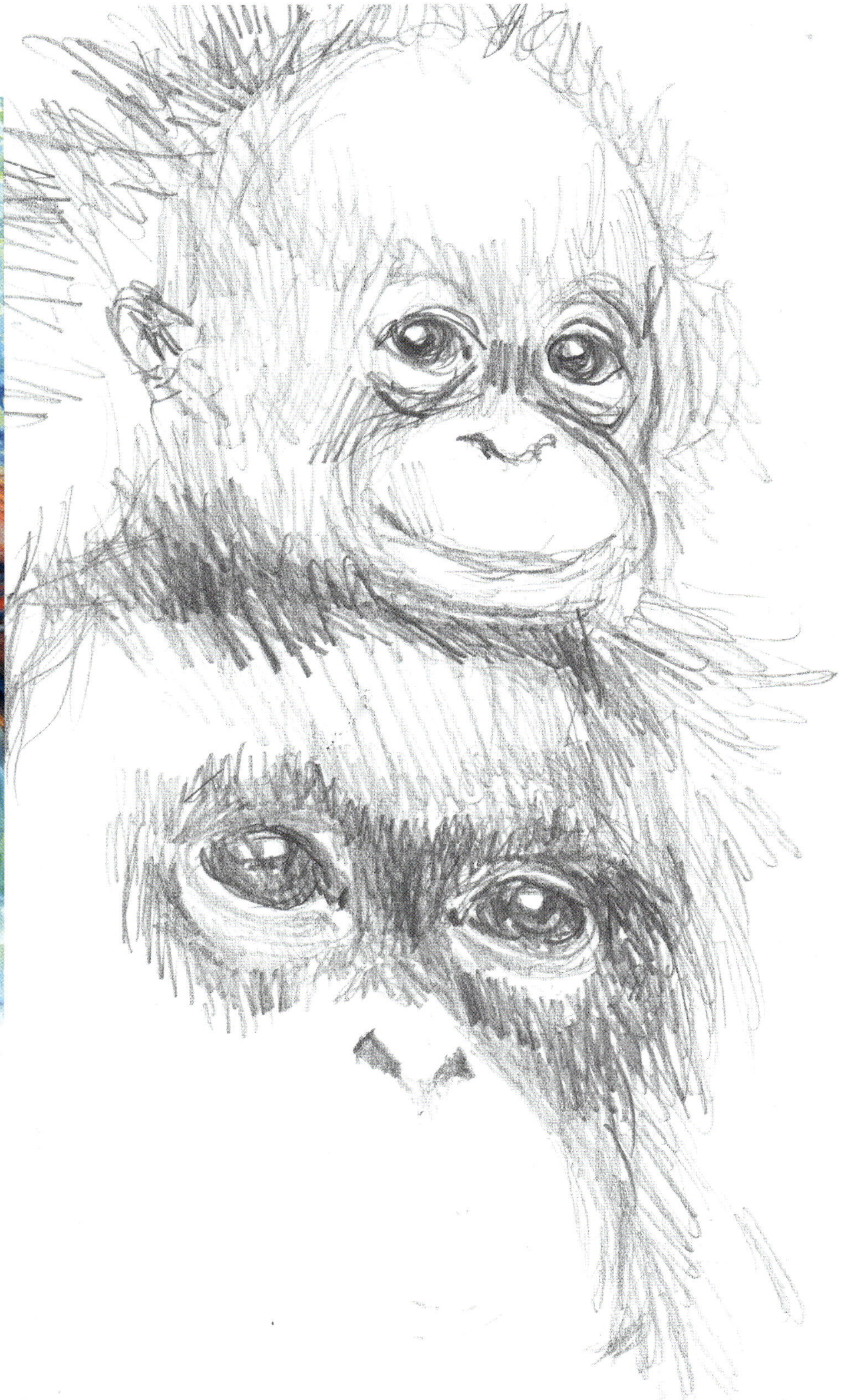

Noel Britten, a member of The Magic Circle, has devoted much of his life supporting the International Animal Rescue Centre for Orang Utans in Indonesia and I contributed this painting of a mother and baby to be sold to aid the funding of this important work. These wonderful animals have suffered much from the hand of man and the charity helps prepare these animals to be released back into protected forest areas which have been acquired for them, away from humans.

The Portraits

"I do not necessarily paint a portrait to look like the person, rather does the person become to look like their portrait."

Salvador Dali

While each artist will have their own objectives in the creation of their work, Dali's quotation at least reveals something of the dilemma faced by the portrait painter; do I create the image the sitter would like to see of themselves or as truthful a rendition as I see them? "Warts and all" as Samuel Cooper was instructed by Oliver Cromwell.

I suppose a more interesting question might be "Why portraiture?" and the answer is rather more difficult to put into words. In the pages following there is a roughly chronological selection of the people whose portraits I have been fortunate to paint. But even my earliest sketchbooks are almost entirely devoted to capturing the human form. For me it has always presented the most fascinating and challenging aspect of being an artist.

As that master of portraiture Jean-Auguste Ingres stated, "drawing is the true test of art" and certainly in my years at the Regent Street Polytechnic and later at Brighton College of Art this was fundamental to the teaching practice. As my earlier sketchbooks reveal it was capturing people on paper that was always the strongest impulse.

But my work has included all aspects of painting and examples of my landscape and still life work appear later in the book.

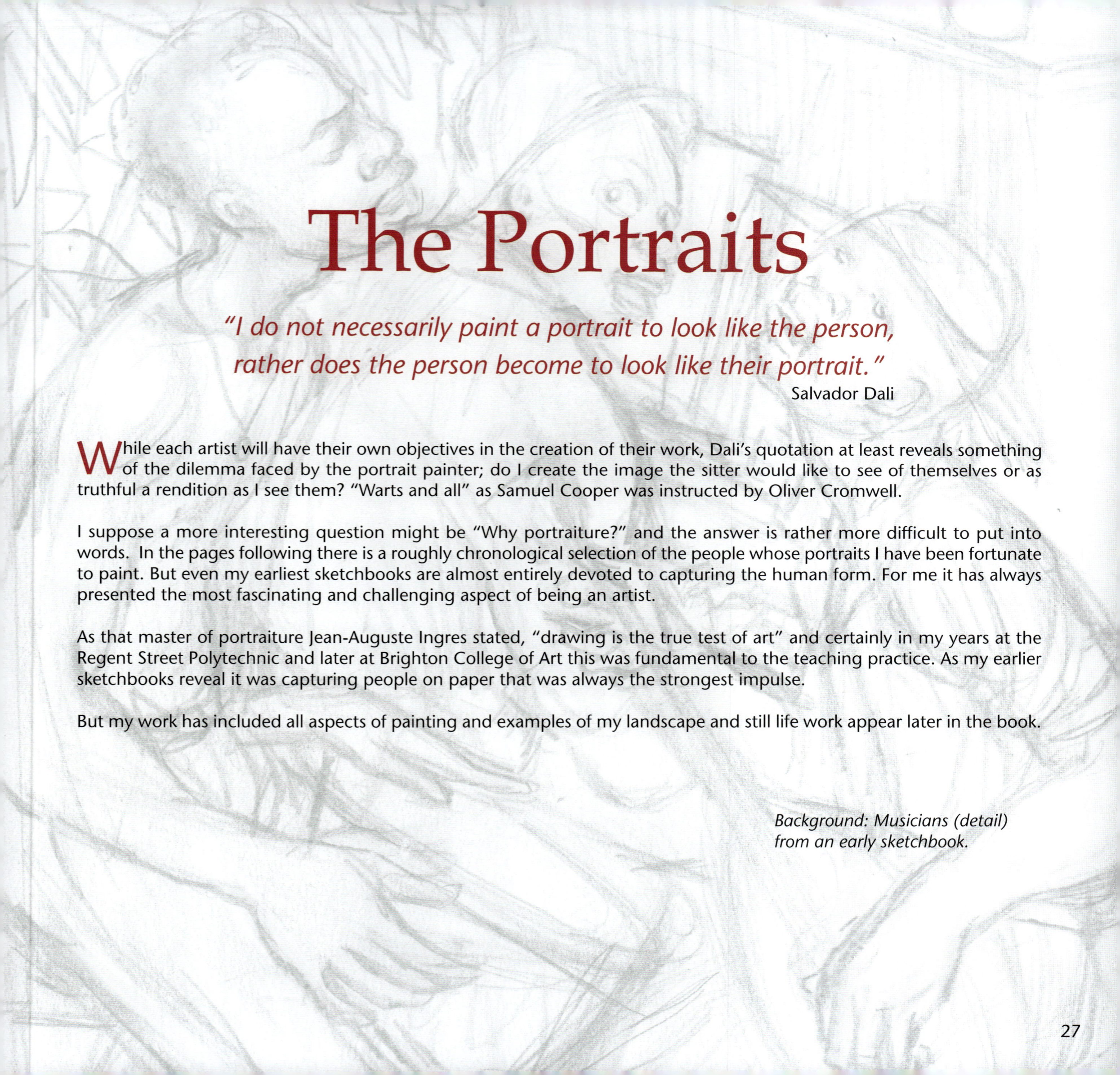

Background: Musicians (detail) from an early sketchbook.

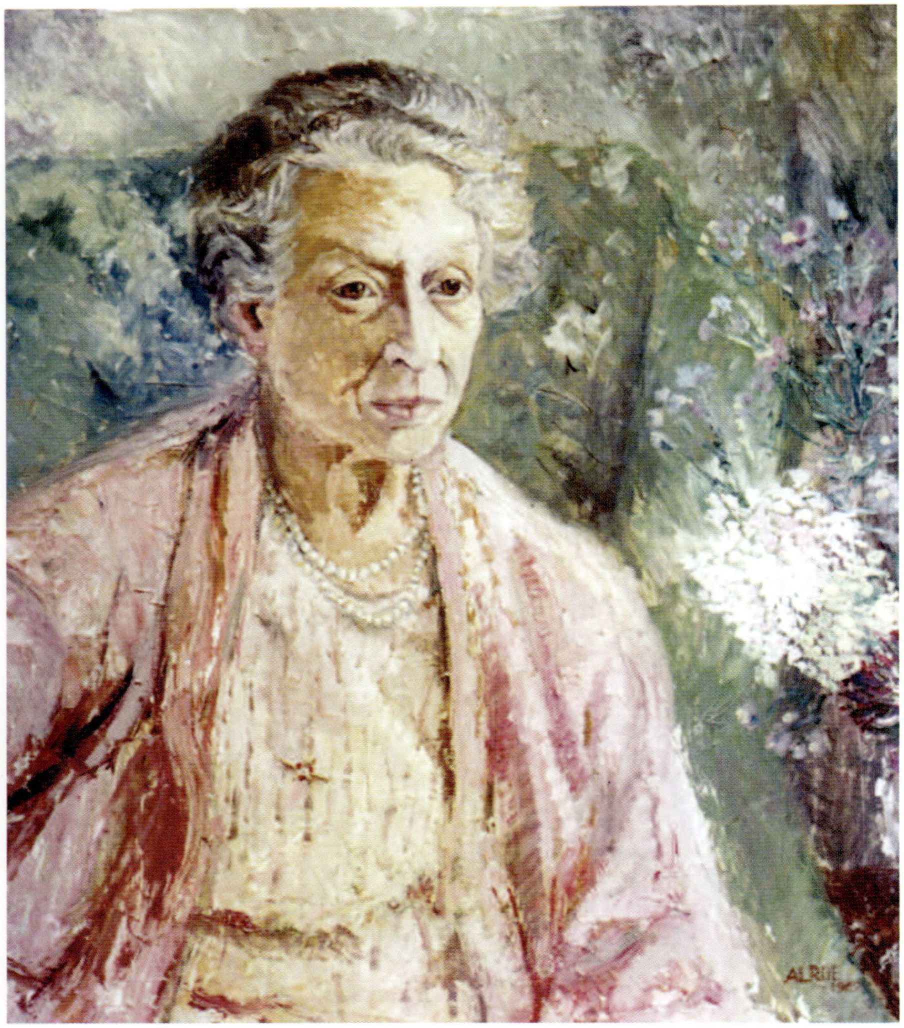

MAY SKINNER. May once told me that her husband had been related to the famous Lieutenant Colonel James Skinner, known as The Father of the Modern Indian Cavalry. We had purchased Oroolong House from this fascinating and formidable elderly lady. In her youth she had played tennis at Wimbledon, an image of her which I could never quite get out of my mind! May told us with pride of the numbers of young men who had fallen in love with her whilst she was in India.

May came over for several sittings, and always arrived bearing excellent curries and rice while we supplied her favourite drink which was whisky. We bargained over payment for this portrait which was exchanged for a sundial in the garden. On purchasing Oroolong House I bartered with May for a large carpet, coming as we did from a much smaller house.

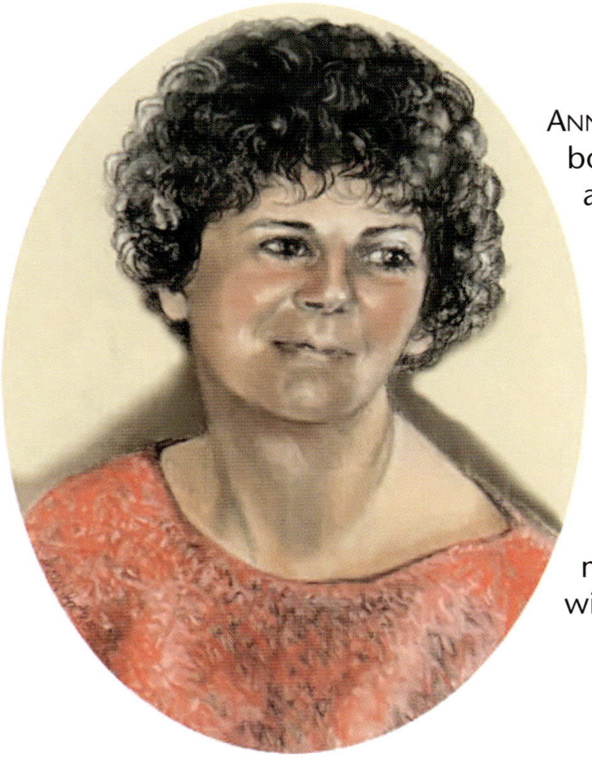

ANN AND MIKE MARSH were both colleagues of ours at Colyton Grammar School and we all retired at the same time. I have made four pastel portraits of them and their daughters. There are so many good memories of our times together and I hope for many more, but sadly without my Alan.

Mike had first attended the Grammar School as a boy, later becoming a teacher there and retiring as the school's Deputy Head. The school gave us all a good farewell retirement party including music by the school's jazz band!

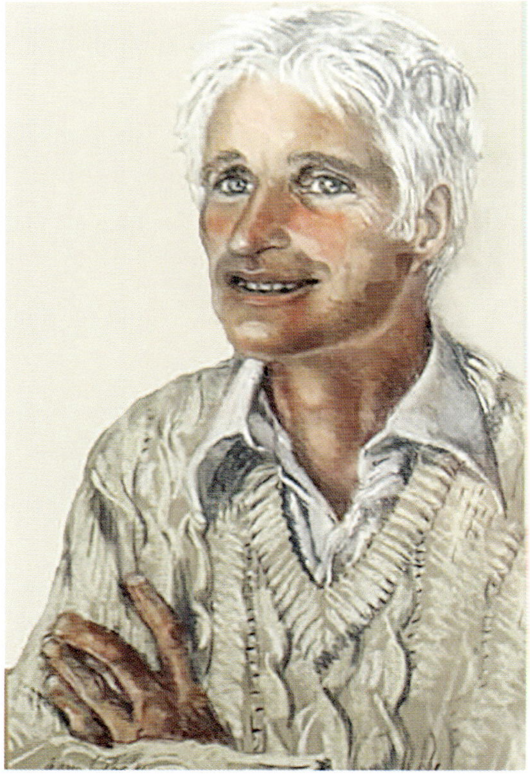

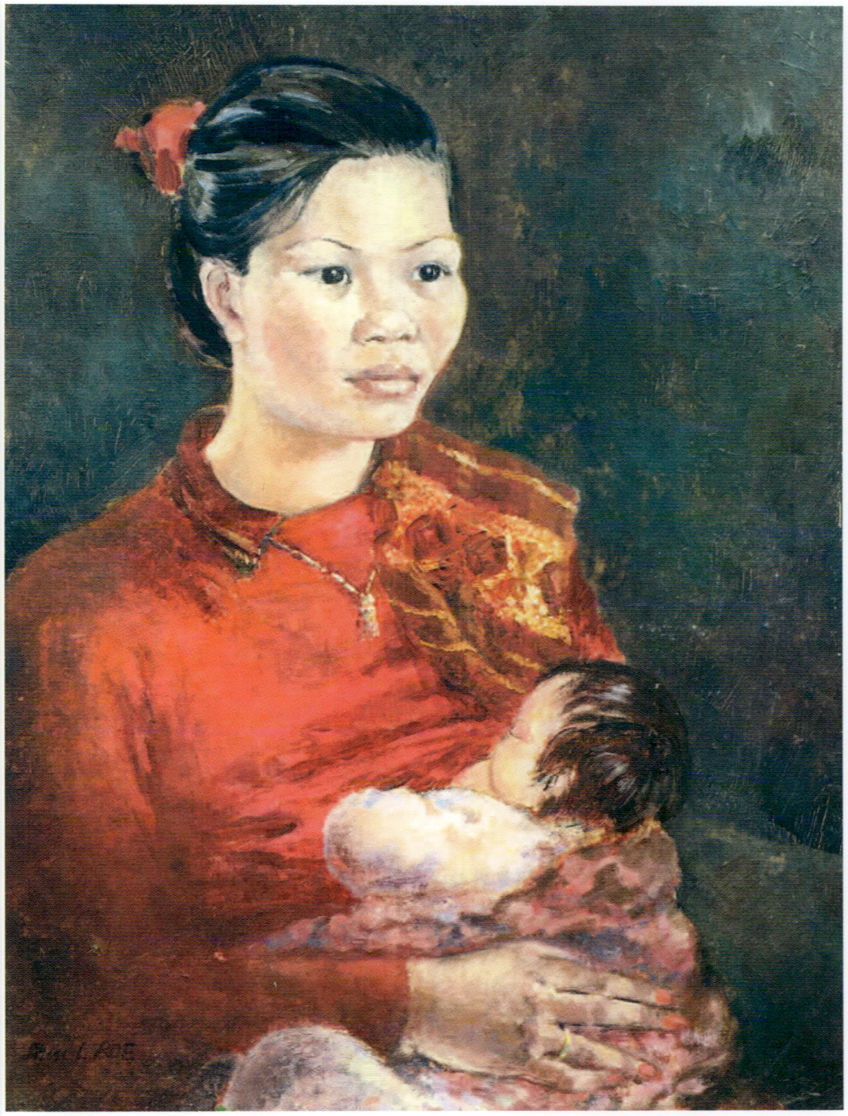

MRS VANNITHORNE. The courageous story of a Laotian artist is told through this portrait of his wife. The Laotian Civil War was waged between the years 1959–1975. Laotians who could escape the country faced dangerous journeys and awful reprisals if caught. The Vannithornes managed to escape at dead of night across the Mekong river carrying their two small children. Reaching the relative safety of neighbouring Thailand, there they were held in a refugee camp where conditions were poor.

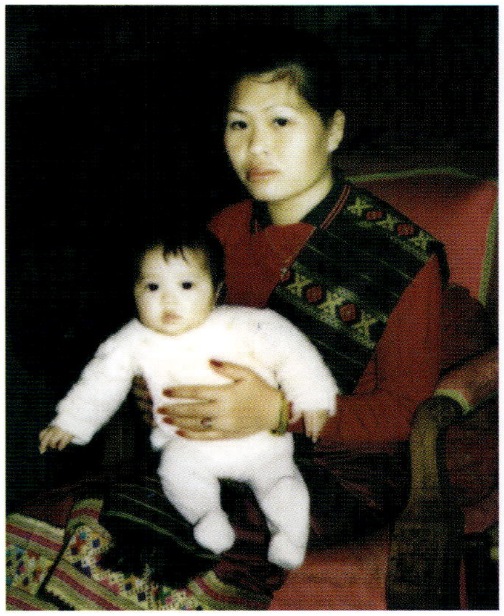

When the Vannithornes had lived in Laos they had made friends with the British Ambassador, so Suon decided to write a letter to the Ambassador in London asking for help, resulting in the family being brought to London.

Having read about their bravery and seen some of Suon's artwork in the Sunday papers, Alan and I contacted the family and just before Christmas they came to stay with us in Colyton for a few days.

I painted Mrs Vannithorne and her small baby. I also painted another of her children. Patrick Larkin, an artist friend, came to visit and he too painted the family. They were all very charming and had never seen a Christmas tree before. This fascinated their little boy who tried to eat one of the glass baubles, but fortunately I managed to get it from him before any disaster happened.

The follow up to this story is that the Vannithornes now own a restaurant in Hythe, Kent, and after sending them a letter, they have recently contacted me and and I am hoping to receive a further update about their lives in the UK. Suon told me that he was still painting, although not every day now. I am looking forward to the chance of meeting this amazing family once again.

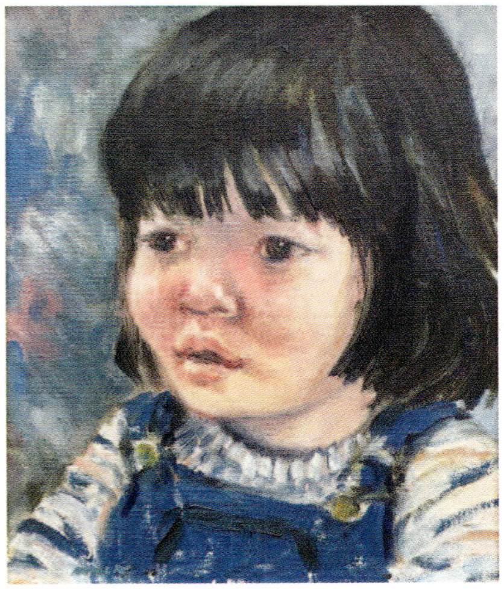

Top left: Mrs Vannithorne with her baby, painted in our Devon home at Christmas.

Top right: A Polaroid photo taken during the family visit.

Right: The Vannithorne's elder daughter.

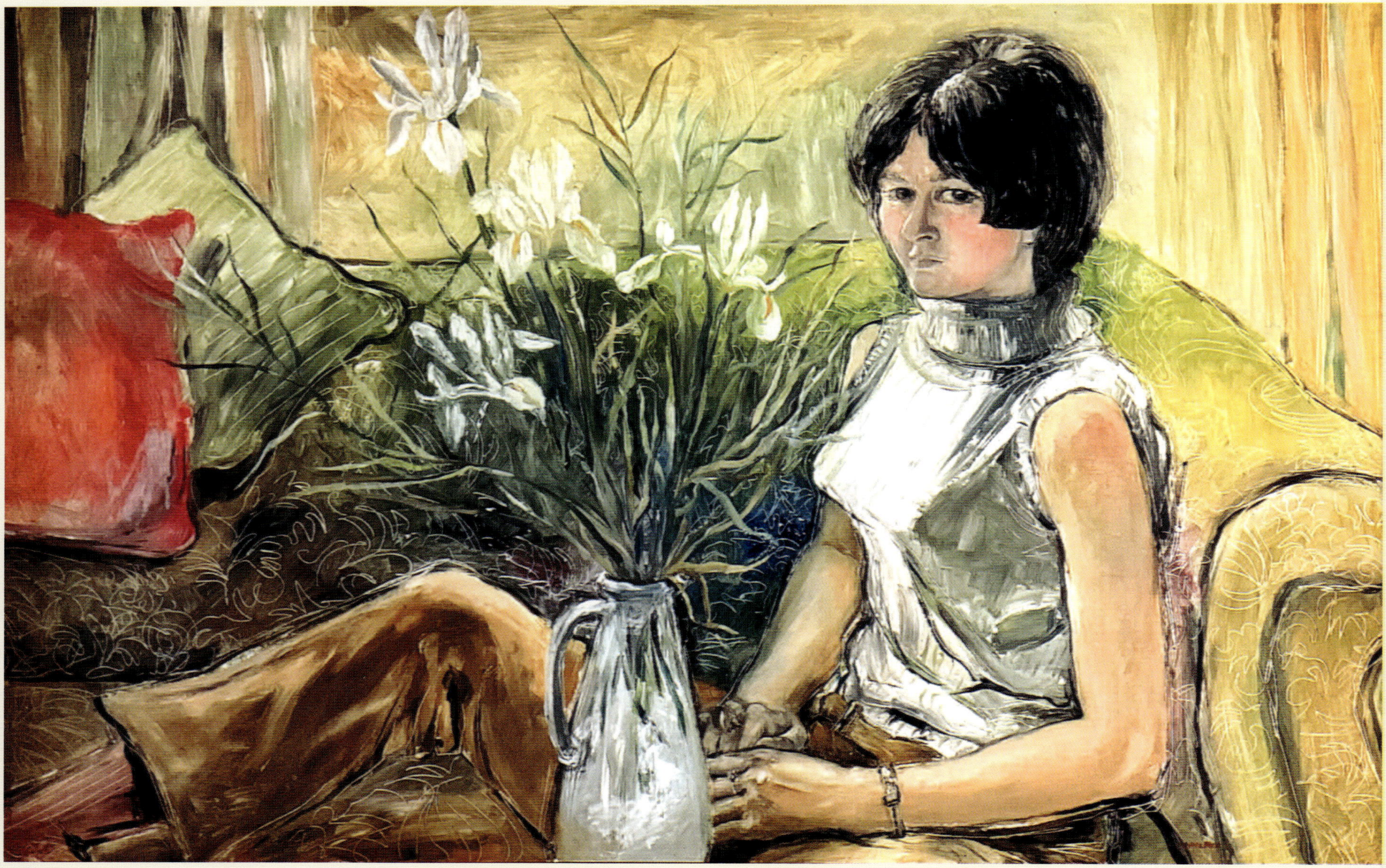

GLENDA BOARD was in the sixth form at Colyton Grammar School. She babysat for my children, Adrian and Lolo when they were young. Glenda married Dougie Board, a builder, whose family have contributed so much to the improvement of buildings in Colyton, including Oroolong House and the Kingfisher Pub. Following the successful fund-raising for the Elefriendly charity at the school, the Board family looked after the papier mâché elephant (for which Dougie built the frame) in one of their fields, allowing other charity events to follow. I have painted Glenda and many of her amazing family members over the years.

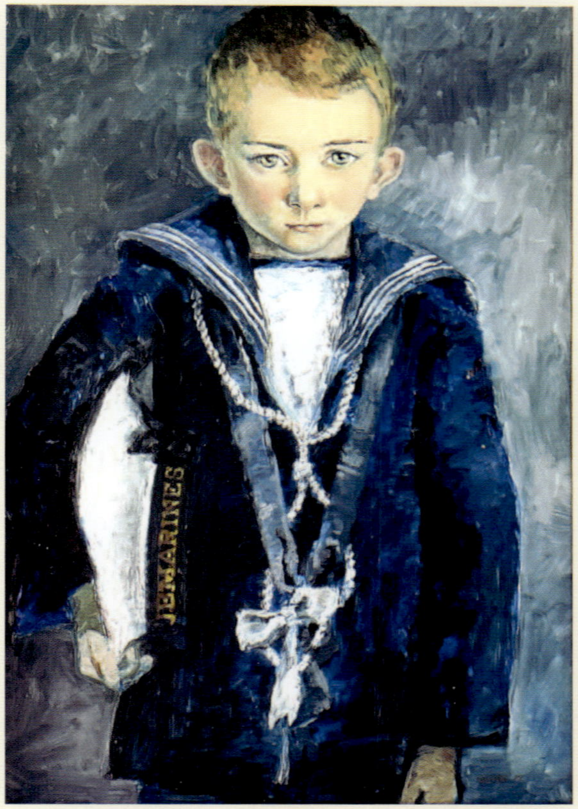

Reuben Board, Glenda's youngest son.

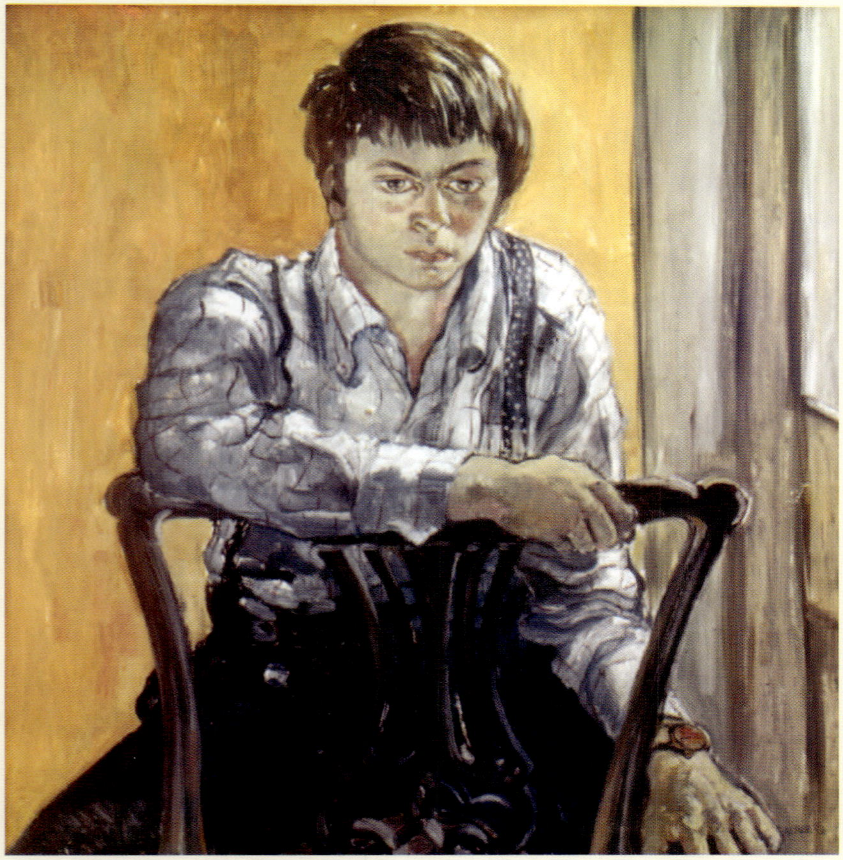

Glenda's brother, Ronnie.

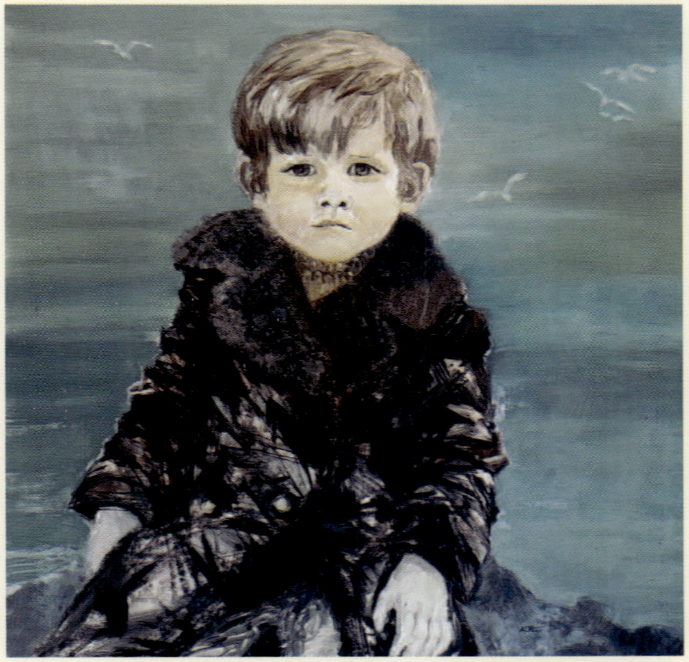

Lee, Glenda's eldest son.

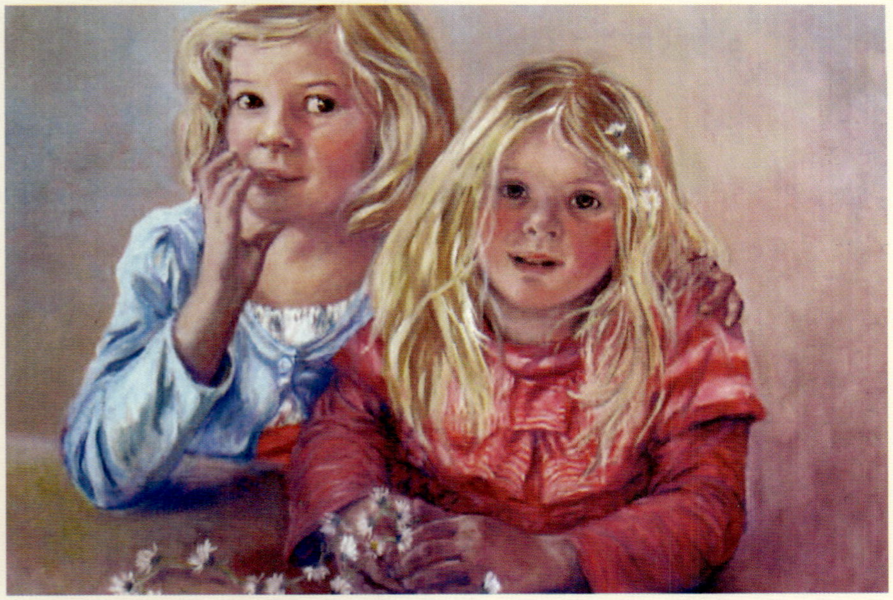

Glenda's sisters Paulette and Joanne.

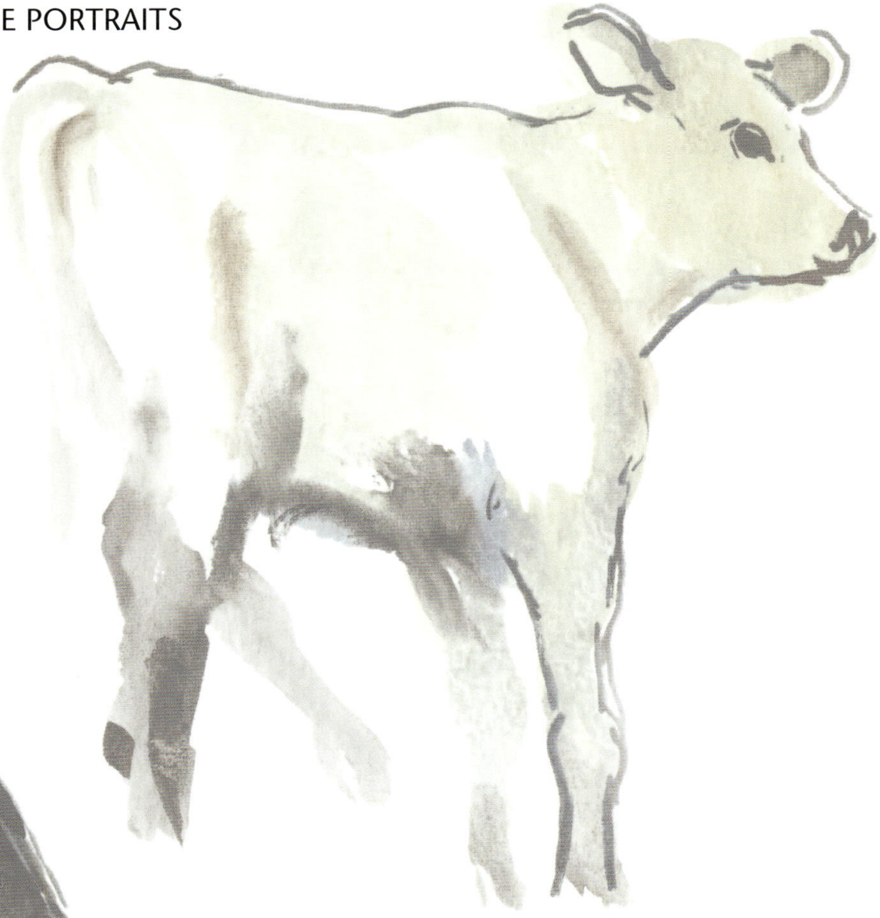

THE PADY FAMILY. Colin Pady was a keen landowner and conservationist of much of our unspoilt and beautiful East Devon farming countryside. The Padys were a remarkably talented musical family and I painted a number of their portraits. Sadly Colin died in November 2024.

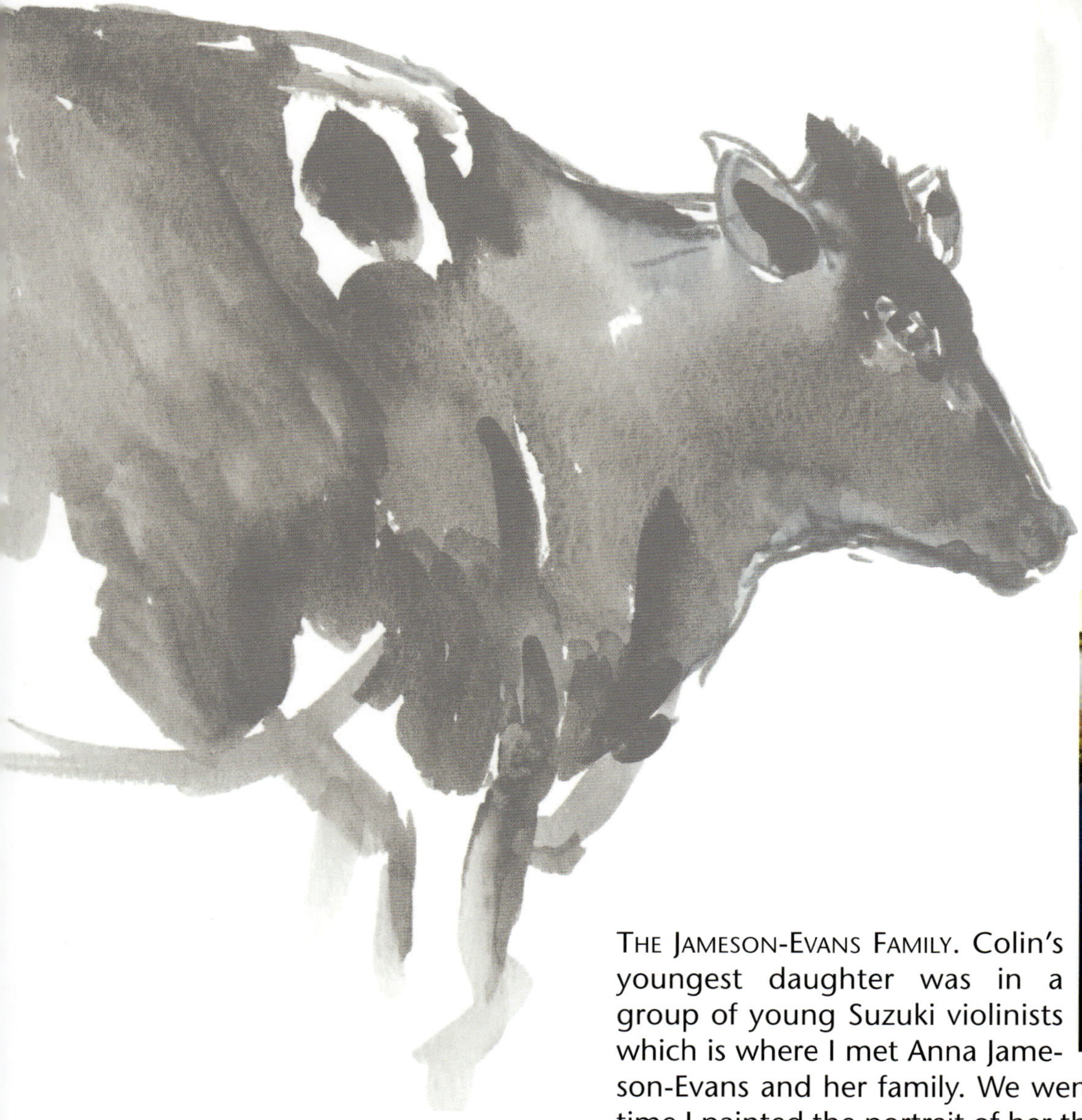

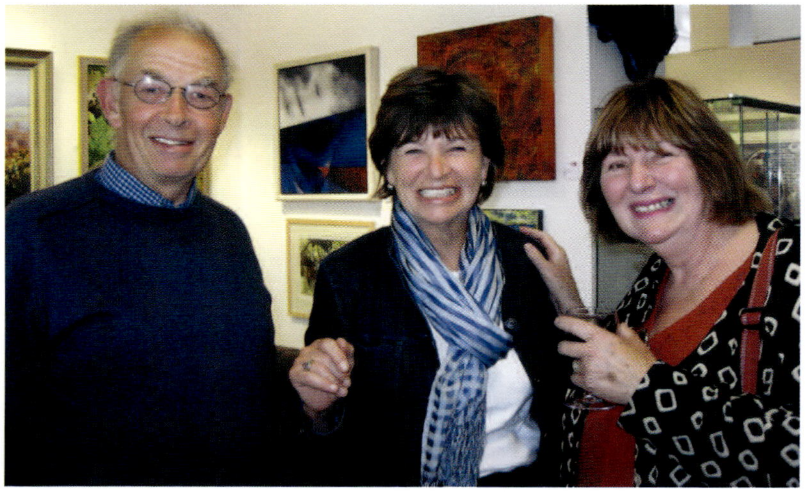

THE JAMESON-EVANS FAMILY. Colin's youngest daughter was in a group of young Suzuki violinists which is where I met Anna Jameson-Evans and her family. We went on a Suzuki course together in Cork and around that time I painted the portrait of her three children playing their instruments (shown opposite). They were a delightful family. Their father was an ortho-paediatrician and always said he could fix my arthritic knees! Somehow we never got around to it and now I am too old!

Background: watercolour sketches of cattle in the Devon countryside.

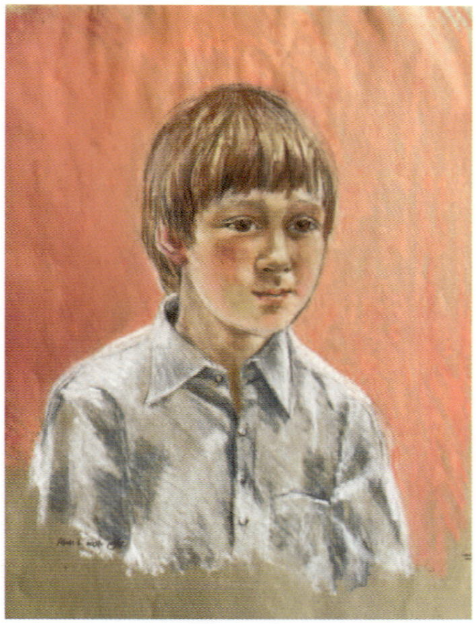

Robert Pady.

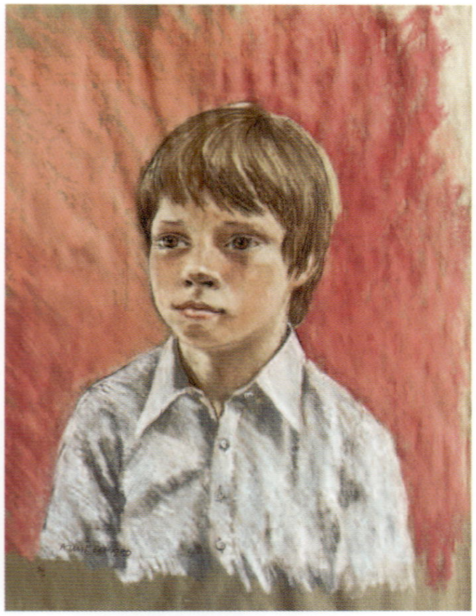

Julian Pady.

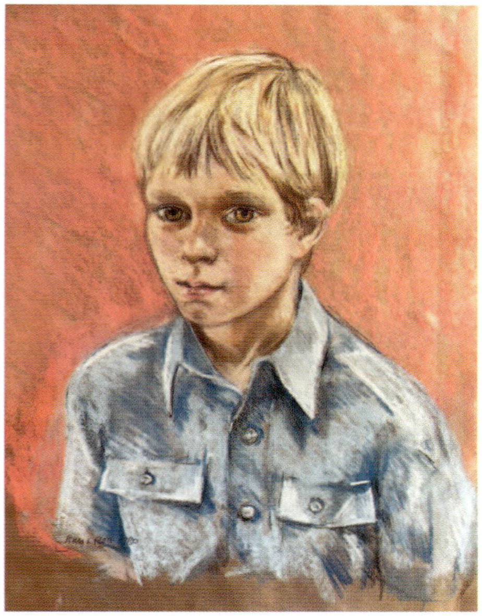

Crispin Pady.

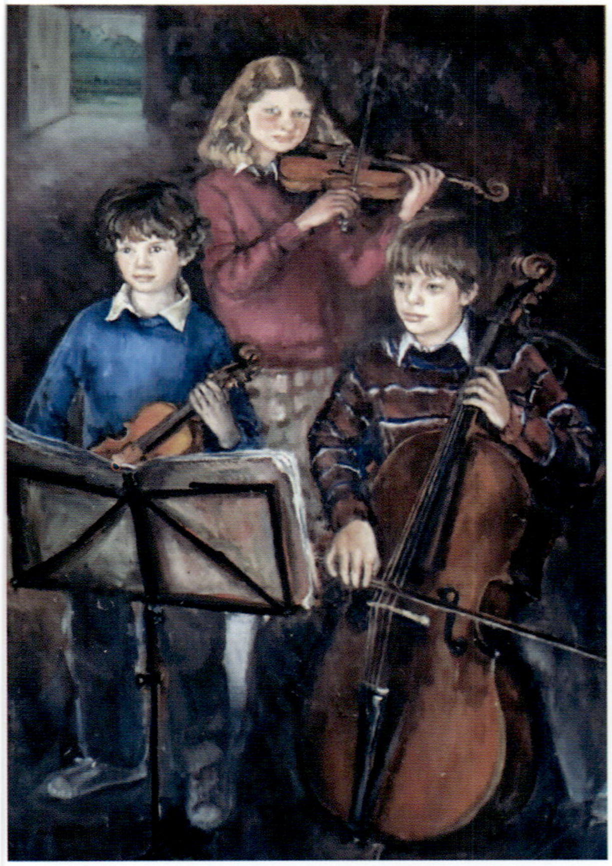

The Jameson-Evans children.

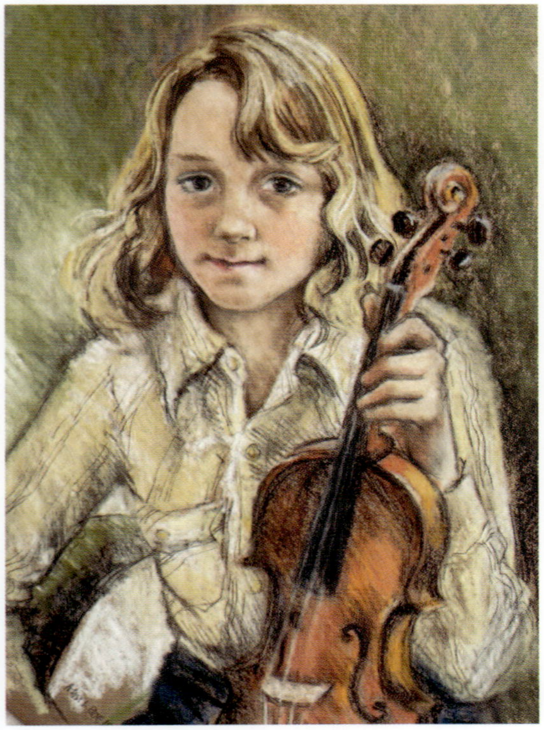

Tamsin Pady.

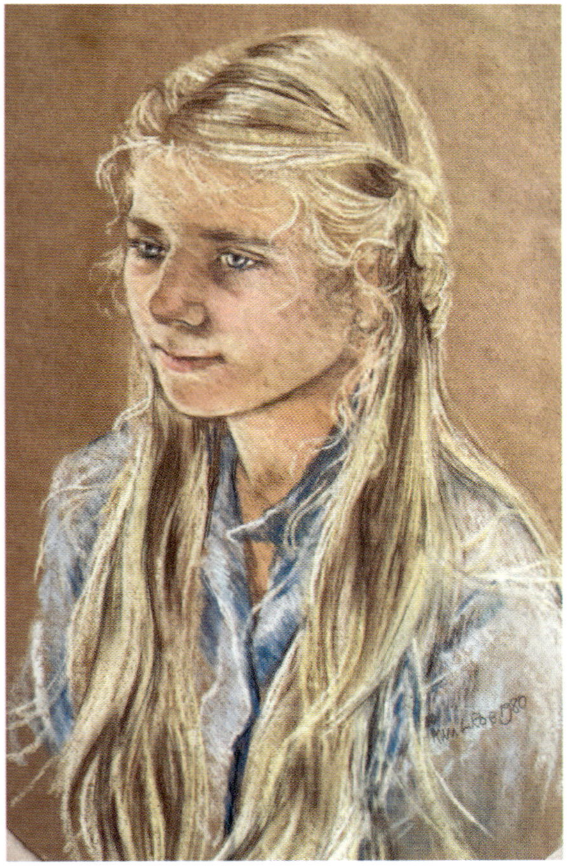

Debbie Pady.

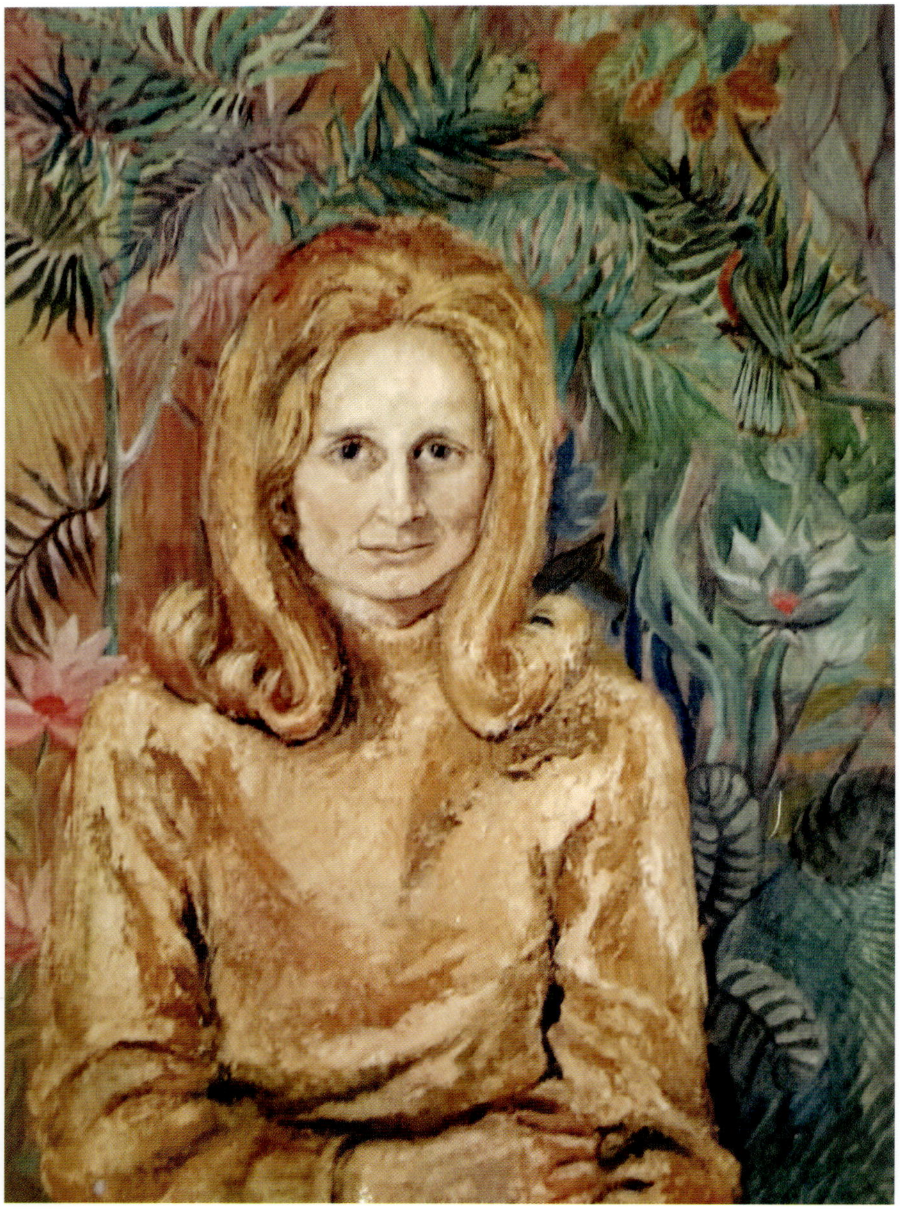

JANE GODBEER (left) and David Shaw were two vets who visited regularly to attend to our numerous animals. From 'Penguin', a borrowed horse who came to stay one winter, to 'Willy Grout', a pet pink pig rescued by Adrian when he worked on a farm one summer holiday. We also had many dogs, a cat, rabbits, a guinea pig and birds (the birds mainly for Alan's magic shows). Jane's was one of my earlier portraits made when I moved to Devon. I suggested a well-respected framer in Kensington and Jane's husband told me that, in the end, the frame was more expensive than the painting!. Jane thought the portrait was in my 'Gauguin' phase!

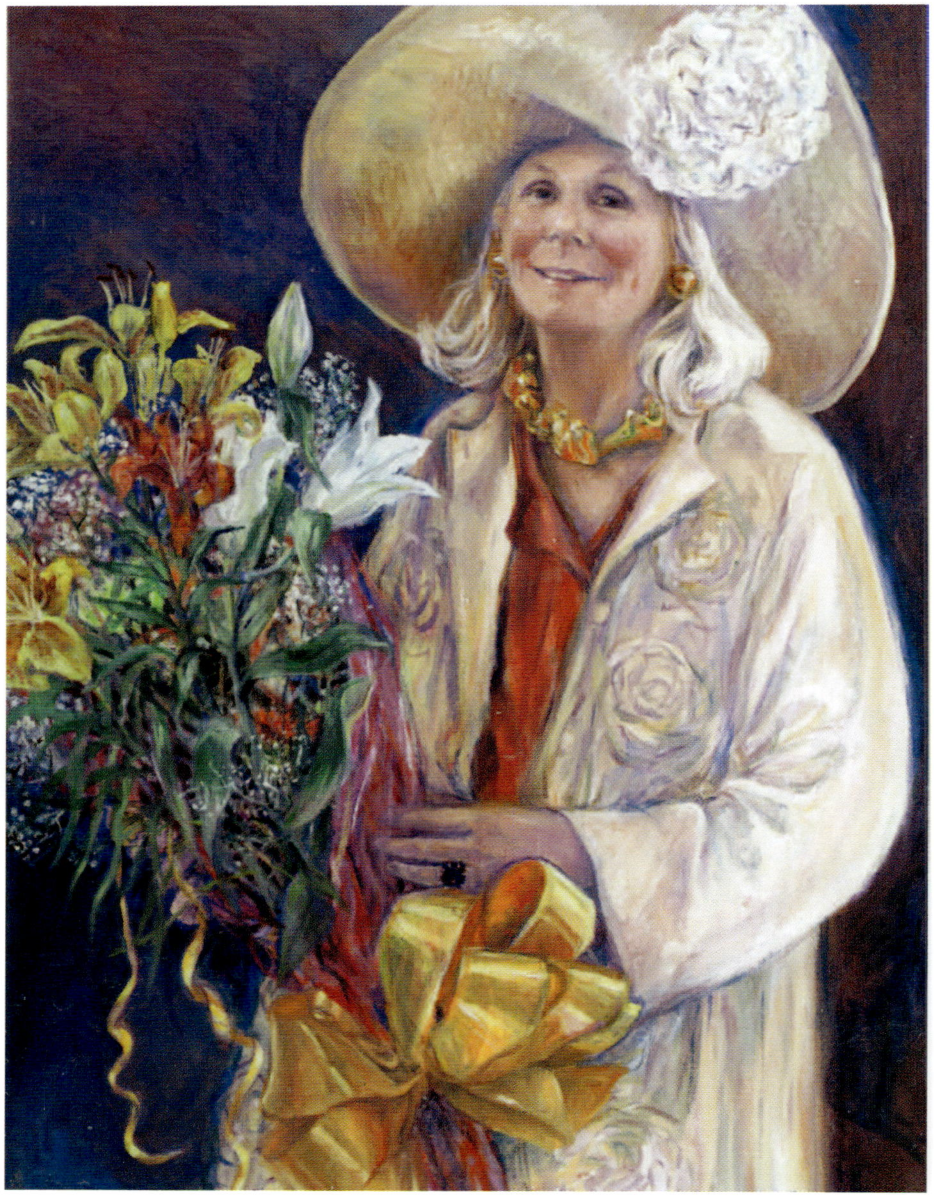

SALLY SEDGMAN (right) calls herself the 'Lady Who Lunches'! I painted two portraits of this effervescent lady who is an excellent speaker and broadcaster as she showed when opening one of the South West Academy's exhibitions. Sally is also well known for wearing wonderfully flamboyant hats and in both my portraits she is shown wearing examples of her 'trademark' headgear.

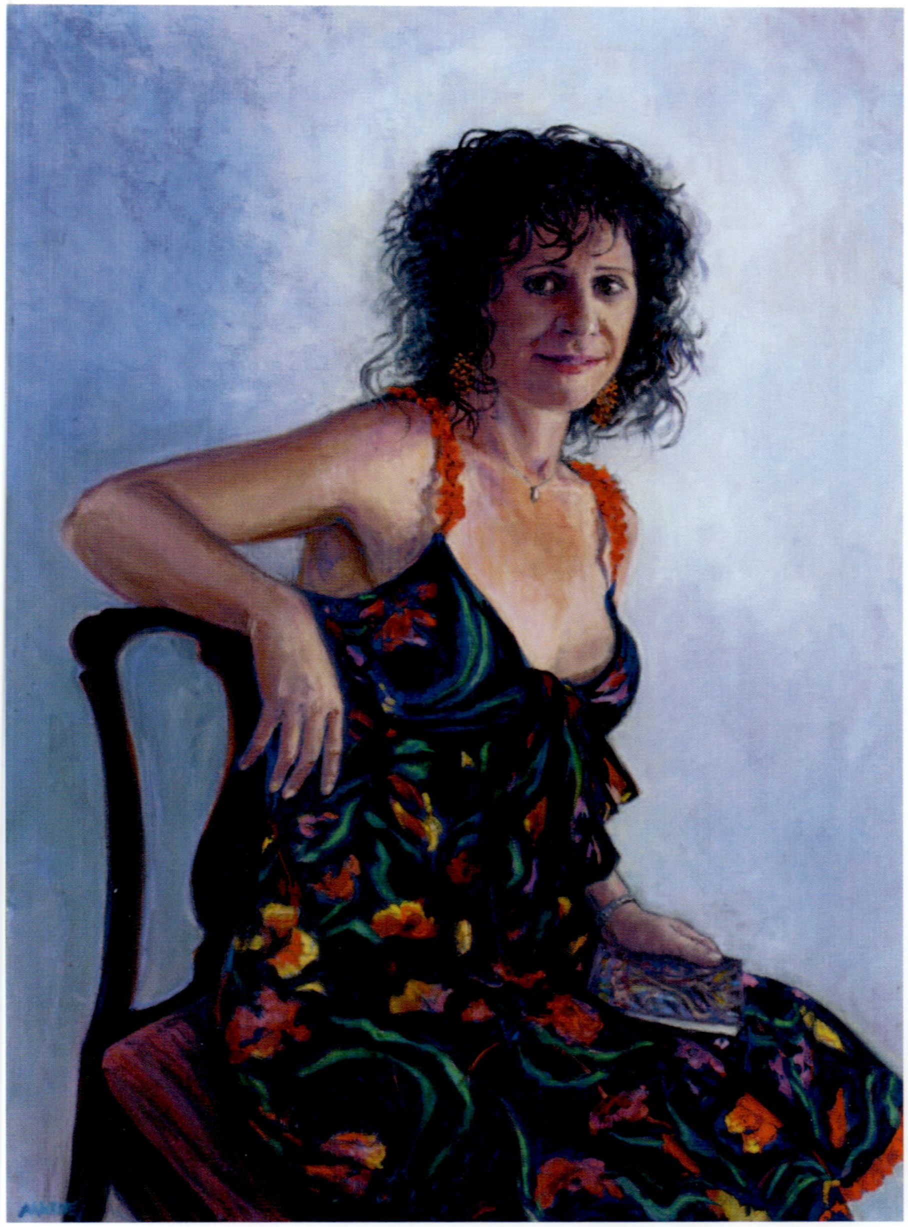

Left: A dancer who sat for me.

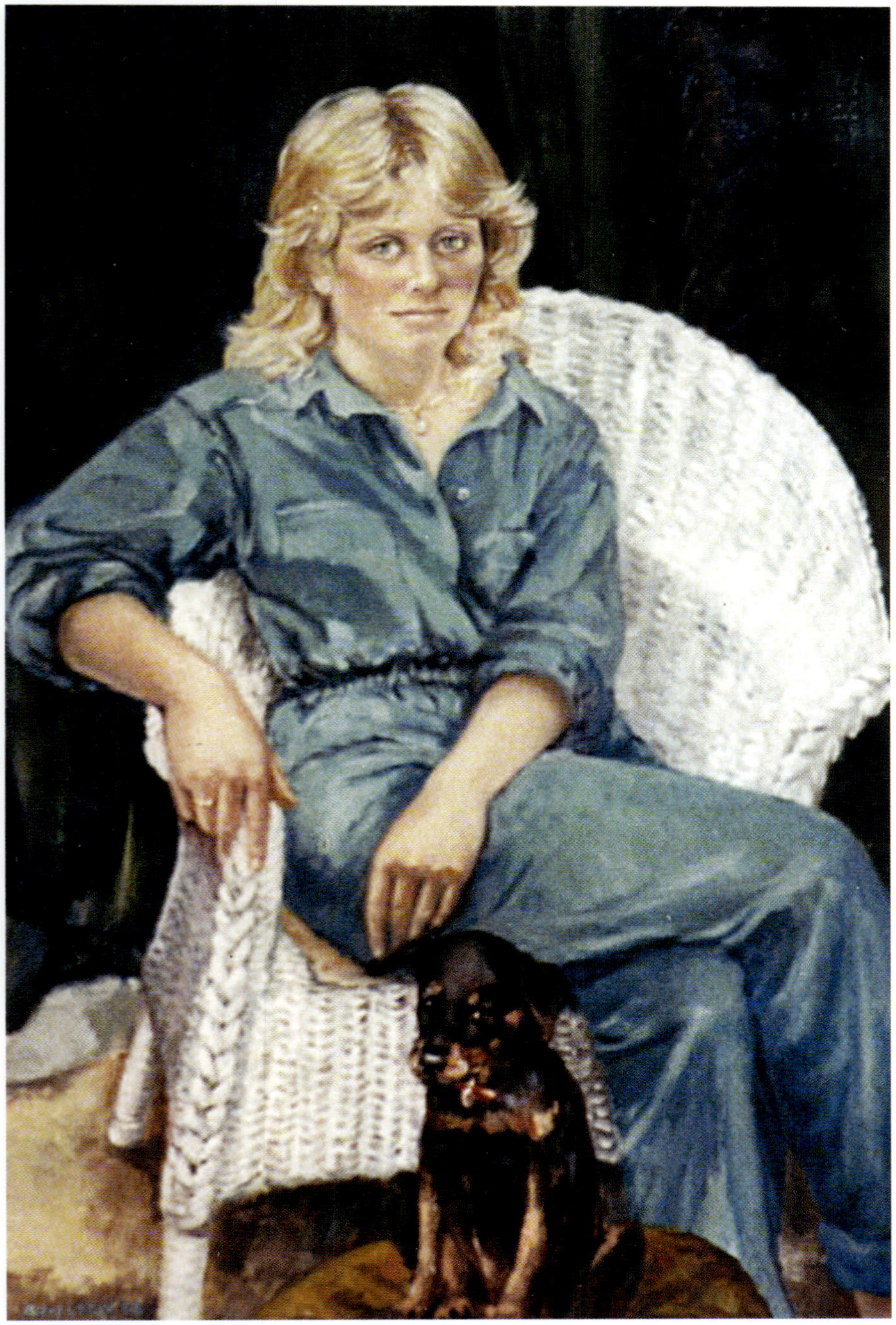

Right: Laurie Keeler with her close companion.

KARIMA ZITOUNI came from Paris and stayed with us to improve her English. She was a beautiful girl from a French mother and North African father. She was very happy to pose for me and I completed two paintings, one of which was sold in France when I was working as a portrait artist at an annual event in Normandy.

The Foire de Caen celebrated links between Devon and Normandy. Alan also attended and performed magic shows all in French. He had just two months to prepare his acts in French and he performed them brilliantly!

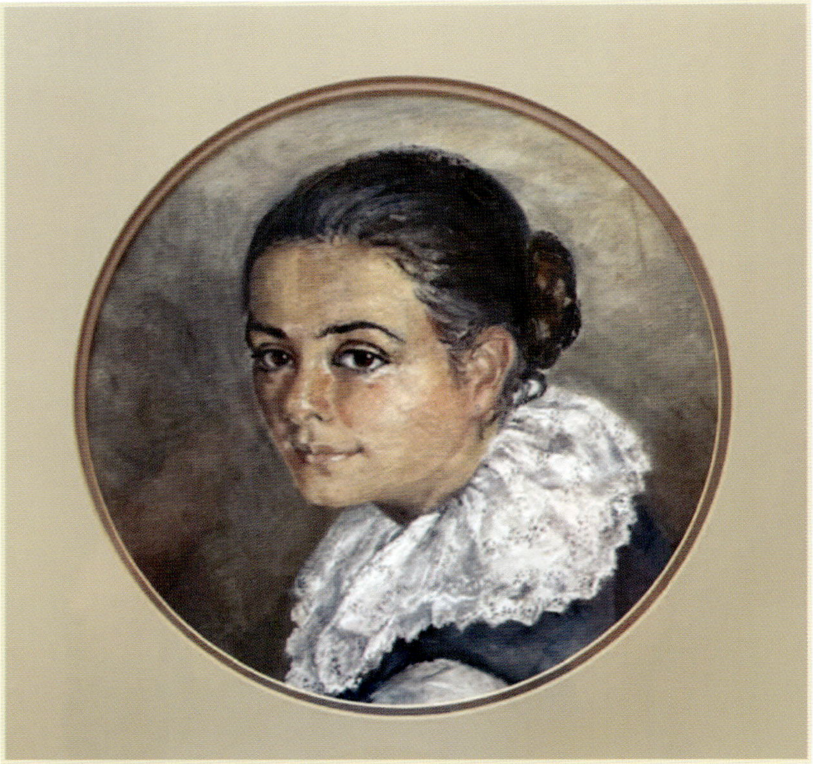

My part at the Foire was representing Devon through art which involved my painting instant portraits of those attending. The pictures then formed part of an exhibition of work open to visitors and offered for sale.

The second portrait I painted of Karima, showing her brushing her long hair and looking in a mirror, was sold at the Foire. We last met up with her in America near to Boston where she was studying at University and Alan and I were able to take her out to lunch.

Left: My portrait of Karima.

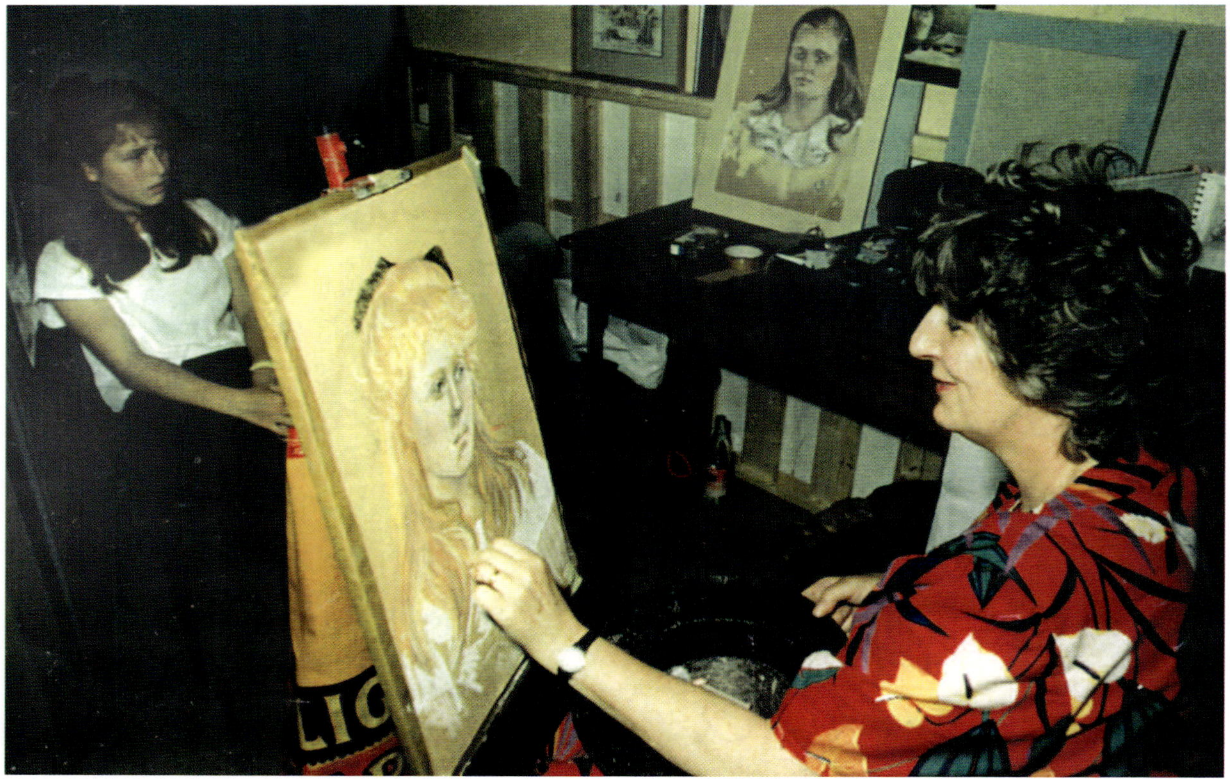

Here I'm painting an inpromptu portrait at the Foire de Caen.

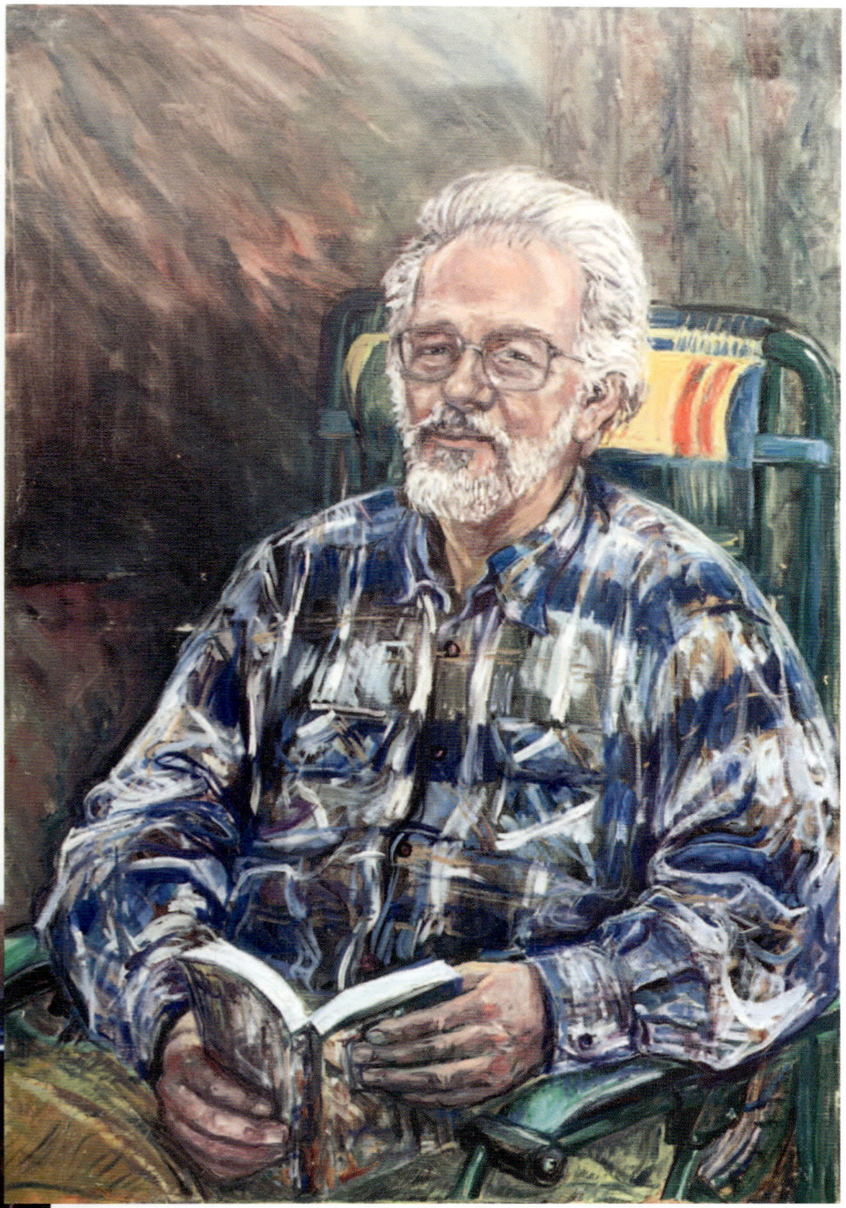

Tristan's finished portrait.

Tristan de Vere Cole was a TV director (now retired from TV programming). He produced programmes such as Z Cars and Dr Who. I met him when my Italian sculpture friend, Fiore, died and Tristan spoke about her at her memorial service. We met again later at the Chelsea Arts Club where we, plus others, all had dinner together. Opposite me at the table was Henry Moore's daughter, who had a shop, I think, nearby in Kings Road.

Tristan sat for me when he came down to visit us. He always introduced himself as "Augustus John's bastard son"!

Zoe Hicks, an actress and sister of Tristan (and another offspring of Augustus John), came down to Exeter to perform in a play and later gave a talk in our studio to a packed audience. Zoe spoke of a day she spent posing for her father. She was an excellent speaker. Strangely she arrived at our front door with no shoes on, saying that she could not find them! She then crossed from our house to my studio over wet grass and sharp gravel but took it all, literally, in her stride!

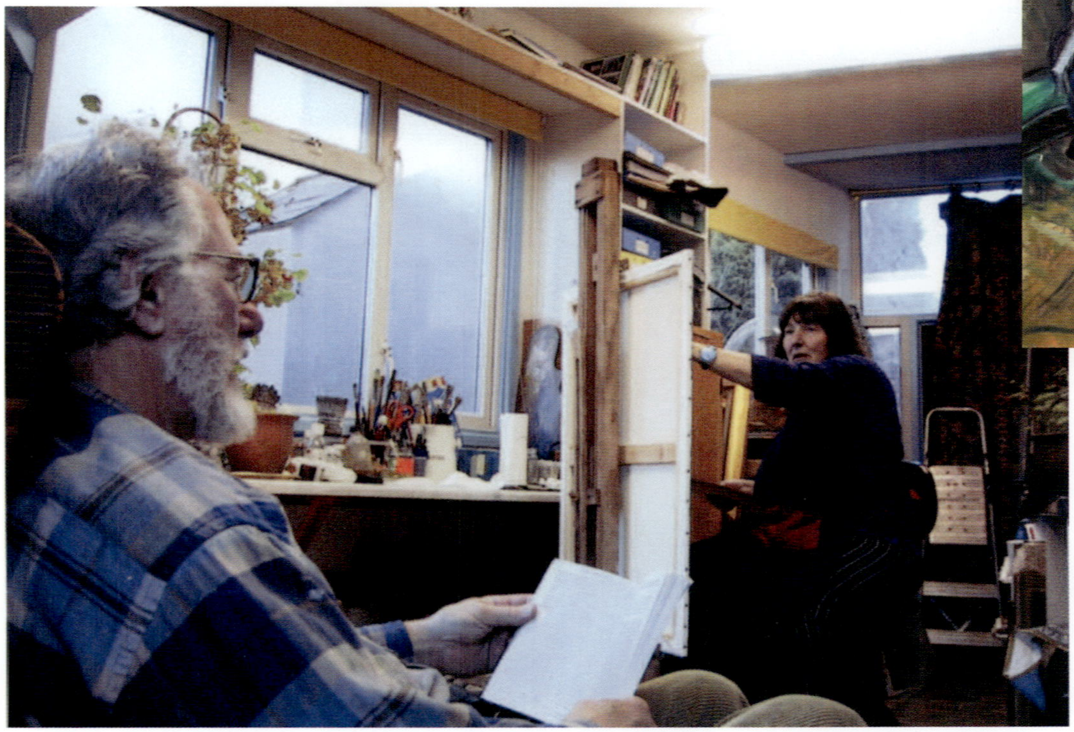

Tristan reads a book while I work at the easel in my Colyton studio.

A CHANCE MEETING: THE CHELSEA PENSIONERS

London is a city full of so much of everything, it became an utter joy for us to visit from time to time, living as we do in a peaceful part of Devon. We were wandering around Peter Jones in Sloane Square one day in 2008 and Alan called out "I recognise that stable belt". This is how we first met Bob Toplis, a retired Royal Army Medical Corps soldier as Alan had also been, but Bob was now a Chelsea Pensioner. We became firm friends and this is how I came to paint three of the pensioners, Bob, Michael Allen and Fred Bland in their glorious red uniforms. Bob and Michael came and stayed with us in Devon (Fred was abroad at the time).

My portrait was exhibited in the Royal Clarence Hotel in a South West Academy Exhibition and after the launch we took Michael and Bob for lunch in the restaurant run by Chef Michael Caines. It was a great event, and our two guests looked magnificent in their red outfits and tricorn hats, which they had to get special permission to wear as generally it was only for occasions involving royalty! We were honoured.

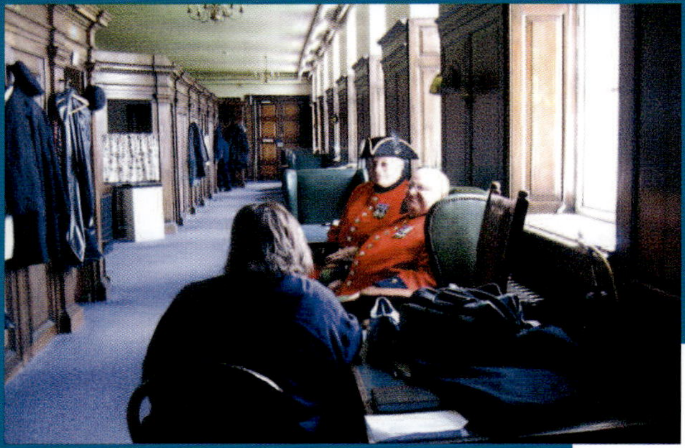

Left: At the Royal Chelsea Hospital working up preliminary sketches of Michael and Bob.

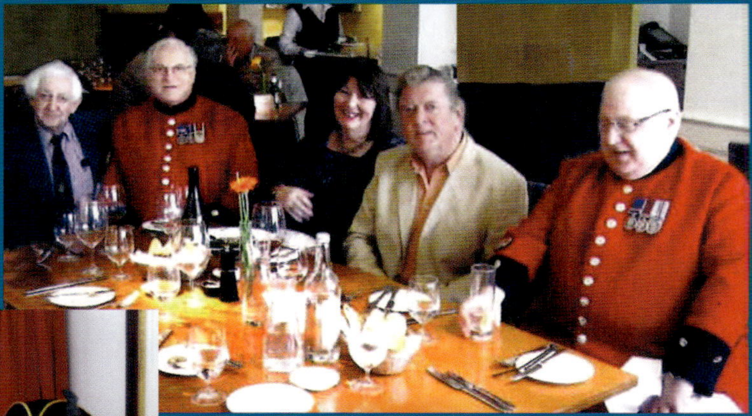

Above: Lunch at the Royal Clarence Hotel in Exeter with l-r: Alan Jones, Michael Allen, myself, fellow artist Alan Cortton and Bob Toplis.

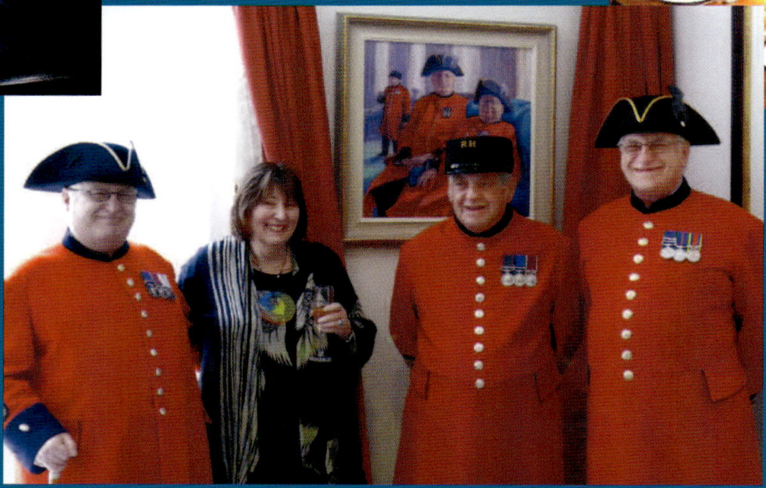

Right: Unveiling my portrait of Bob, Fred and Michael at the Royal Chelsea Hospital in 2009.

Opposite: The finished portrait of (l-r) Fred, Michael and Bob.

Alan and I were invited to various events at the hospital, one being when Princess Alexandra came for Founders Day, she was charming. Later in the day we had lunch at the little tables on the lawn when suddenly, to our surprise, belly dancers in colourful outfits were gyrating around the tables to the great delight of the pensioners. At that time there were only one or two women pensioners, things may have changed now?! We were also invited to the Chelsea Flower Show the day before it was open to the public. It was a busy day as all the exhibitors were putting their final touches to their exhibits. A marvellous experience. My painting was unveiled by the Governor of the Royal Hospital, Chelsea, General the Lord Walker. He was a charming fellow, surrounded by Brigadiers.

Michael Allen's humorous hospital Christmas Cards are always the first to arrive each year. Thank you Michael.

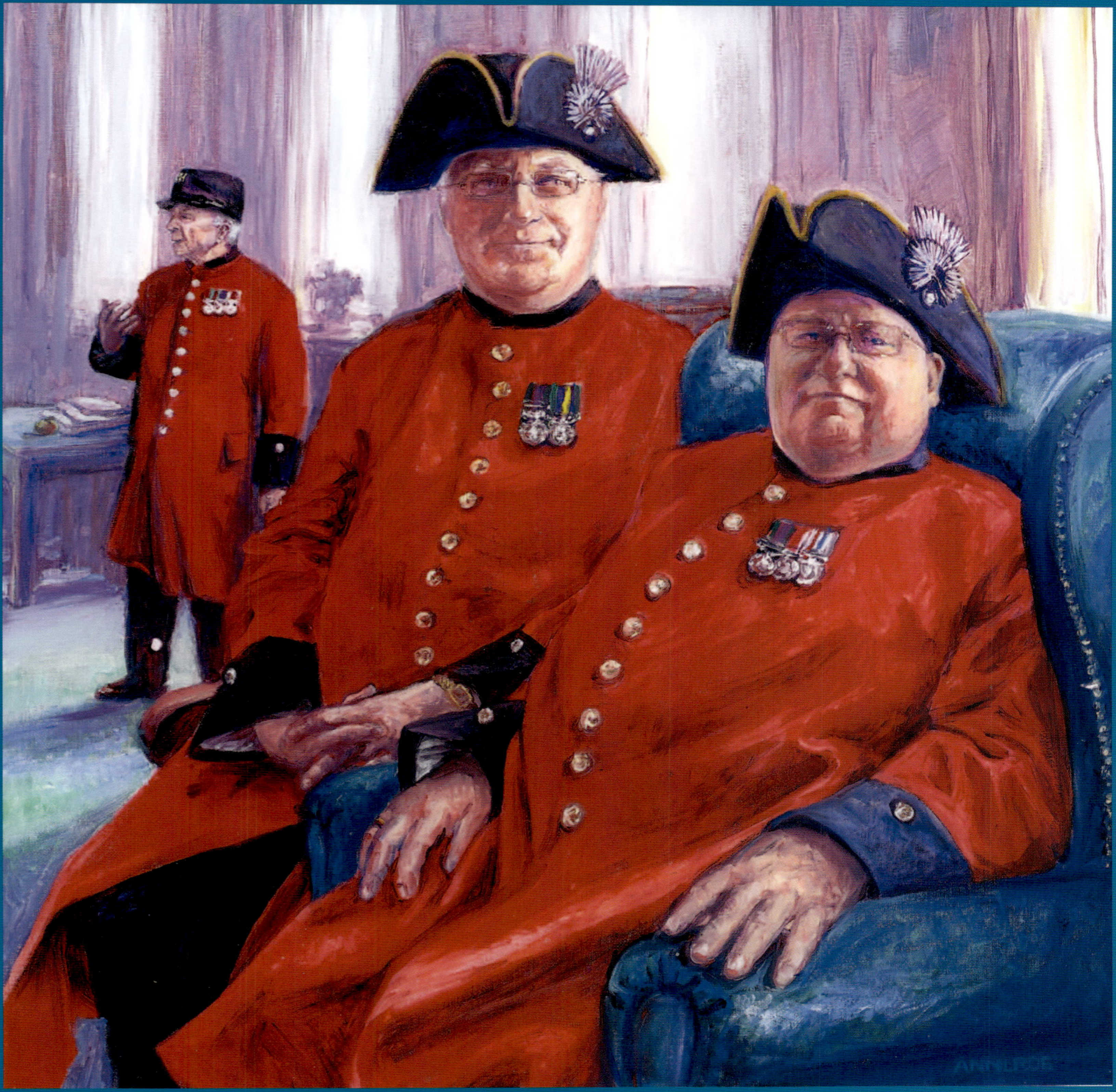
ANN L ROE

THE FRIEDMAN FAMILY

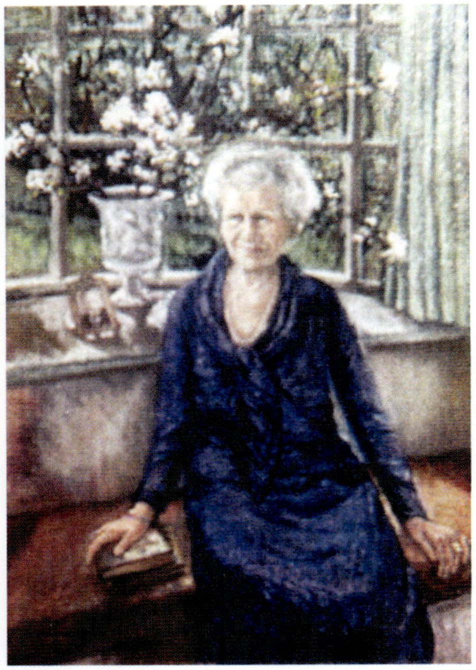

Kathleen Sims.

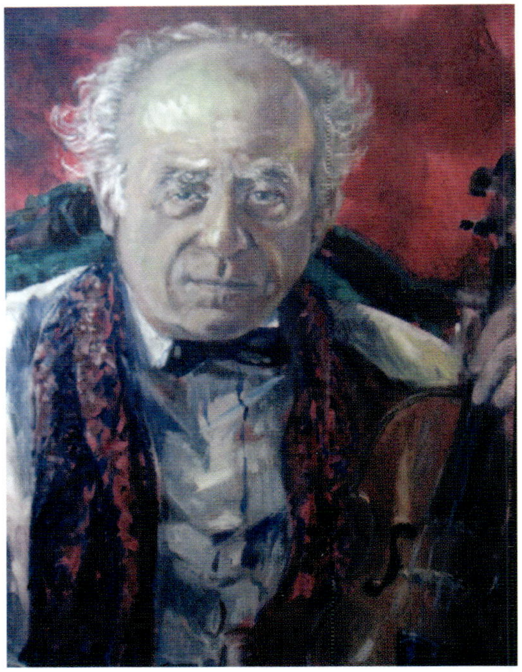

Leonard Friedman.

I've been fortunate to paint or draw a number of my lovely Friedman cousins, including Kathleen Sims who was my mother's brother's wife. I painted Kathleen in the sitting room of my mother's cottage in Brockenhurst. Her son-in-law Leonard Friedman went to music college in London with my lovely cousin Claire, a pianist whom he married. Leonard was a world-class violinist, and a friend of Prince Philip as I found out when he was playing with his son Richard, also a violinist, in Dartington Hall. I invited them to come and stay, but Leonard had a previous invitation on that night with Prince Philip at Buckingham Palace! I painted and drew Leonard when he did manage to come and stay with us, together with a pianist and singer. He gave us one of his last ever (very personal) concerts before he died. Leonard had four children with my cousin Claire, but I only managed to paint a portrait of Maria and Sonia. Both girls are in the musical theatre sphere. Maria is a singer, actor and director, having won many Olivier awards, and Sonia has many accolades for her work as a producer in musical theatre, for which she has received a CBE. Sarah the eldest daughter, veered towards the Sciences and is a Senior Research Fellow at the University of Limerick but, so far, I have not managed to paint her.

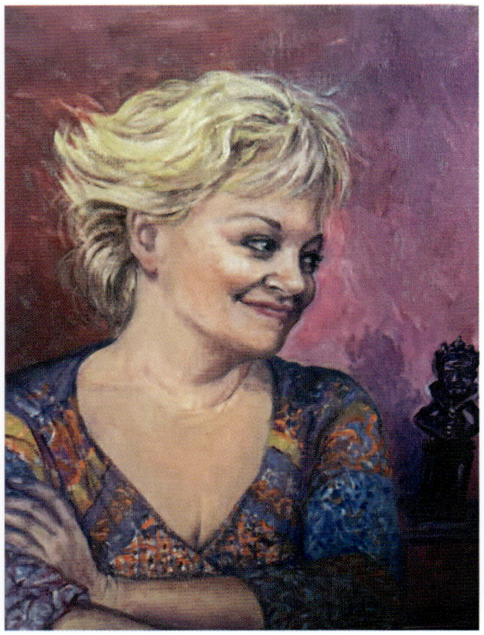

Maria.

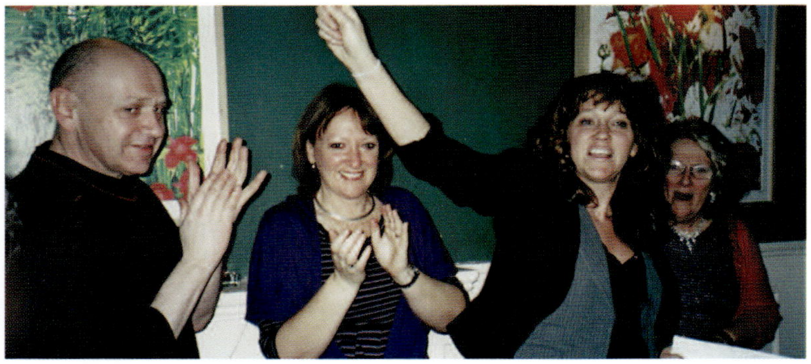

Ricky, Sarah, Sonia and Claire Friedman.
Opposite page: Sonia Friedman.

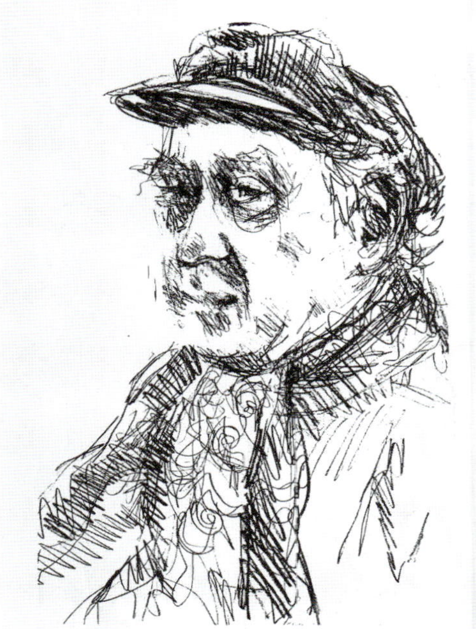

Leonard Friedman from my sketchbook.

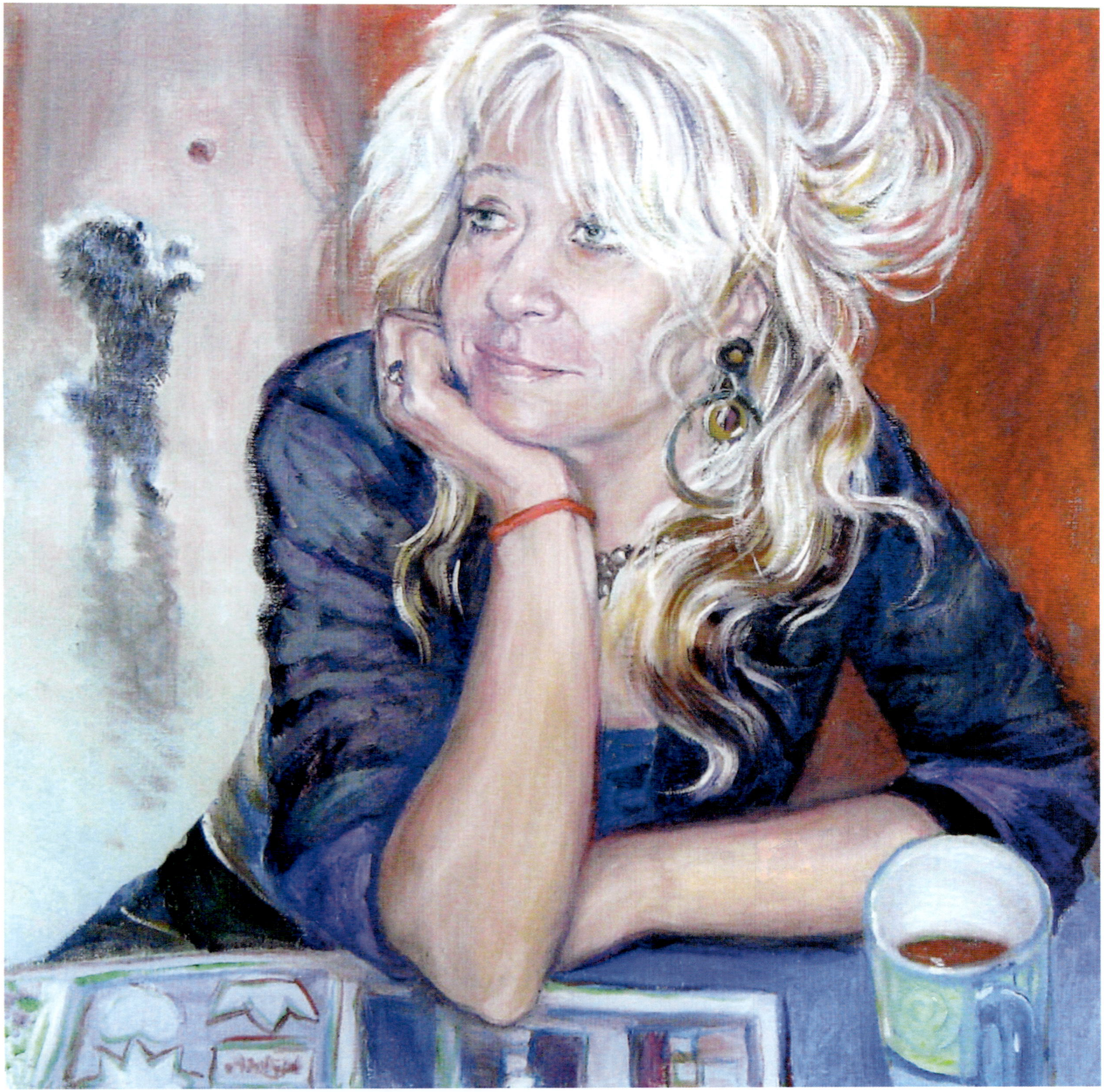

School Days

My thirty years at Colyton Grammar School form a vital part of my life both as a teacher and an artist. It was also where my husband, Alan, and I worked among the superb teaching staff and pupils many of whom I drew or painted and who became lifelong friends. Examples of the work that the school, its staff and students inspired are included throughout this book and here are just a couple of examples of the many sketches made – some while attending various staff meetings which were not always the most interesting part of the day!

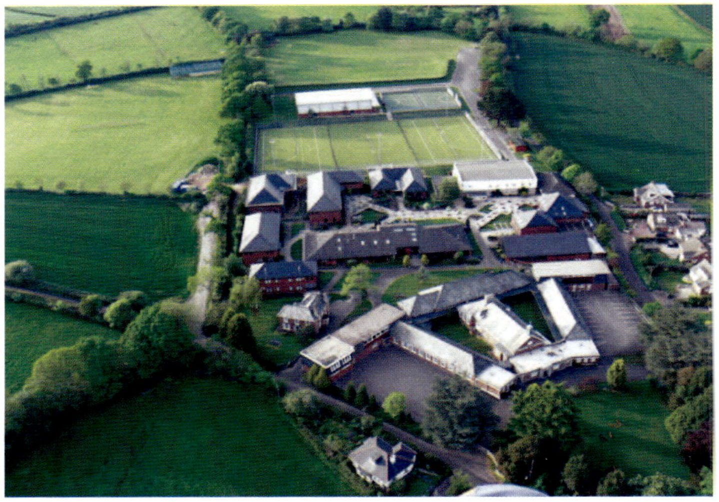

Colyton Grammar School an aerial view.

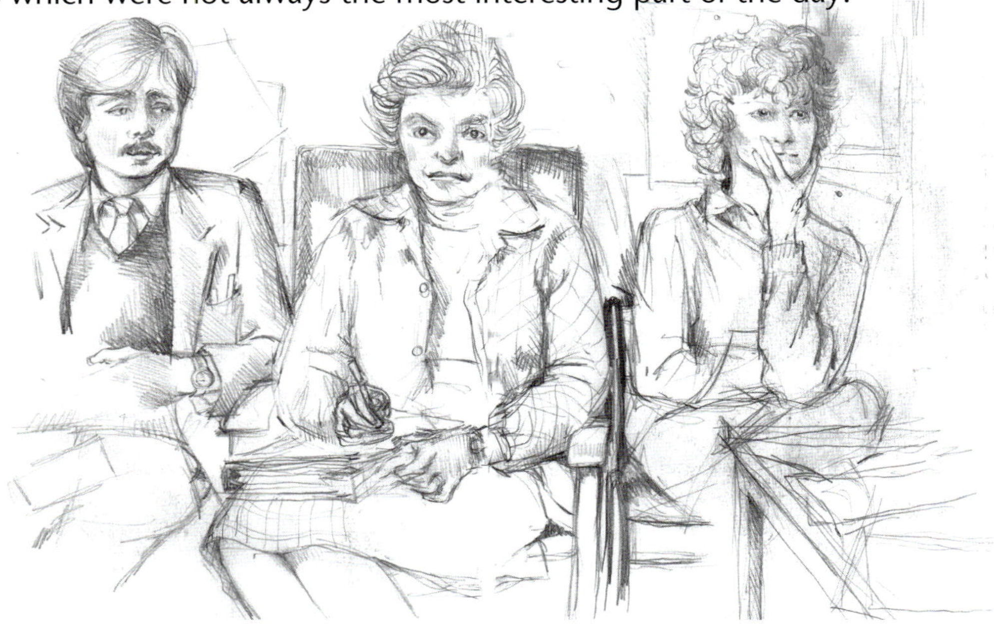

Staff meetings at Colyton Grammar School from my sketchbooks.

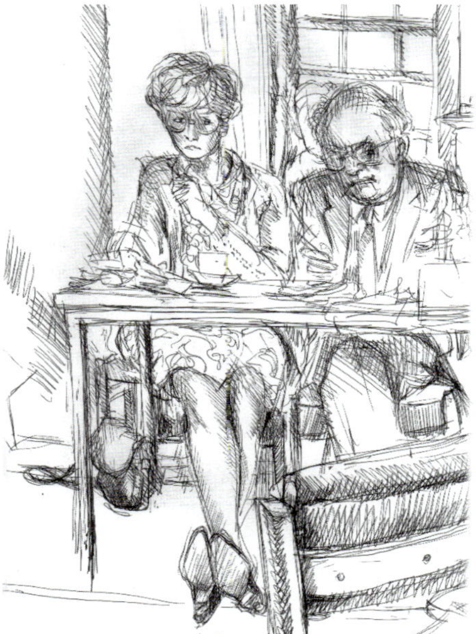

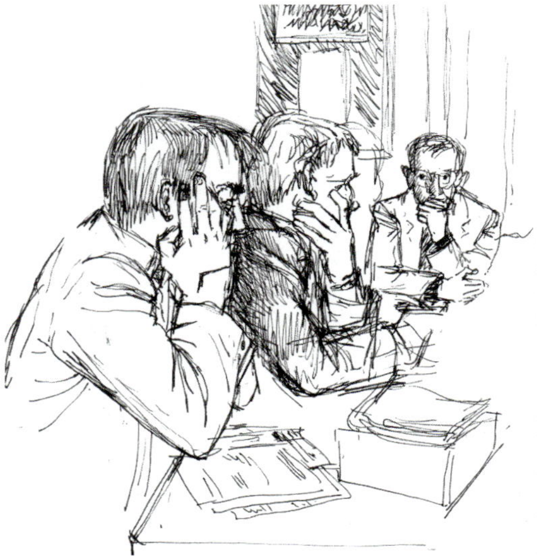

Right: My portrait of Professor Bob Clements who was the Art Advisor for Devon County Education Service.

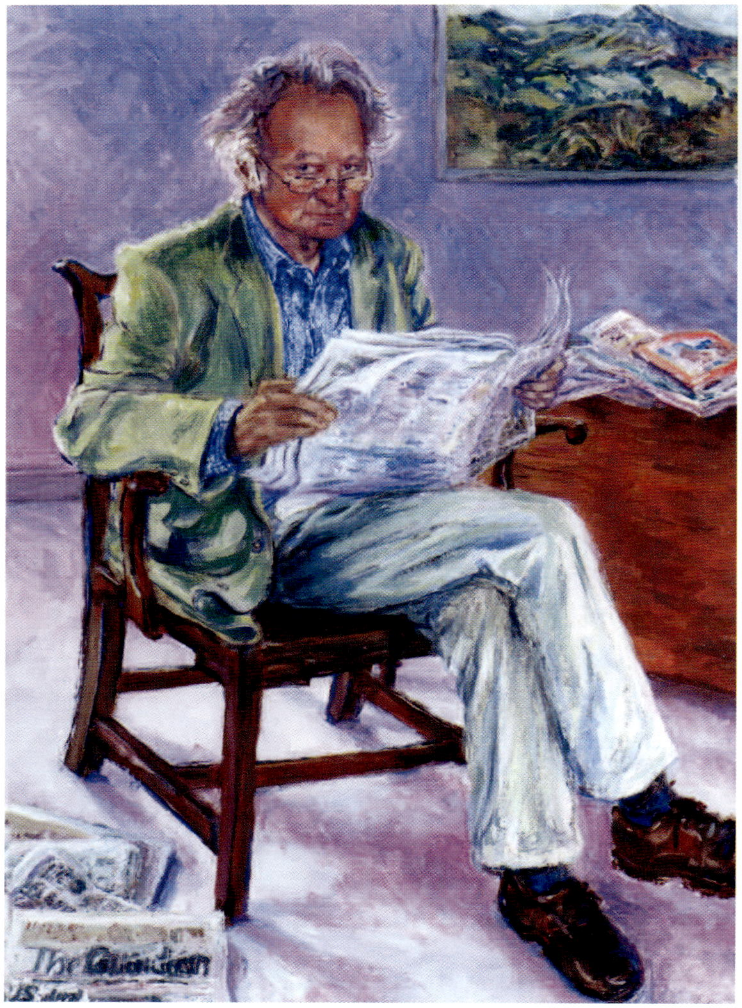

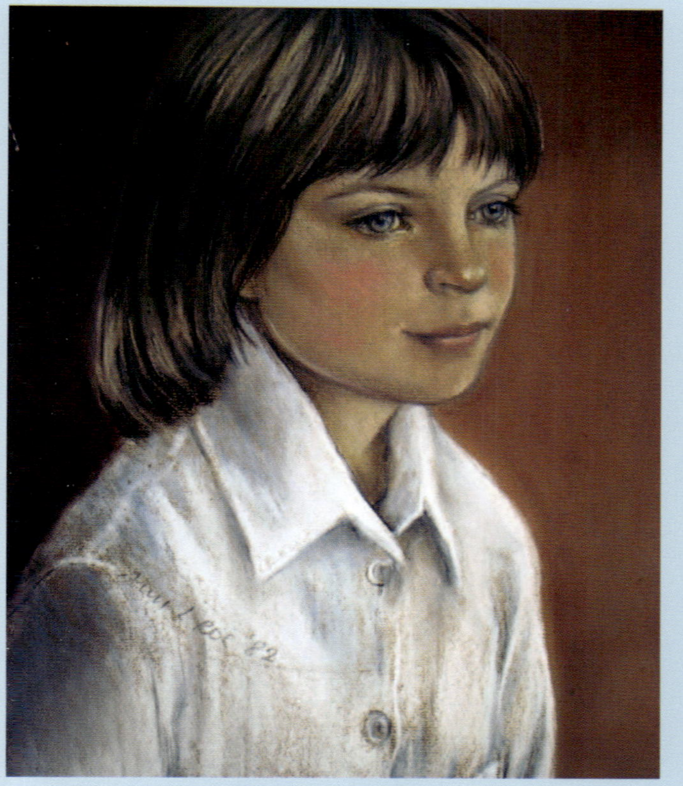

A pastel of student Karin Fox.

I was Head of Art and Design at Colyton Grammar School for nearly 30 years, while Alan was head of Biology for almost 46 years! During that time I painted portraits of a number of our students and teachers, examples of which appear throughout this book.

At weekends, for a short while, I worked with a business producing instant portraits for public school students. This meant staying at the school while I completed the students' portraits, working in different media including oils.

The completion of each portrait was limited depending on the medium. One hour for a drawing, up to four hours for an oil painting. On one occasion I was drawing a girl when I discovered that her family had been great friends of my parents when I was young. We chatted a great deal and my portrait was a disaster. The parents did not buy it and I was not surprised. You need a lot of concentration to produce a successful portrait!

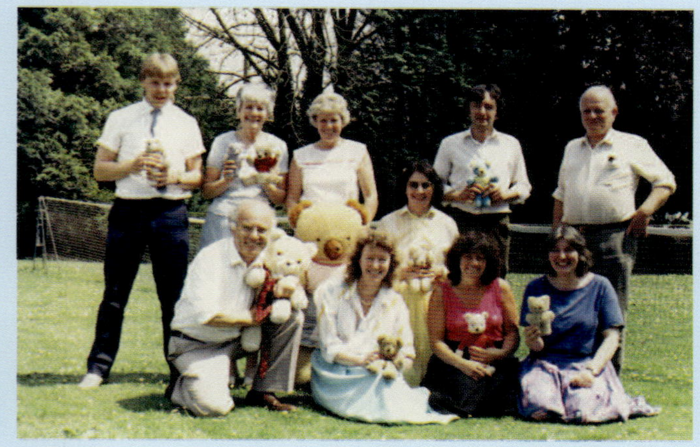

Above: A group of teachers at CGS (me front row right). Here we are holding small teddy bears – one of the many charity events we took part in.

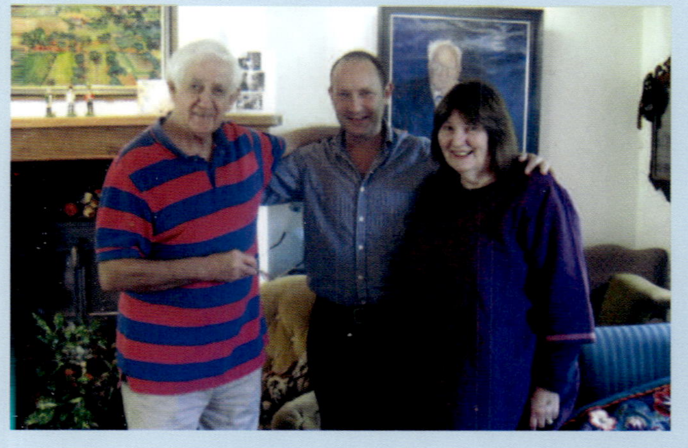

Above: Nick Sargeant, a former student and good friend who attended Colyton Grammar School with our daughter Lolo. Now himself a talented artist, here he is visiting Alan and I in our home.

Right: Patrick Morrison, former Head of CGS standing in front of his portrait.

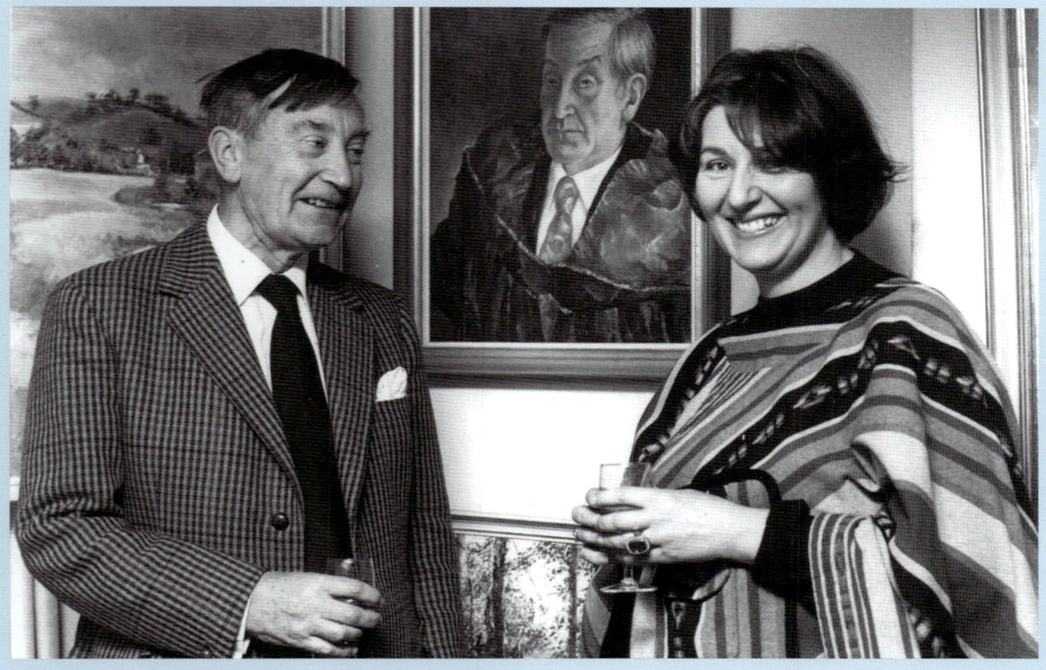

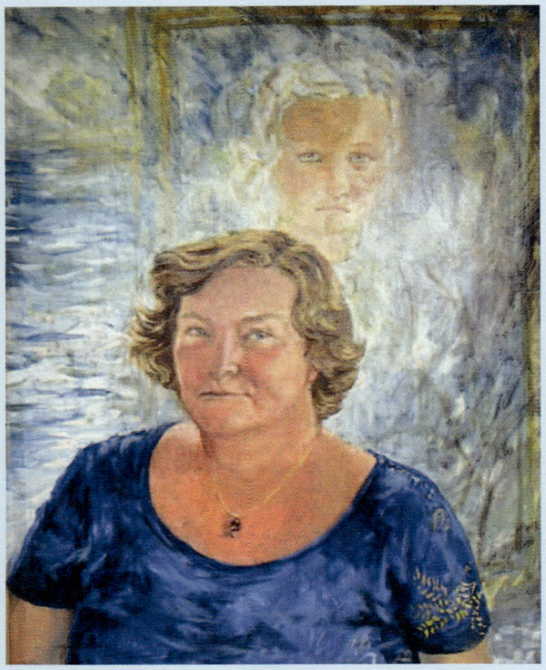

My 'double' portrait of Margaret Clark.

I taught at Colyton Grammar School with Margaret who was in charge of the Music Department. We collaborated in some very exciting musical events. One such collaboration was West Side Story where Ernie Fox (Headmaster) and Mike Marsh (Deputy Head) took on major roles very successfully. But a memorable moment in our friendship was when Margaret fell off her bicycle outside our cottage – just in time for breakfast.

Having known Margaret for many years I decided to paint her in front of an earlier portrait to show her as she is now. The two-in-one was fun to do and she was also an excellent sitter. During our time at CGS Margaret managed to invite some superb musicians to play for a series of concerts. One was the violinist Nigel Kennedy who came twice. On one occasion he was deciding on buying a 'fiddle', and set out on the floor of the hall a selection of some priceless violins from which he would pick one! On both occasions he came back to our home to have supper in Oroolong House, a great privilege for us all. Margaret's niece was also a very good sitter. I did two portraits of her in pastel, a medium I found gave an instant vibe of colours. I used beige paper which worked well with pastels.

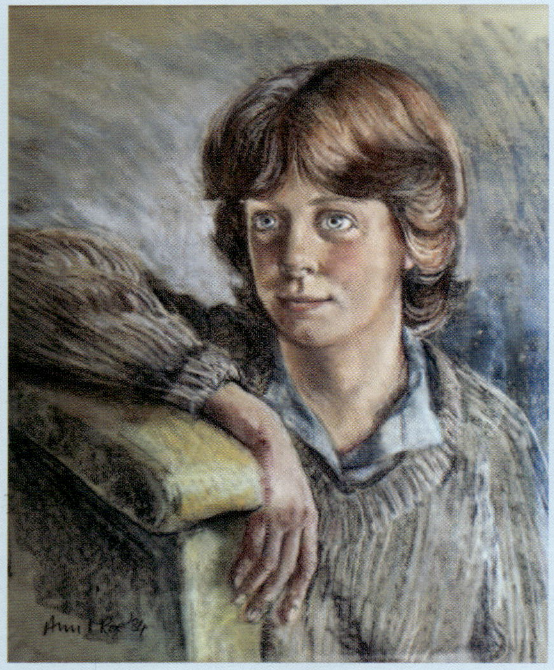

Margaret's niece Astrid Press.

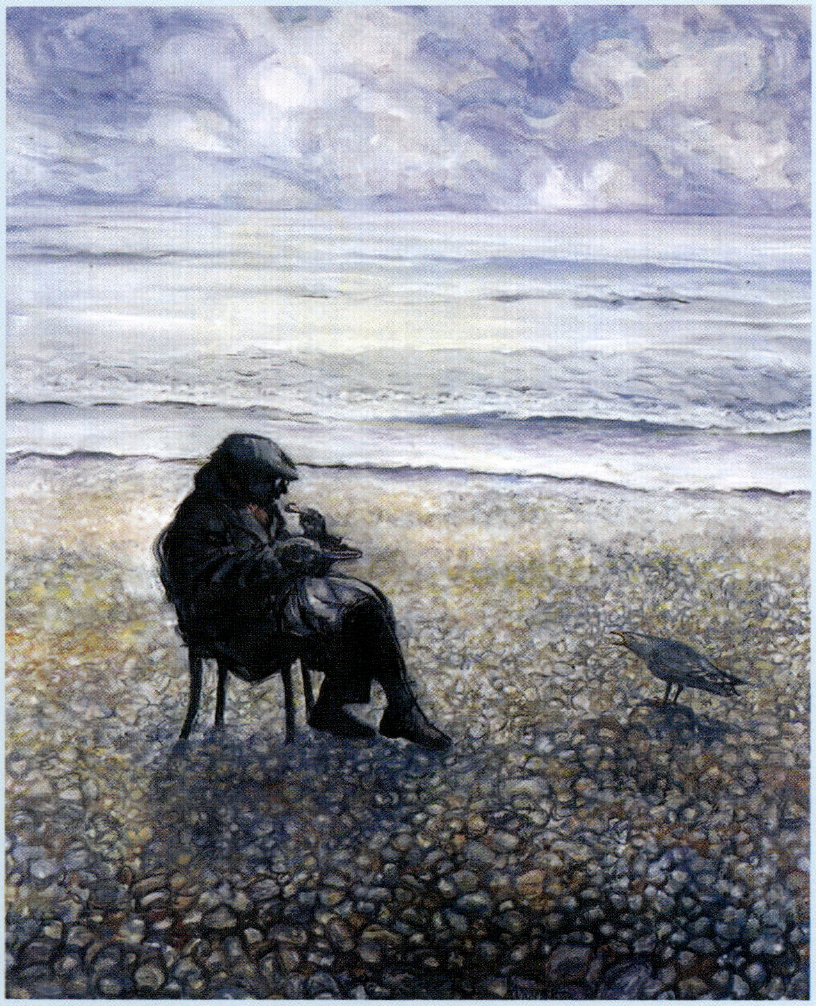

A fun painting made following a chilly day celebrating Margaret's 4th July birthday on a windy beach at Seaton.

A PRIME MINISTER'S SECRET VISIT

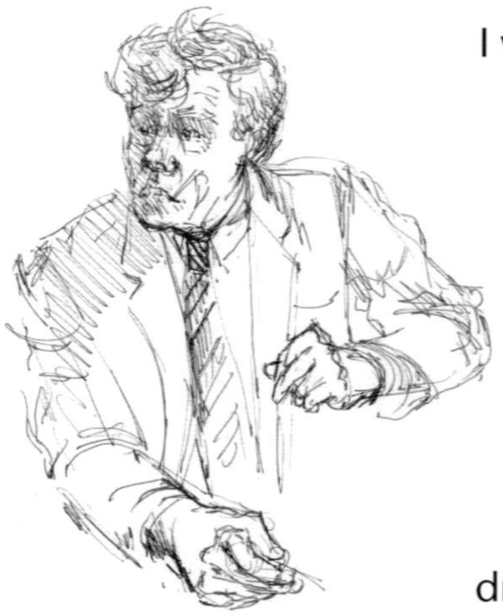

Barry Sindall, Head of Colyton Grammar School

I was away from teaching due to a painful back when a call came from the headmaster, Barry Sindall, to do a cartoon of a VIP. A visit to the school was in the offing but the happening was a top security secret so at that point the visitor remained nameless. I was eventually told who it was, the then Prime Minister John Major, so (apart from lying flat to improve my back problem which did not work!), I went about finding source material which was quite difficult as there was no internet in those days. I sat at a table and started drawing with a minimal amount of visual information just to get some ideas down on paper, again without the advantage of an iPad and other tech.

On the day of the visit John Major arrived and although I never met him, Alan did, and to much hilarity presented him with a balloon animal. He was also presented with a framed image of my cartoon. In the drawing for his November 5th visit, I put fireworks in the background, plus part of the school and John Major dressed in a cricketing outfit with masses of children snaking away in the background. Here is his charming thank you letter.

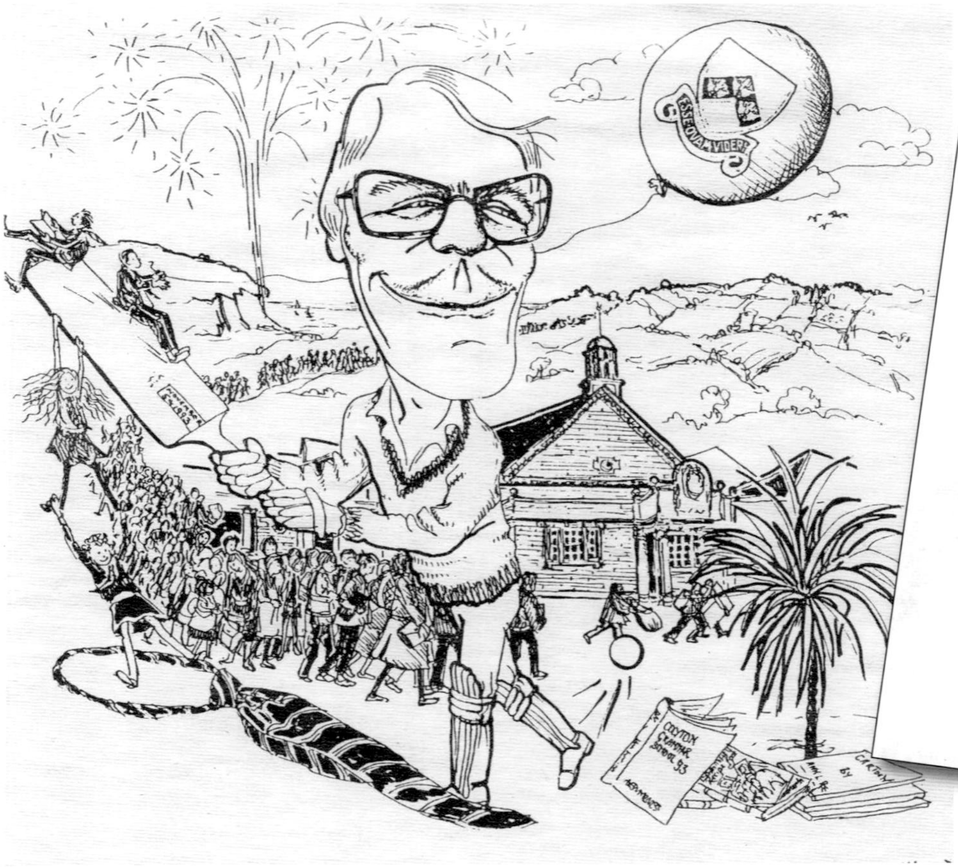

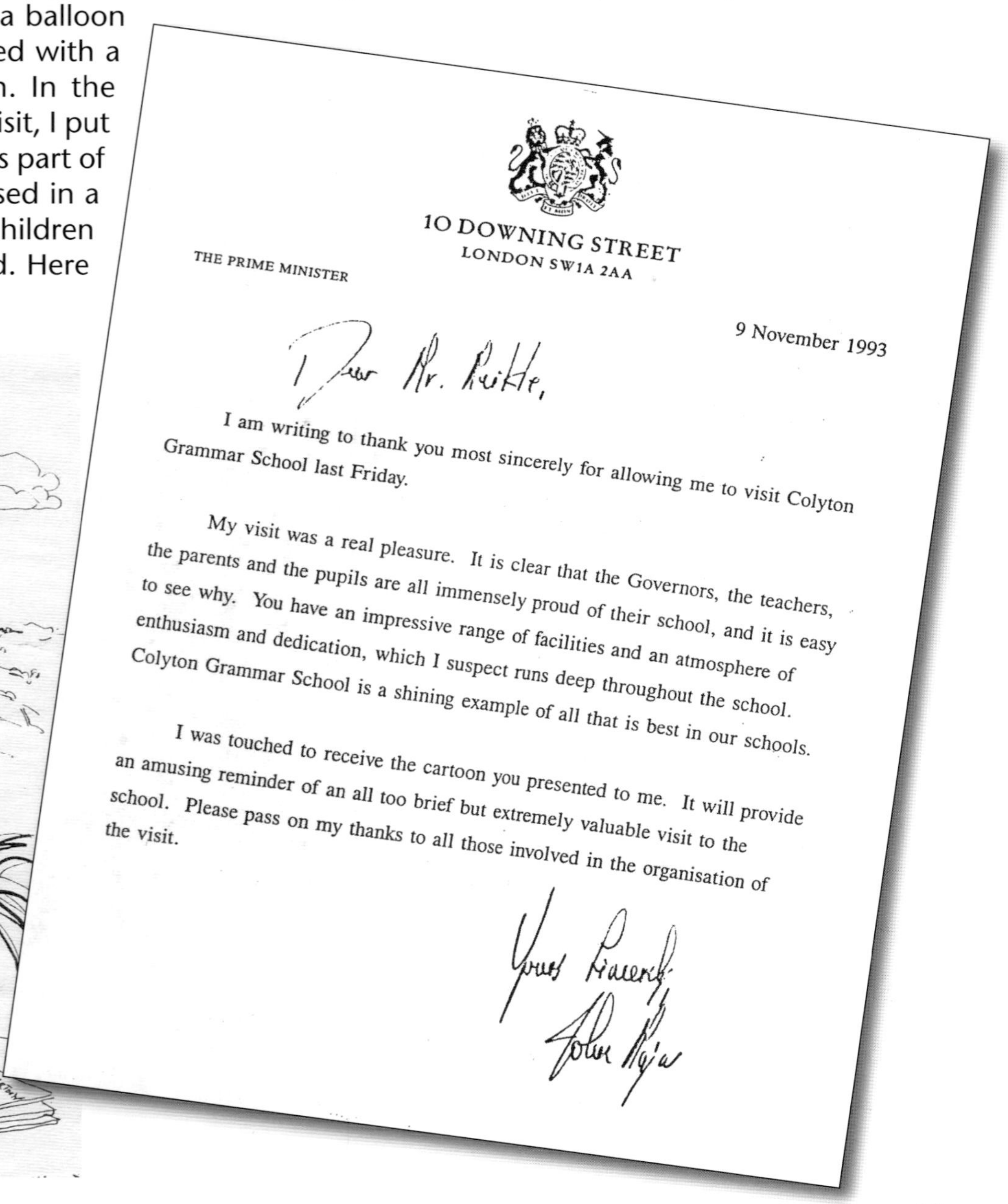

10 DOWNING STREET
LONDON SW1A 2AA

THE PRIME MINISTER

9 November 1993

Dear Mr. Pickle,

I am writing to thank you most sincerely for allowing me to visit Colyton Grammar School last Friday.

My visit was a real pleasure. It is clear that the Governors, the teachers, the parents and the pupils are all immensely proud of their school, and it is easy to see why. You have an impressive range of facilities and an atmosphere of enthusiasm and dedication, which I suspect runs deep throughout the school. Colyton Grammar School is a shining example of all that is best in our schools.

I was touched to receive the cartoon you presented to me. It will provide an amusing reminder of an all too brief but extremely valuable visit to the school. Please pass on my thanks to all those involved in the organisation of the visit.

Yours sincerely,
John Major

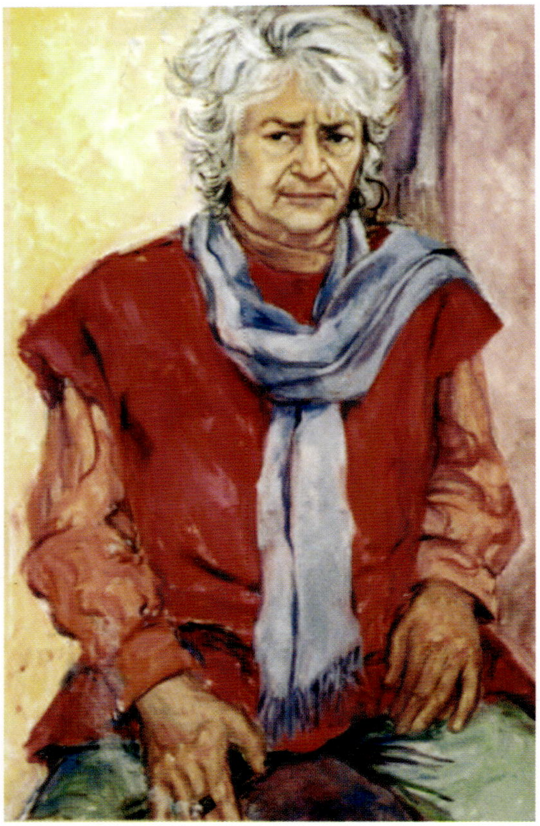

FIORE DE ENRIQUEZ. Unexpected things happen in life and meeting Fiore was one of them. Alan had started painting and liked the idea of finding a painting course. Then, after seeing many advertisements for painting holidays, I came across Derek and Di King who were running courses in desirable venues, all over Europe. When I phoned them, they told me about the one they were about to run in a Tuscan hilltop village, Peralta, owned by an Italian sculptress. We thought that sounded wonderful, and so it turned out to be. Fiore de Enriquez had renovated a crumbling group of buildings and gave talks and demos about sculpture. Fiore's plan was to rebuild Peralta into the charming artistic venue which it is today.

I painted three portraits of Fiore, one in her studio and two when she came to visit us here in Devon. One was bought and was last seen being unveiled in her studio attended by a crowd of artists including Derek and Di, all drinking champagne.

Fiore's life in Italy was unusual in many ways; she was a very striking and tall young girl and could easily be mistaken for a boy, as she generally wore an outfit of colourful knee-high leather boots, a sleeveless waistcoat and vibrant shirts and trousers. When young she slept on the beach and was taught by her brother how to disarm mines which the Allies had laid at sea, a dangerous task she later undertook toward the war's end. A courageous thing for a young girl to do! Fiore smoked cigars in her later years which were specially made for her. Early in life she had been commissioned to create a sculpture in Sicily. For the unveiling of the completed piece Fiore decided to wear a dress but when she showed up the locals, believing her to have been a man, were so outraged they blew up her sculpture. At this, Fiore took the first flight out of Italy arriving in London penniless. A lady who was sitting beside her on the flight offered her accommodation, which she gladly took.

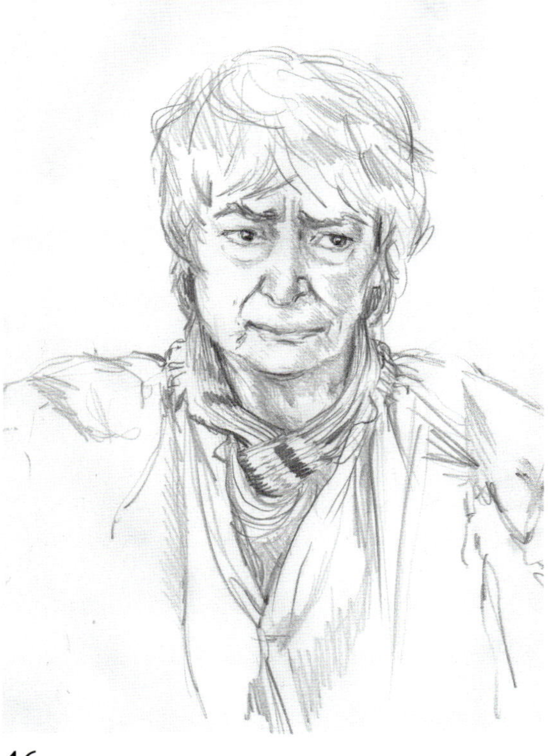

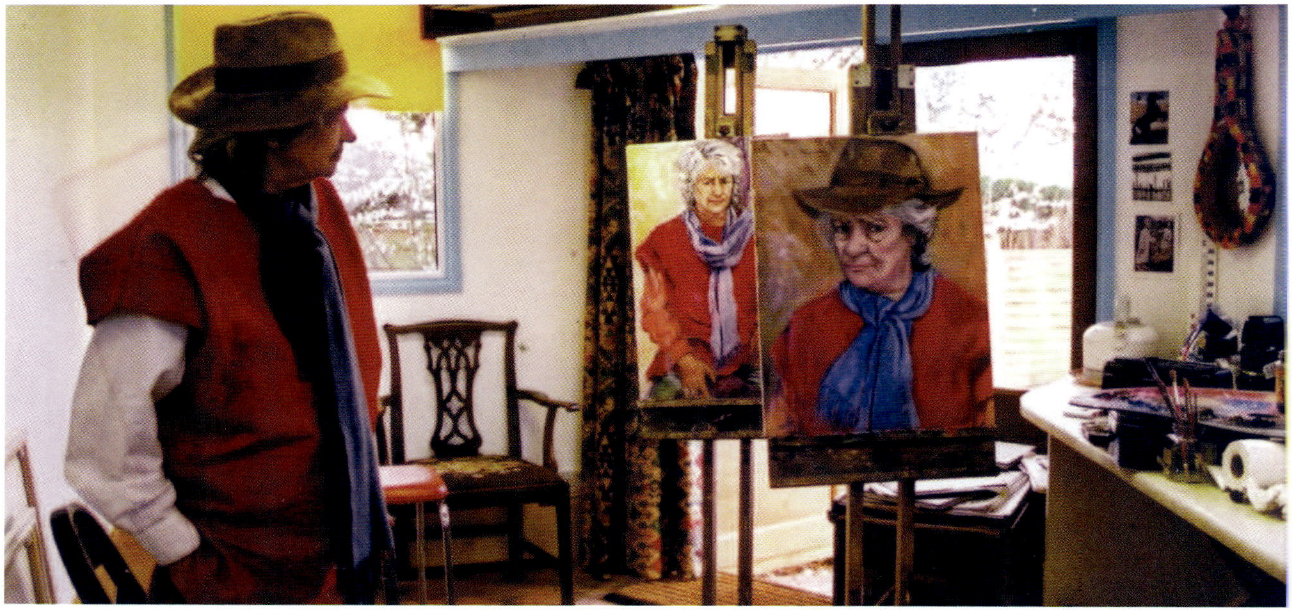

Above left: One of two portraits I painted of Fiore in my studio. Left: A preliminary sketch.
Above: Fiore standing back to consider the two portraits in my studio.

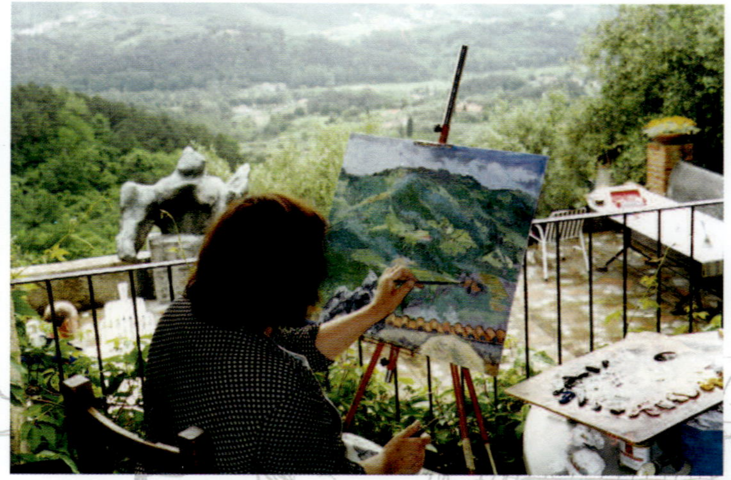

We met up with Fiore much later when she was living in Chelsea in a small but lovely studio owned by Lord Cadogan. She had sculpted many famous people by this time, including President Kennedy (just before he was assassinated), and the Queen Mother with whom she was a good friend. The day she vacated her Cadogan studio she had a party and we all signed her visitors' book; the page before ours was signed by the Queen Mother.

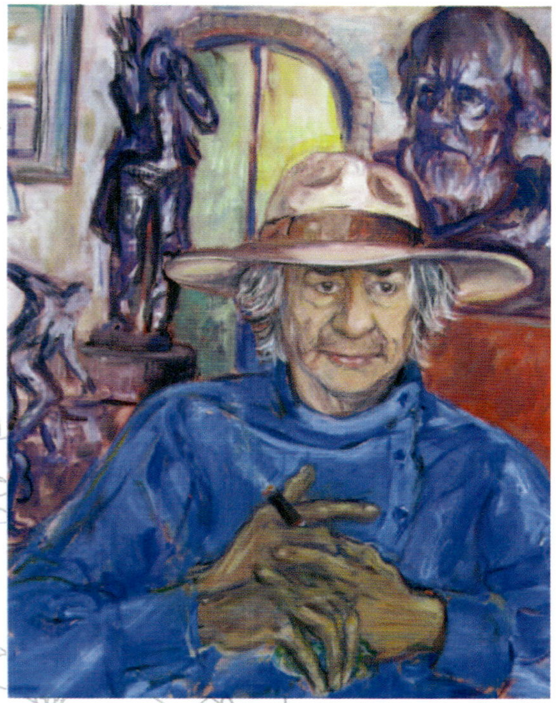

Above left: Painting the scene from the balcony at Peralta. Above: My portrait of Fiore painted while we were in Italy. Background: Pencil sketch of Peralta in Tuscany.

Fiore's charismatic personality was infectious and at times challenging. When she stayed with us she interspersed sitting for me and sculpting Alan at the kitchen table. This sculpture was unfinished and she took it with her back to London. It was never seen again!

We last saw Fiore when she was in a coma in her room in Peralta with her dearly-loved operatic music playing in the background. She died the following day. We were so privileged to have known such an unforgettable person. The background to one of my portraits of her included a sculpture she had made of her friend Augustus John whose illegitimate son, Tristan de Vere Cole (whose portrait appears earlier in this book), gave a talk about Fiore in the Chelsea Arts Club following her death.

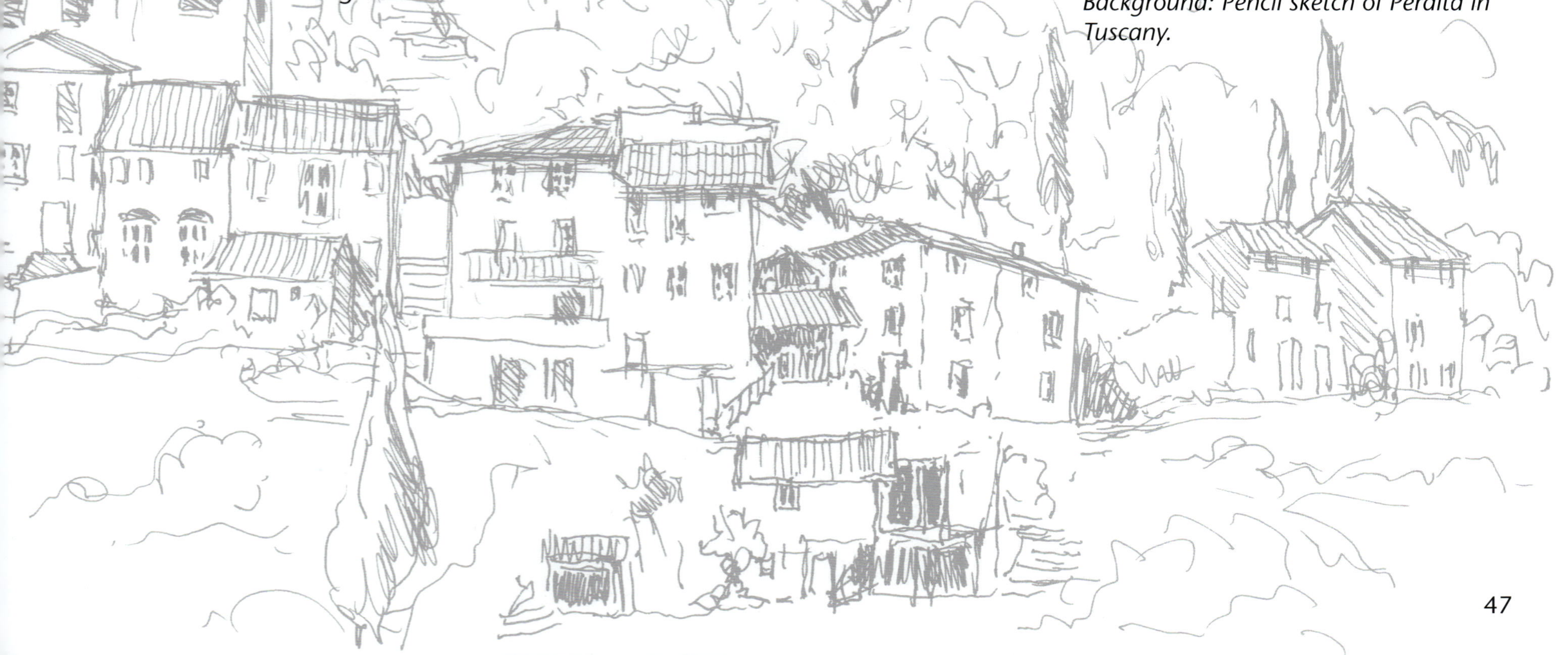

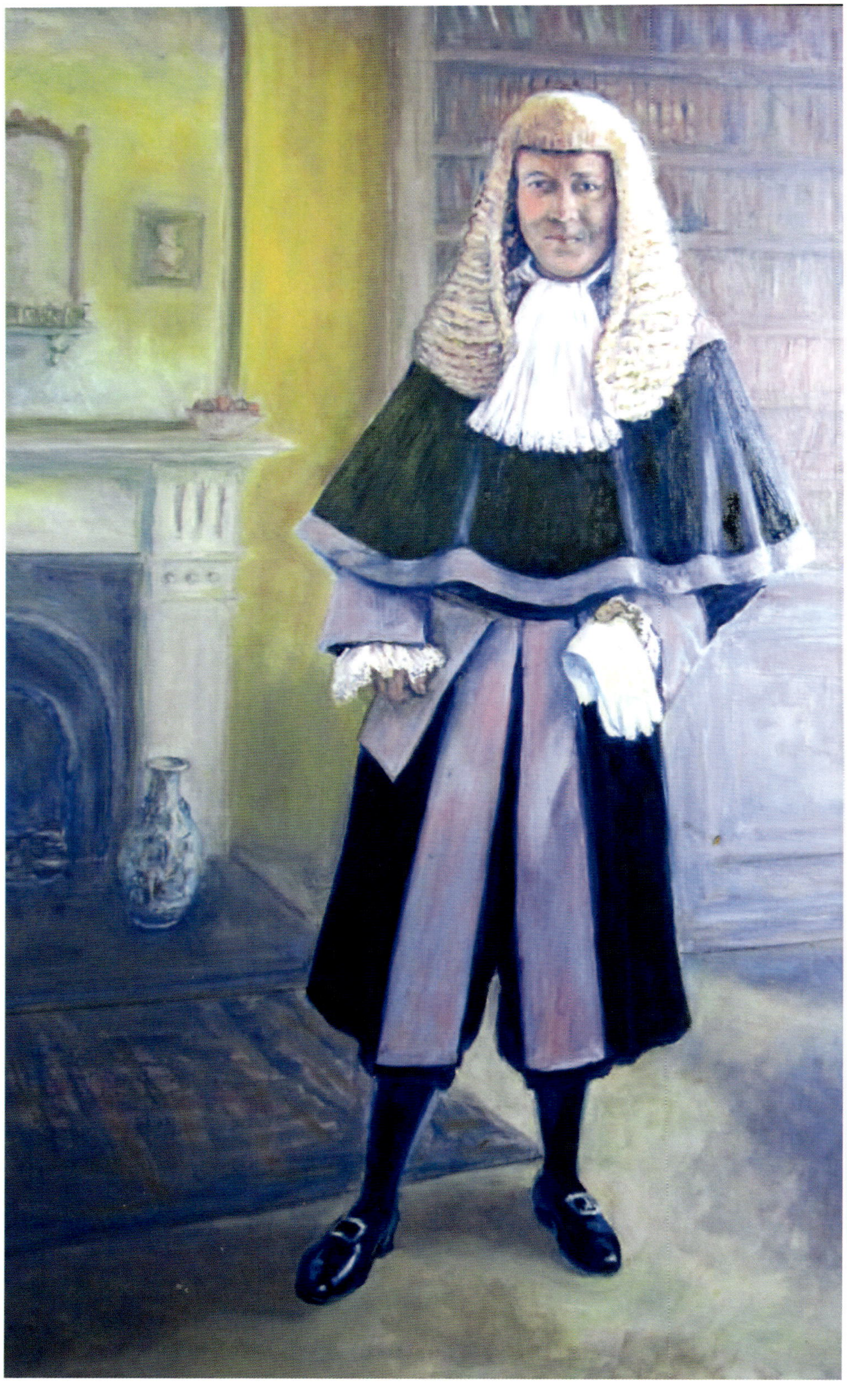

JUDGE PAUL COOK. It was at the home of our dear friends Mo and Frank Thursby that we first met Paul. He was a delightful young judge, full of life and interested in so many things, including painting. By the end of our lunch party we had decided to paint a portrait of Paul in all his official regalia and so arranged to have a special sitting. He provided a superb lunch in his charmingly restored home, where his parents lived in a flat downstairs. His glamorous mother helped Paul to dress in all his legal robes (he had to keep his wig in a freezer to preserve it from moths!). Each item of his dress had to be put on separately, including lace cuffs and collar, and when he was fully garbed he posed in his sitting room. Alan took a selection of photos, while I created a variety of drawings. Paul invited us to stay, but I was eager to get home to start on his portrait.

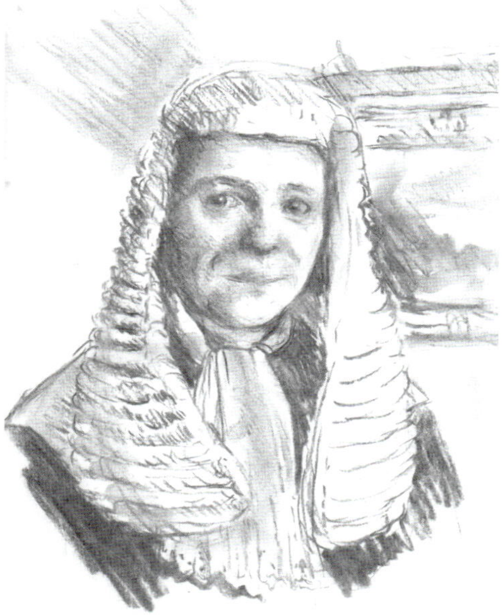

Often I paint two portraits to get the feel of any sitter. Paul was standing, as it best showed off his regalia. Once finished we arranged a meeting to unveil the portrait. This is always a moment of great tension in case the subject does not like the portrait. Fortunately it was a great success and Paul's mother is always telling me how much she loves the painting.

Paul suffered from rheumatoid arthritis when he was young. For many people this might have stopped them from doing so many things, but not Paul. He has been up ladders and working on the restoration of his house, goes camping in France with friends, and enjoys cycling. A lovely man, who I am sure is compassionate and just in his professional life.

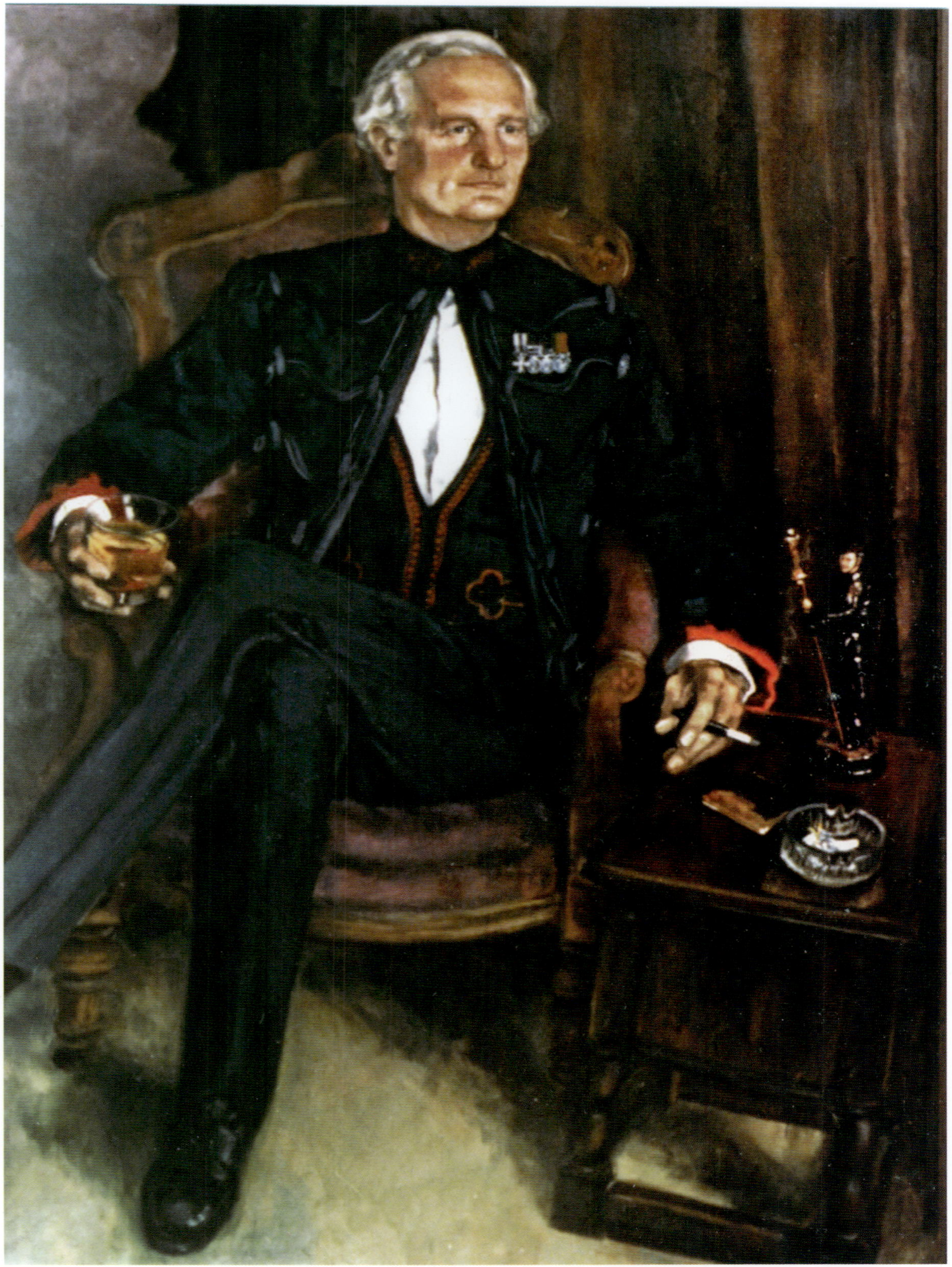

Lieutenant Colonel Digby Willoughby

Digby Jeremie Willoughby was born in India in 1934, the son of an army officer. Educated at Blundells and at Sandhurst he was commissioned into the 2nd Gurkha Rifles and served in Malaya. Outside his military career he is perhaps best known for his love of winter sports and in particular downhill tobogganing having set a world record in 1961 for the two-man bobsleigh on the Cresta Run.

Some years earlier I received an invitation from Lieutenant Colonel Digby Willoughby to paint his portrait. He had a tradition of family portraits going back generations, and he wanted one of himself in his regimental dress uniform.

He was an amazing sitter, as any part of him which I was painting would remain completely motionless, such as the glass of whisky in his right hand. This extraordinary skill, he told me, had been learned in the jungles of Malaya while serving with the Gurkhas who would need to remain motionless and hidden from the enemy for long periods of time.

You can just see in the corner a little Gurkha on the table – a gift given to him by the Gurkhas on his retirement – and a very treasured object. Lt-Col. Willoughby died in 2007.

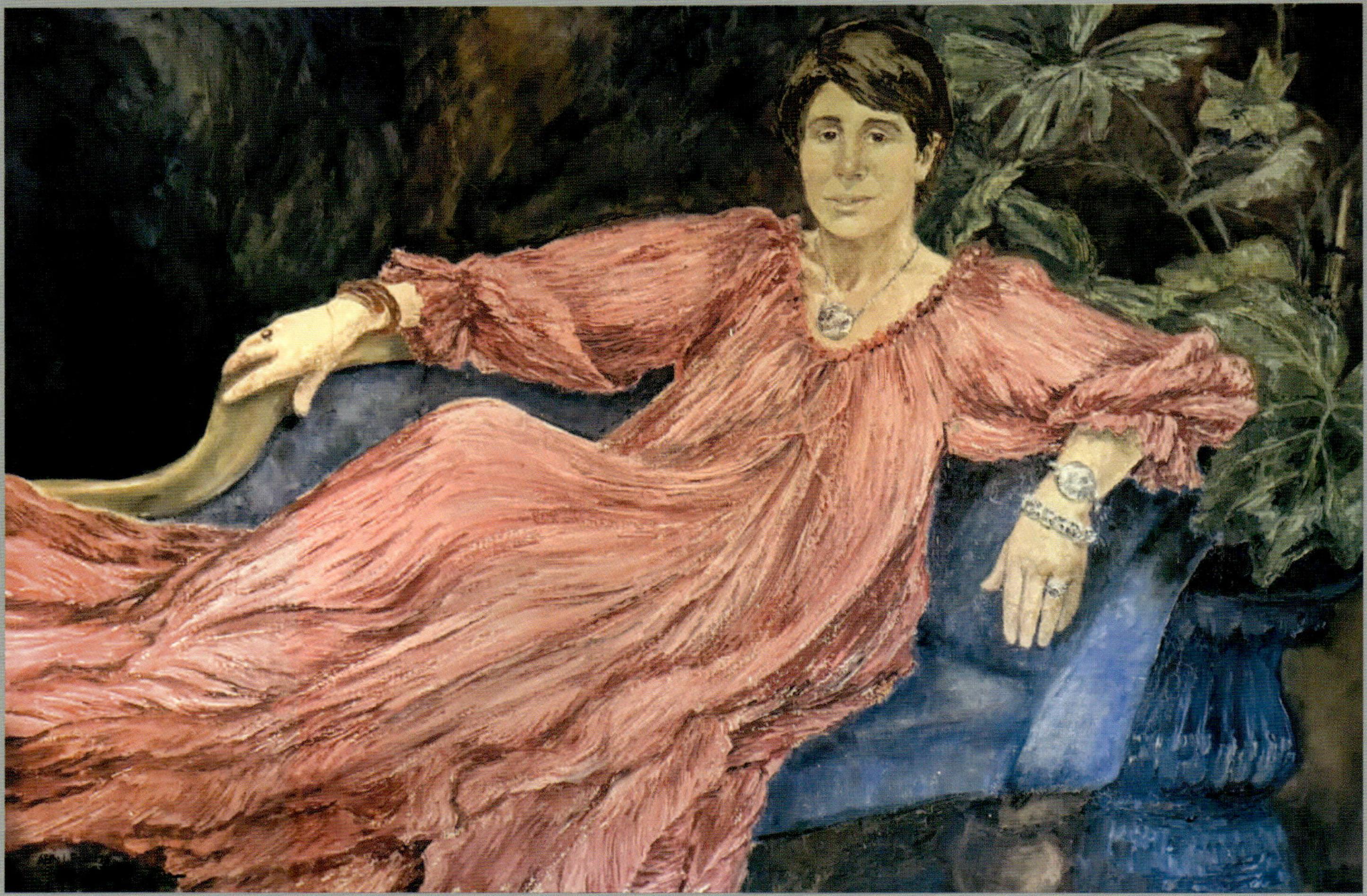

Isabell came to my front door with a baby (Kate) in her arms. I opened the door with a baby (Xanthe) in my arms. An interesting start to a lifetime of friendship. Isabell's family ran an English language school in Bilbao which her father had started. He was a Yorkshireman and Isabell's mother was Spanish. Isabell at the time ran the UK side of the business bringing Spanish children over to England and placing them with families to learn English during the summer. Consequently we had many lovely children staying with us. Two of Isabell's children are now carrying on this exchange now that Isabell has retired.

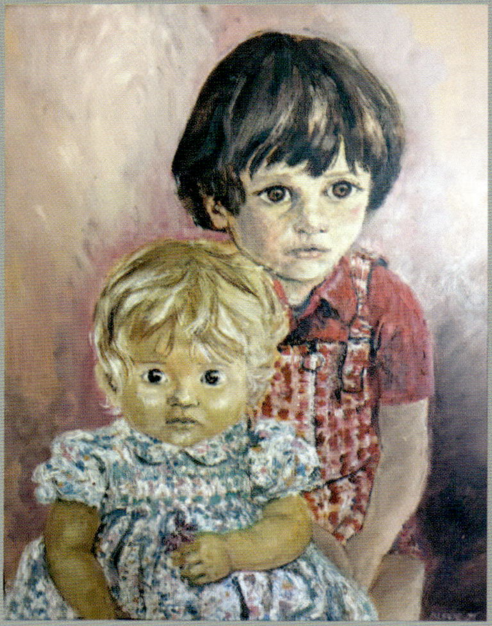

I painted Isabell in this fascinating dress which you could screw up and unravel uncreased without any ironing being necessary! This painting hangs in her sitting room in Chideock, Dorset, along with the painting of her two young girls, Harriet and Kate.

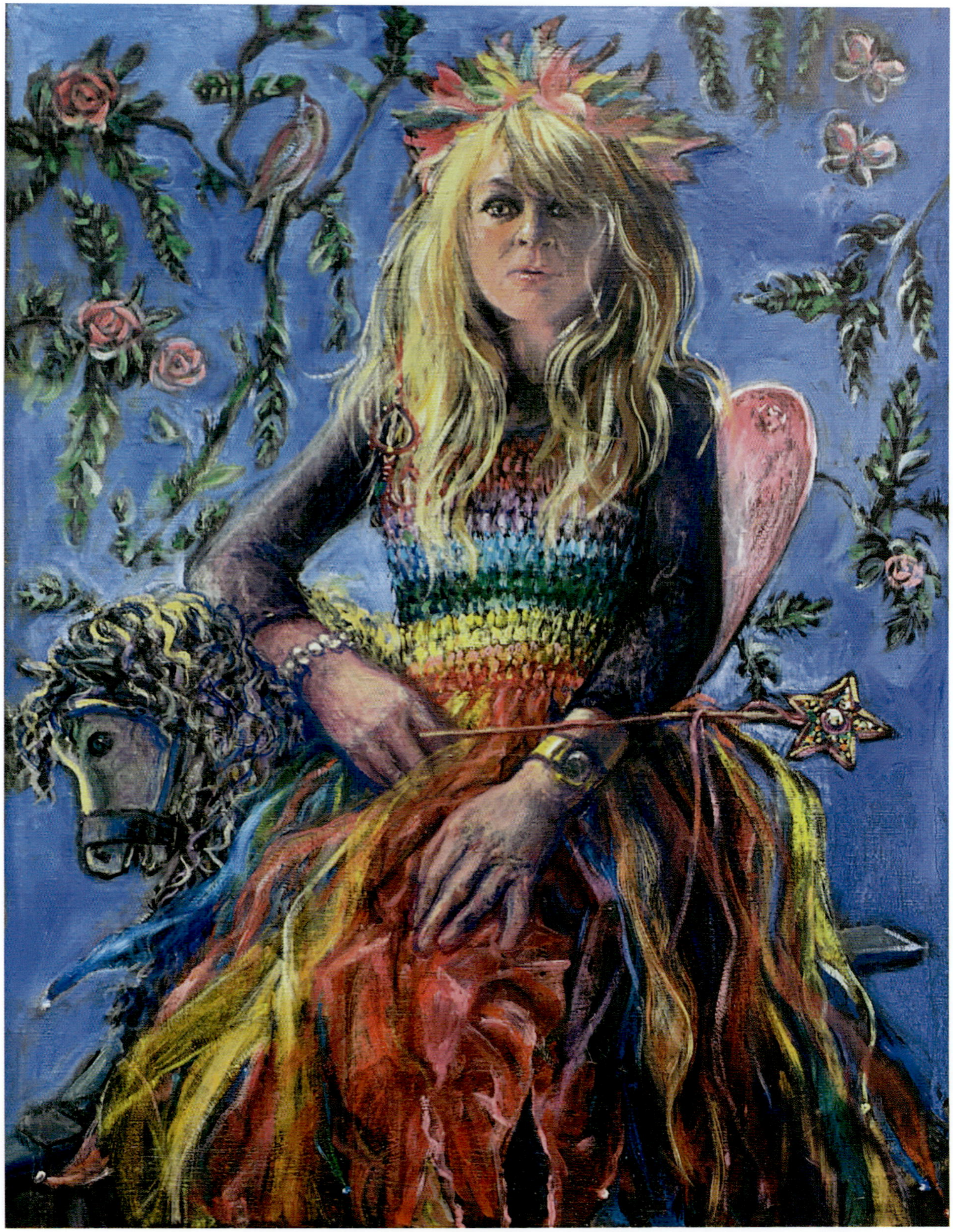

TERRY BOSWELL. The beautiful Terry is an artist and another lifelong friend. Although I do not see her that often, when we do meet up it is always a joy.

She very kindly sat for me after she had been to London to see the wonderful Cirque du Soleil at the Royal Albert Hall. At some point during the trip Terry had passed a shop displaying a kind of fairy costume, which she thought was great, so she persuaded her husband John to buy it for her. So this is the costume she is wearing in the portrait. I included a rocking horse she owned and the background is an interpretation of some of Terry's own wall paintings. It was a fun portrait to paint.

Terry and her husband, John, ran Combe House Hotel in Gittisham for many years. It was a treat to go there, as so much of Terry's work was on view: sculptures and paintings.

Some of our best memories are of the parties our family members enjoyed, including going to New Year's Eve dinners at Combe House; much drinking, eating and laughing.

Terry has just moved to Colyton where the transformation of her new home will be a joy to witness. Her colourful imagery will be a delightful and decorative addition to our lovely little Devon town.

LORD BATH. Alexander George Thynn, 7th Marquess of Bath (1932–2020) was a very colourful character whom I kept seeing on TV and I thought that he would be wonderful to paint, so I wrote to him. That was how it started. He was a delightful man and in 2007 he allowed me the privilege of capturing him in paint. Together we sorted through his extraordinary wardrobe to find the right clothes to wear for his portrait. On the top shelf lay a variety of his head gear, on the middle section were his amazingly creative and colourful outfits, and on the lowest level was his footwear, mostly made from embroidered fabrics. I had never seen such a memorable selection of clothes. I remember he was happy to go along with my fun idea for what he should wear for his portrait, and as an artist himself, he was fascinated by what I was doing.

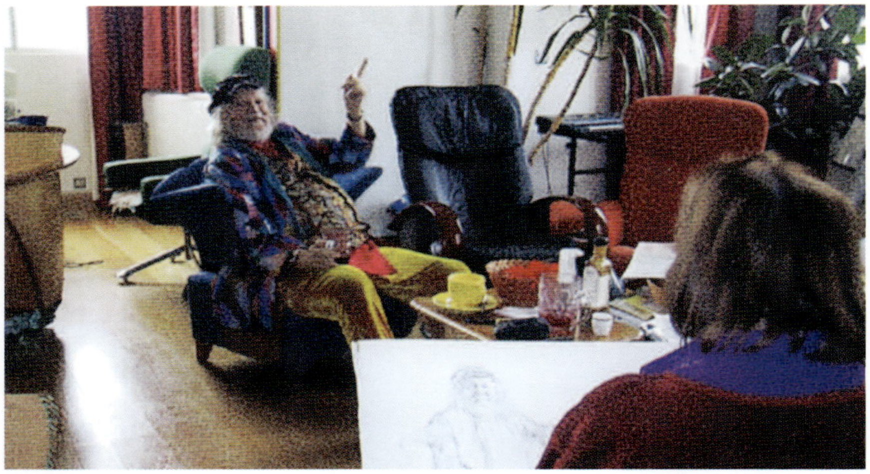

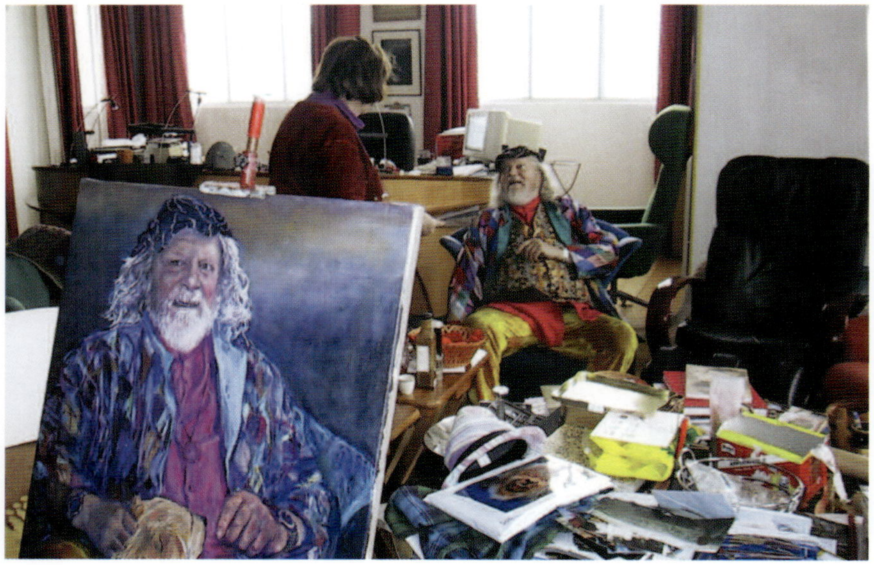

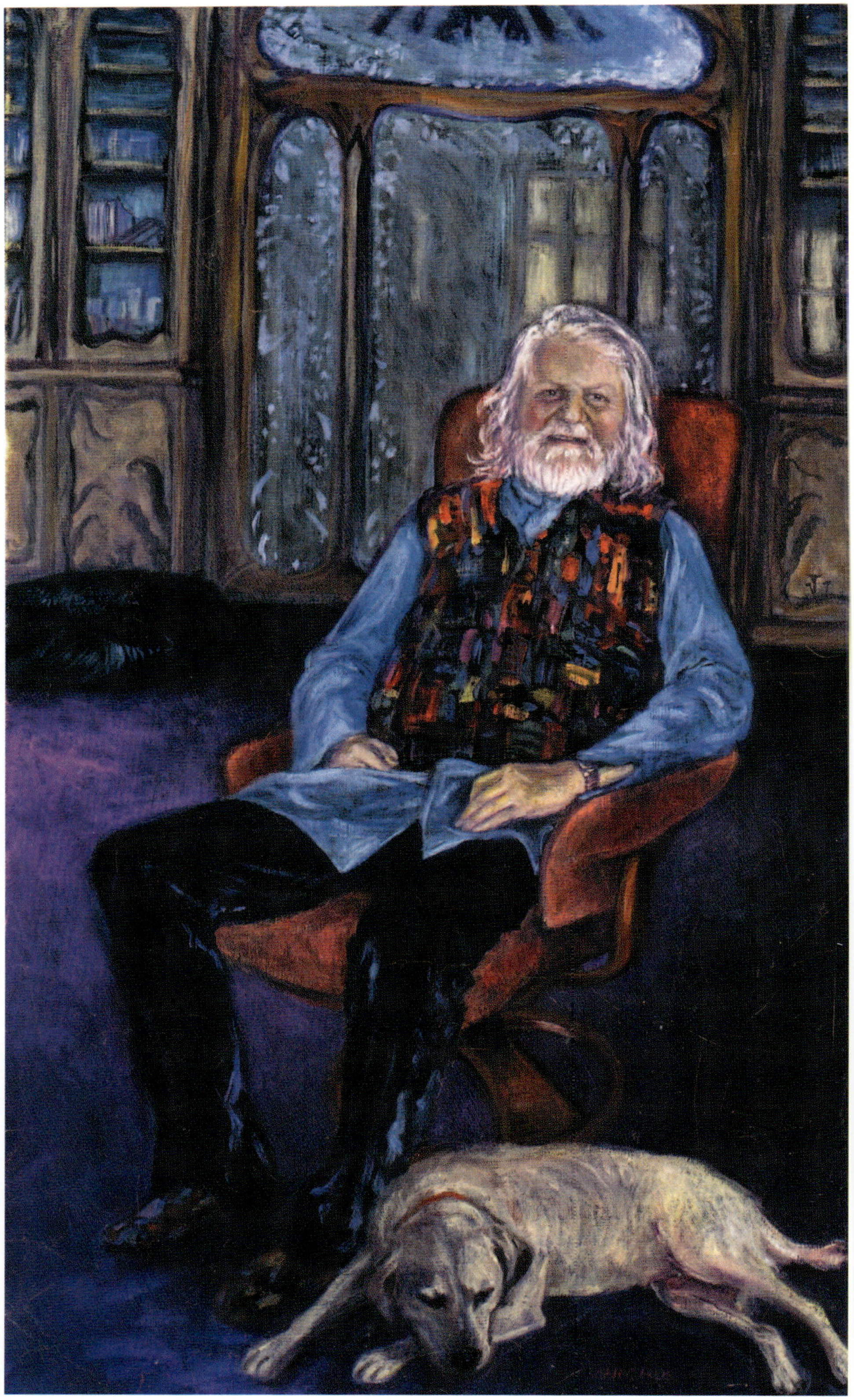

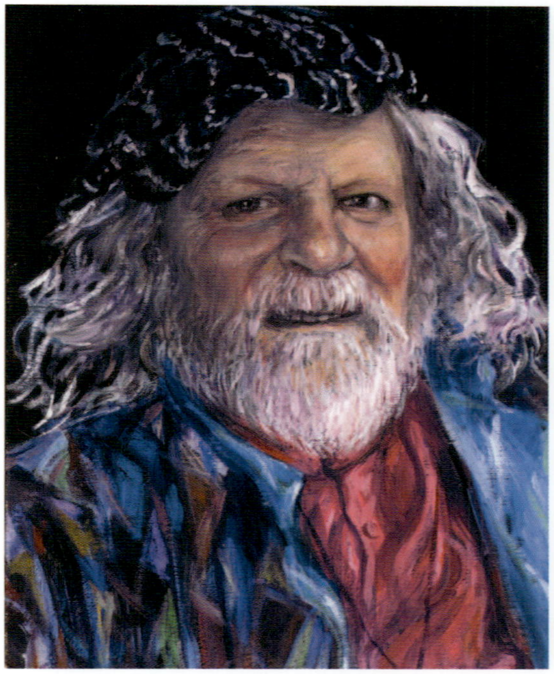

I painted two portraits of him one of which he bought and now hangs in Longleat House. I also produced two greetings cards which were sold in the Longleat gift shop.

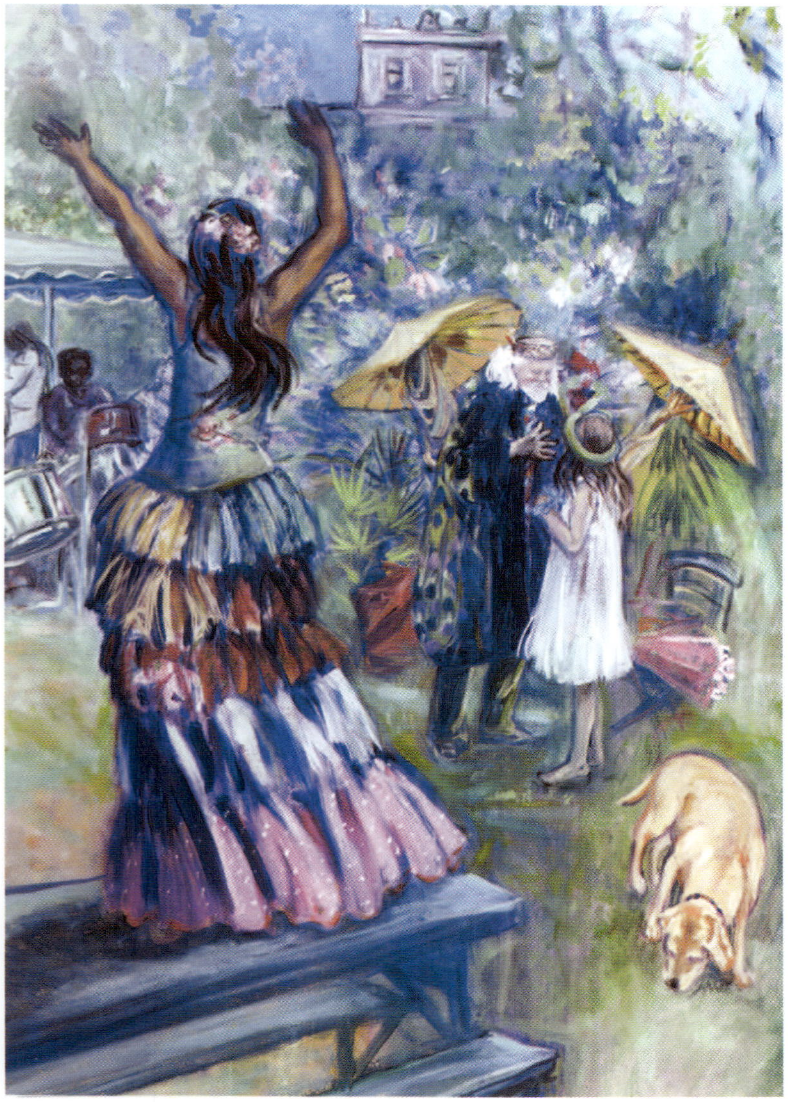

Alan and I were invited to two of his parties. One in his 'secret garden' in the summer where he had a steel band playing and we chose food from an interesting display of picnic hampers. His daughter danced to the music and dogs raced around and swam in the pool. One of his famous 'wifelets' also danced on an empty table top while Lord Bath sat in a tall-backed chair surrounded by birthday gifts from all of us. On another occasion we were shown around parts of Longleat unseen by the many visitors and on descending a spiral staircase we were shown a series of portraits of his wifelets. We were then accompanied by Lord Bath and some dogs and a wifelet number 64. Apparently he was hoping to get up to wifelet 100 one day!

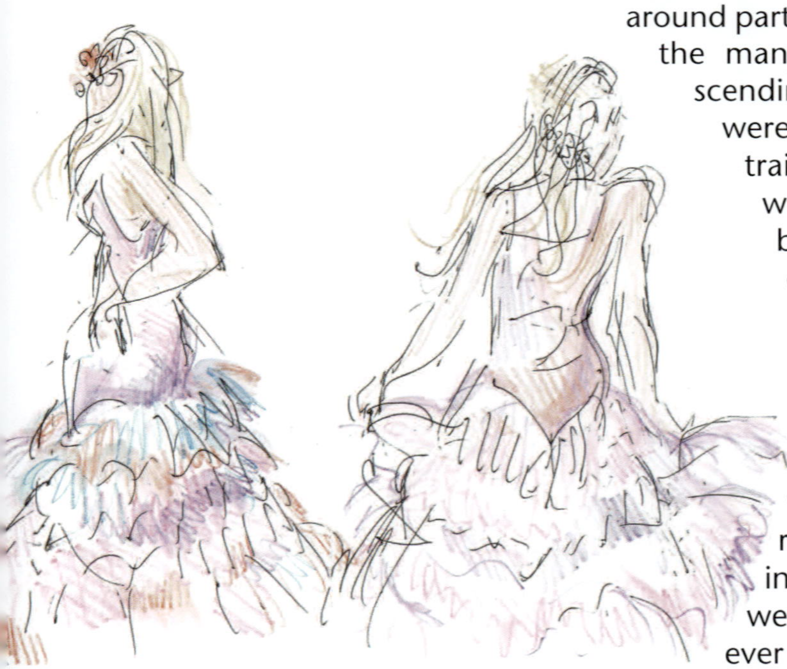

A particularly memorable room was the Kama Sutra room, full of erotica, and while Alan and I looked at everything on display he lay on a couch watching our reactions! Quite an experience! Before the pandemic, another party we were invited to included the artists who had painted him through the years. The portraits were on view and a camera crew were busy filming although I don't know if it was ever broadcast. We were so sad to hear that he died of Covid in 2020.

Opposite Page far left top: Preliminary sketching while his Lordship holds forth on a wide variety of topics. Far left bottom: The head and shoulders portrait nearing completion. Left: The full portrait which was used on a greetings card. Above left: Detail of the second portrait, also used on a card. Above right: My painting of the garden party celebrating his Lordship's birthday with his young daughter in a white dress and bare feet. Inset: From my sketchbook, dancers at the garden party.

Sir Patrick Alfred Caldwell-Moore was an English amateur astronomer who attained prominence in that field as a writer, researcher, radio commentator and television presenter known to millions through the long-running TV show 'The Sky At Night'.

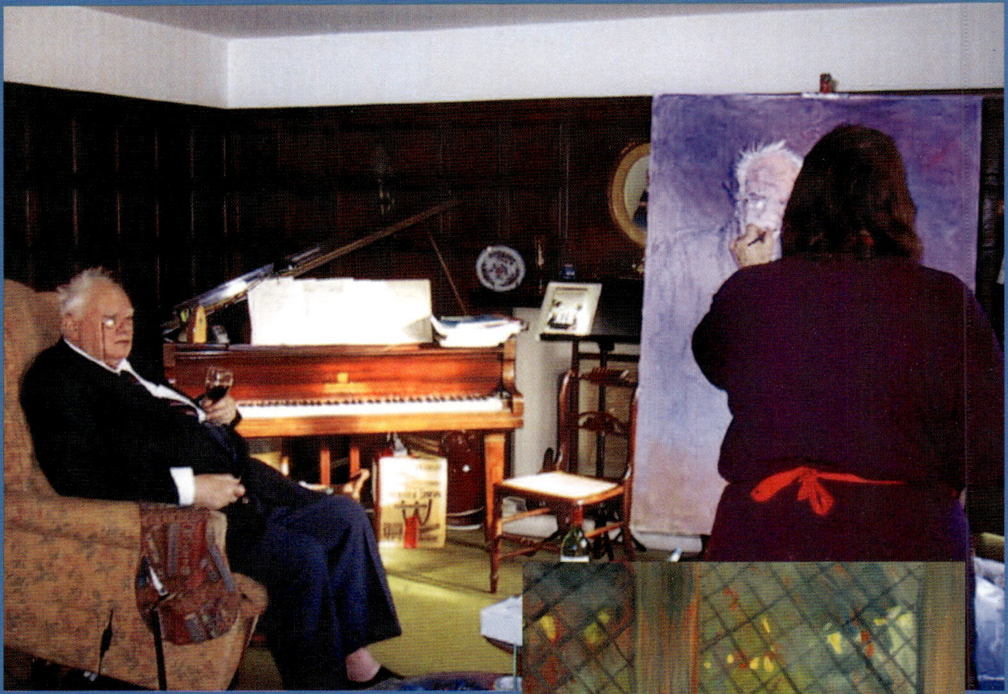

I met and arranged a sitting with Patrick through a friend of mine, Clive Juster, who knew Patrick well. Alan and I drove to Patrick's home in Selsey where we read the directions pinned on the front door, relating to his cat and the care that must be taken before entering the house. Patrick was fearful of the dearly beloved cat being run over by the busy traffic near his house. I later painted a portrait of this cat and gave it to him for a present at his birthday party.

Our sittings were constantly being interrupted by phone calls, asking Patrick to talk to various groups of people and special events. If they picked him up and catered for his wheel chair he generally was very accommodating to such invitations.

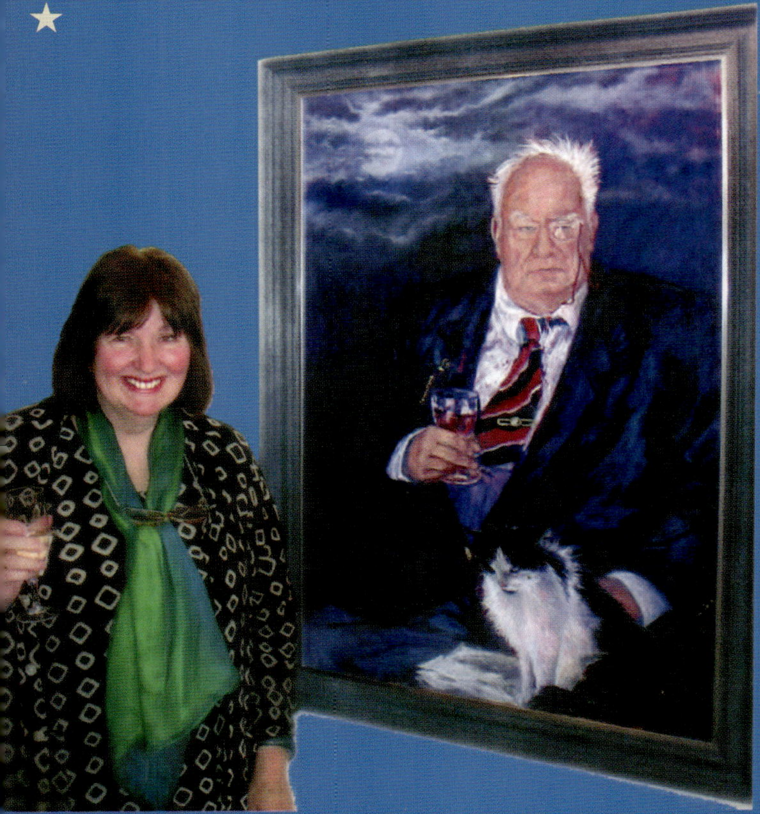

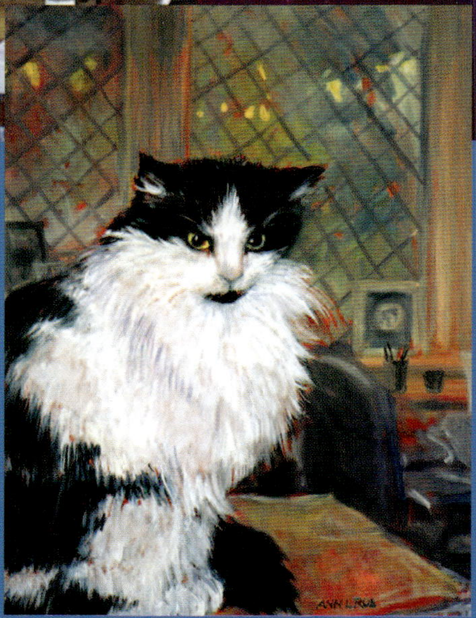

During our sittings several glasses of red wine were consumed and after lunch Patrick fell asleep in his chair while I carried on painting. We were invited to his house many times for sittings, parties and for his birthday. It was always good fun. At one time Alan and I sat talking to him at a 'Sky At Night' party with a man who had very curly hair. Later we were to find out that this was Brian May of the famous band Queen. Brian had written a book with Patrick about the stars and had just completed his degree in astronomy.

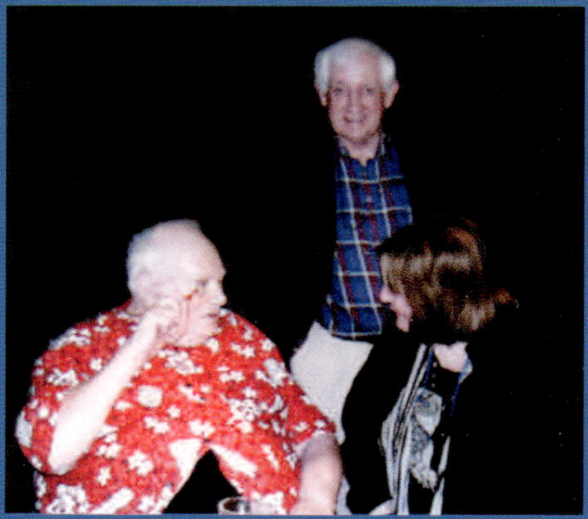

Top right: In Patrick's music room in the early stages of the portrait. Centre right: My portrait of Patrick's cat which I gave to him as a birthday present. Right: Patrick, Alan and I at the party celebrating the fiftieth year of 'The Sky At Night'. Left: Glass in hand at the unveiling of Patrick's portrait. Opposite: The finished work.

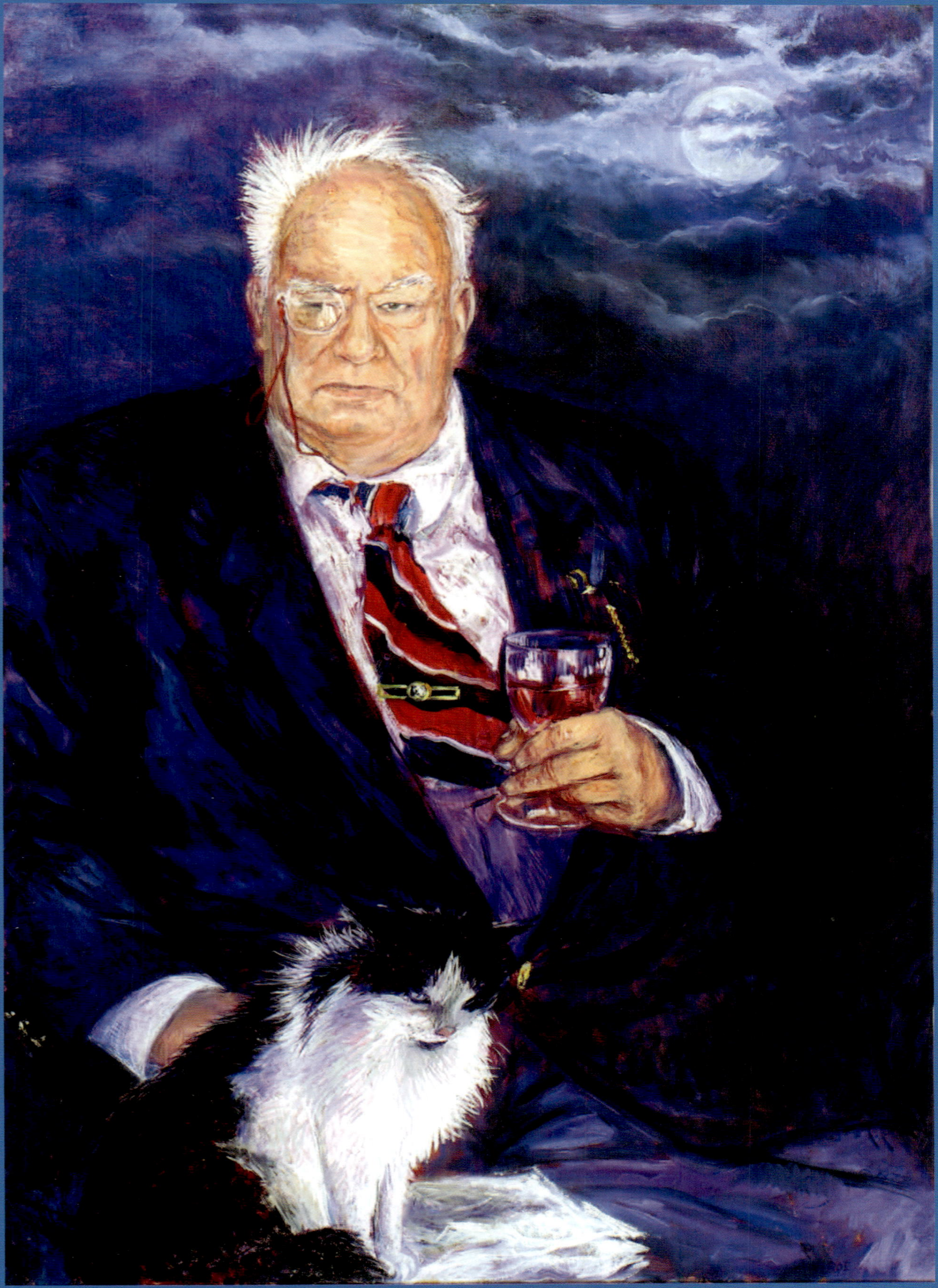

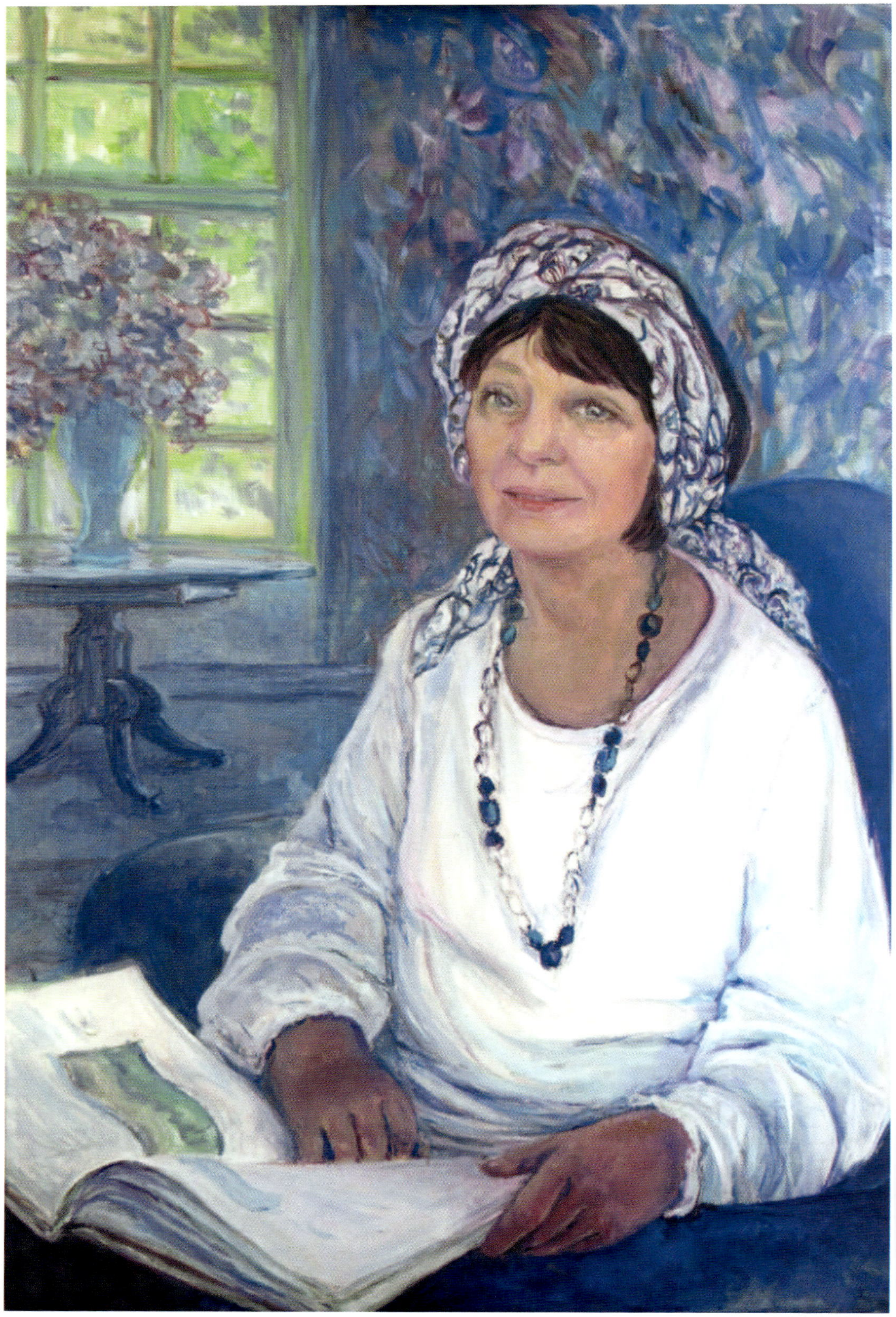

CHRIS MITCHELL. In 2018 in order to celebrate the centenary of the first occasion of women being allowed to vote in a UK general election, the South West Academy of Fine and Applied Arts arranged a special exhibition of paintings by women Academicians. The exhibition was held as part of the Open Exhibition at The Castle in Exeter. A group of women dressed in the green and purple colours of the suffragettes sang a medley of their protest songs.

Alongside the exhibition was a display of photographs from a recently published book *Land Girl Suffragette* by Simon Butler based on the remarkable life of Olive Hockin, an artist and suffragette who during the First World War had been imprisoned for her beliefs. Later in the war she worked on the land in Devon, writing a book about her experiences.

Christine, who was then the Academy's administrator posed for me dressed in the Suffragette colours for her portrait.

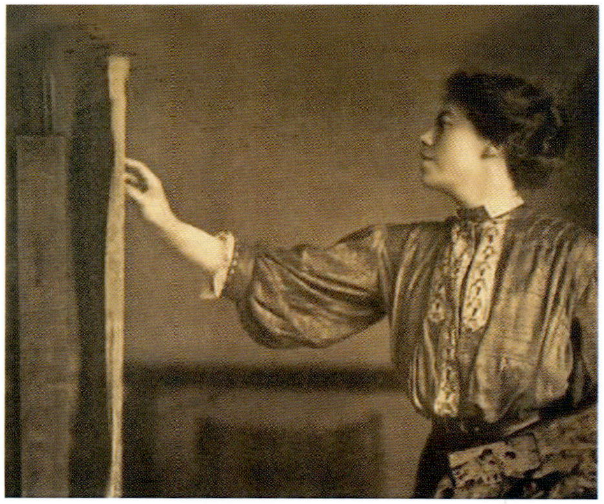

Olive Hockin painting in her studio c.1900.

ANIKA'S Middle Eastern heritage has, among other blessings, endowed her with the most amazingly beautiful brown eyes. After leaving her country of origin and moving to Africa her family then came to Britain. She funded her own studies in London to become a lawyer, telling her father that she needed no financial support from him, and also chose her own husband, which was a breakthrough for a woman with a Muslim upbringing.

When she came to pose for me she brought some amazing outfits. The dress I chose was edged with real gold embroidery and was very heavy. She allowed my granddaughter Alys to try it on. What a thrill!

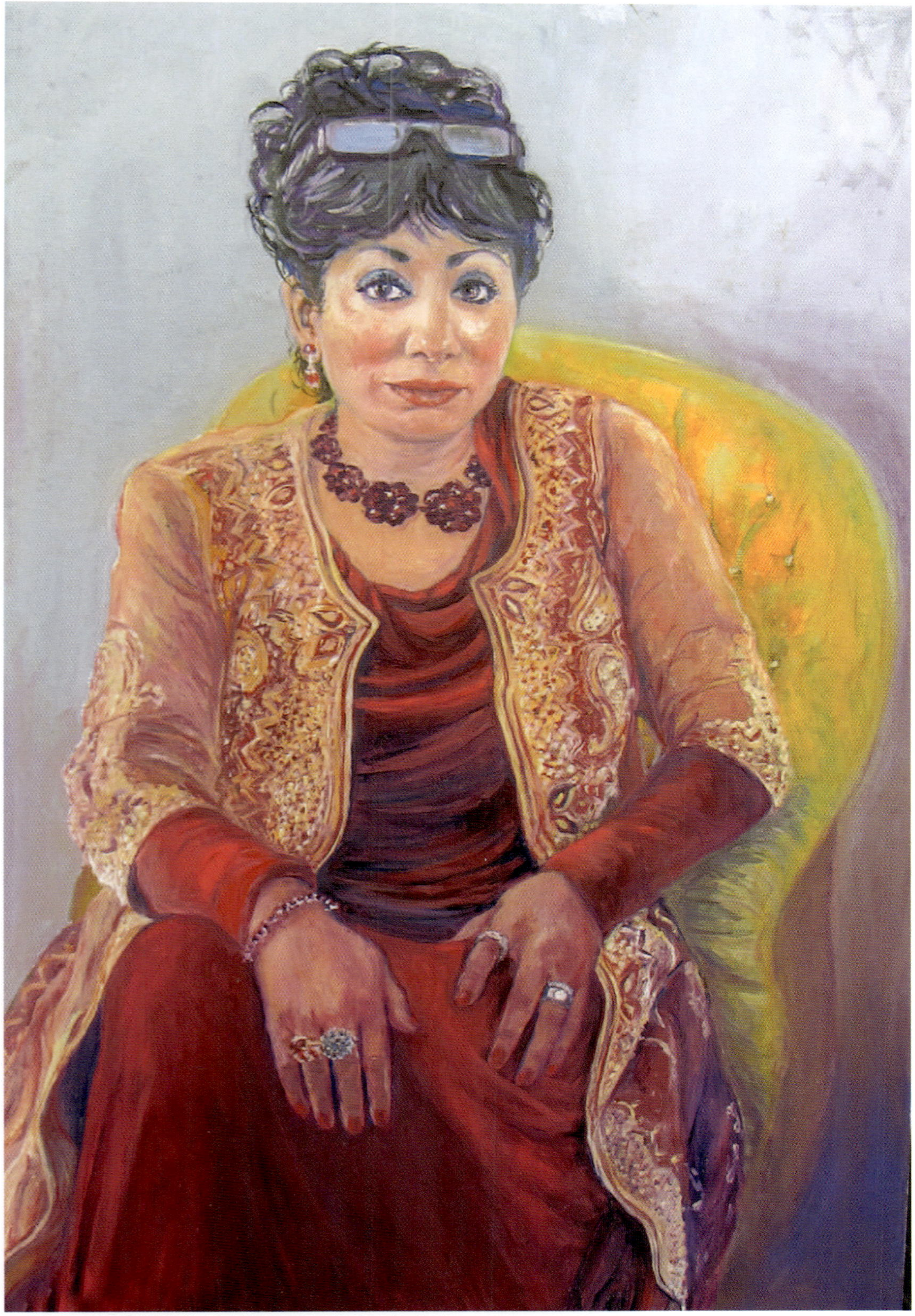

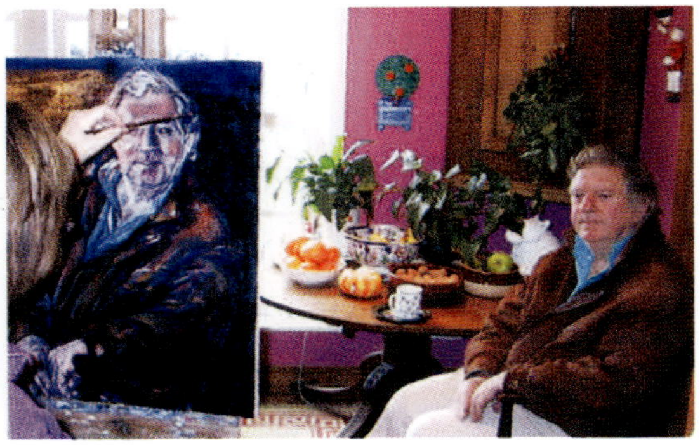

Alan sitting for his portrait.

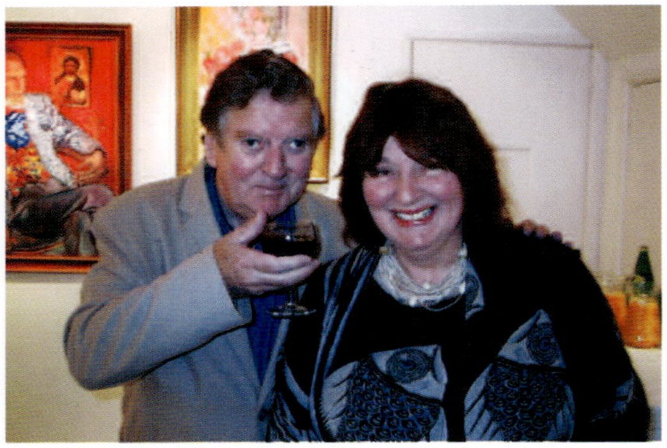

Myself and Alan enjoying ourselves at a SWAc Open private view.

Alan Cotton MBE PP, Hon. SWAc. An important benefit of being an artist is meeting other people with similar interests, as often an artist is working alone, possibly listening to music with the radio as their sole companion. Thus mingling with other artists is important. I was happy to be asked to be President of the Colyton Leisure Painters many years ago. They continue to be a delightful group of people, often coming from a variety of careers but who had always wanted to paint if only they had time. They always produce an interesting variety of work for exhibitions at which I presented a prize every year for singular achievement.

Alan Cotton, whose deserved accolades are many, not least for his excellent exhibitions annually with Messum's in London, produces superb landscape paintings from his travels with a sketchbook, often accompanied by his wife Trish, whose successful first novel *Heartbreak Baby* was recently published. Both of them have been friends with Alan and myself for many years, particularly following the formation of the South West Academy and The Young Artists Exhibitions which were a collaboration with schools throughout the Westcountry. We had a great team of helpers, Professor Robert Clements and Philip Creek who were Art Advisors for the region. Lolo designed the covers to the catalogues for each exhibition. We accompanied Alan and Trish along with Nanette Newman, the actress, at the opening of one of our Young Artists Exhibitions. Alan was wearing his brown jacket and turquoise shirt which suited him extremely well. Later he kindly sat for me to produce this portrait.

The South West Academy is very much Alan Cotton's baby, and he has worked tirelessly to achieve its high standing in the art world, inviting Dame Floella Benjamin to become our Patron and John Nettles OBE, the actor and art collector, who is now our Honorary President. King Charles III has several of Alan Cotton's works in the Royal Collection and, as Prince Charles, asked Alan to accompany him as official artist on a tour of the Southern Hemisphere.

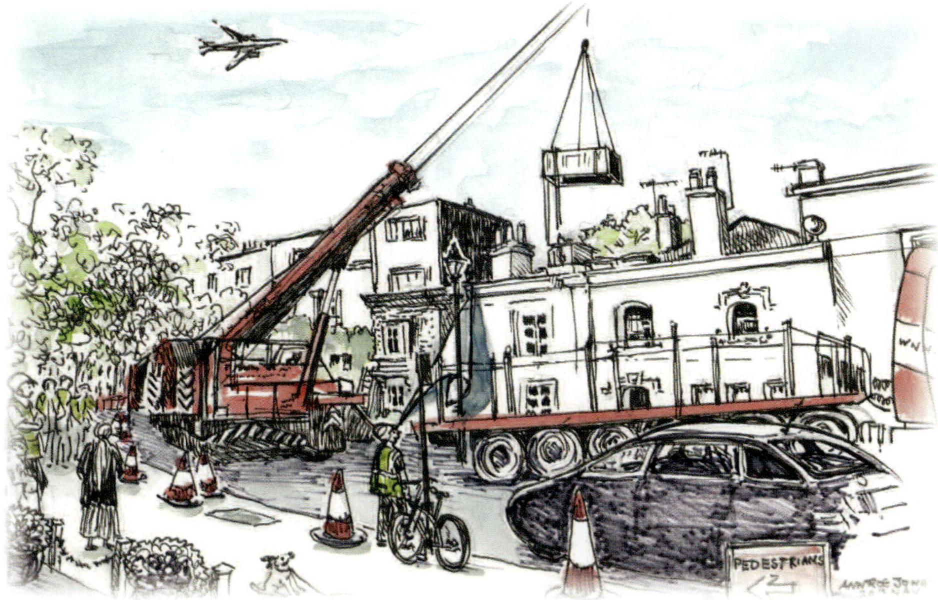

I feel proud to be a member of the South West Academy of Fine and Applied Arts and for some years had been a Trustee mover and shaker along with a team of hard-working volunteers in organising the Young Artists Annual Exhibitions. Alan also encouraged me to apply for membership of the Chelsea Arts Club, which I did. Since becoming a member I have spent many days staying in this delightful venue, and enjoying all the events which are always happening there, from exhibitions, jazz evenings, choral concerts and talks.

A sketch I made in May 2017 looking towards the Chelsea Arts Club as a temporary kitchen was being lowered over the roof while the old kitchen was being renovated.

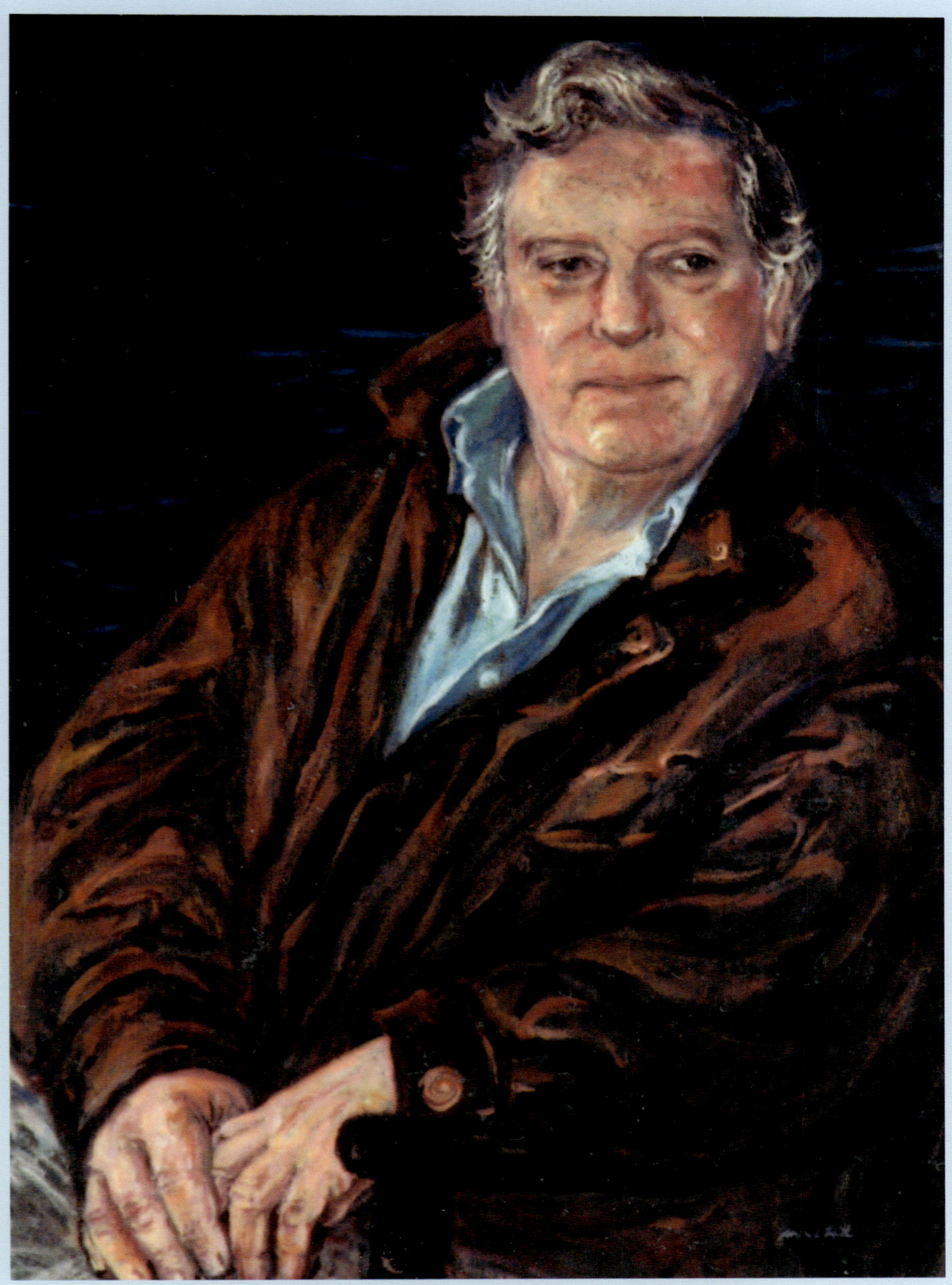

JED FALBY is never without a sketchbook, keeping one on his person at all times. A superb caricaturist, Jed is also an excellent graphic artist as is clear from his graphic novel *Le Train de Michel* based on a true story set in France during the Second World War.

During National Service in the 1950s Jed was a photographer and following art college he worked in TV and film in this country and in the US, Canada, Italy and France, winning the Palme d'Or at the Cannes Film Festival.

After coming to live in Devon, Jed became a member and an extremely active supporter of the South West Academy – at one time its Chair. He is always a joy to be with and it was a real pleasure to paint this portrait.

From time to time we receive postcards from Jed, always featuring his own inimitable cartoon drawings, always funny and always a joy to receive – thanks Jed!

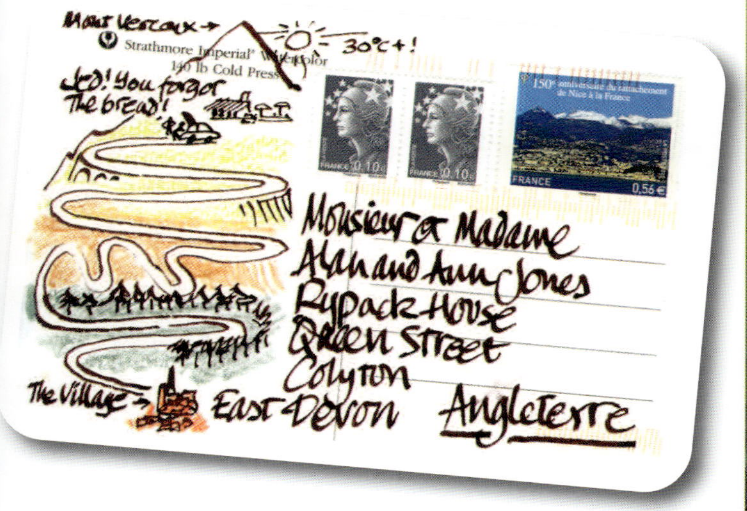

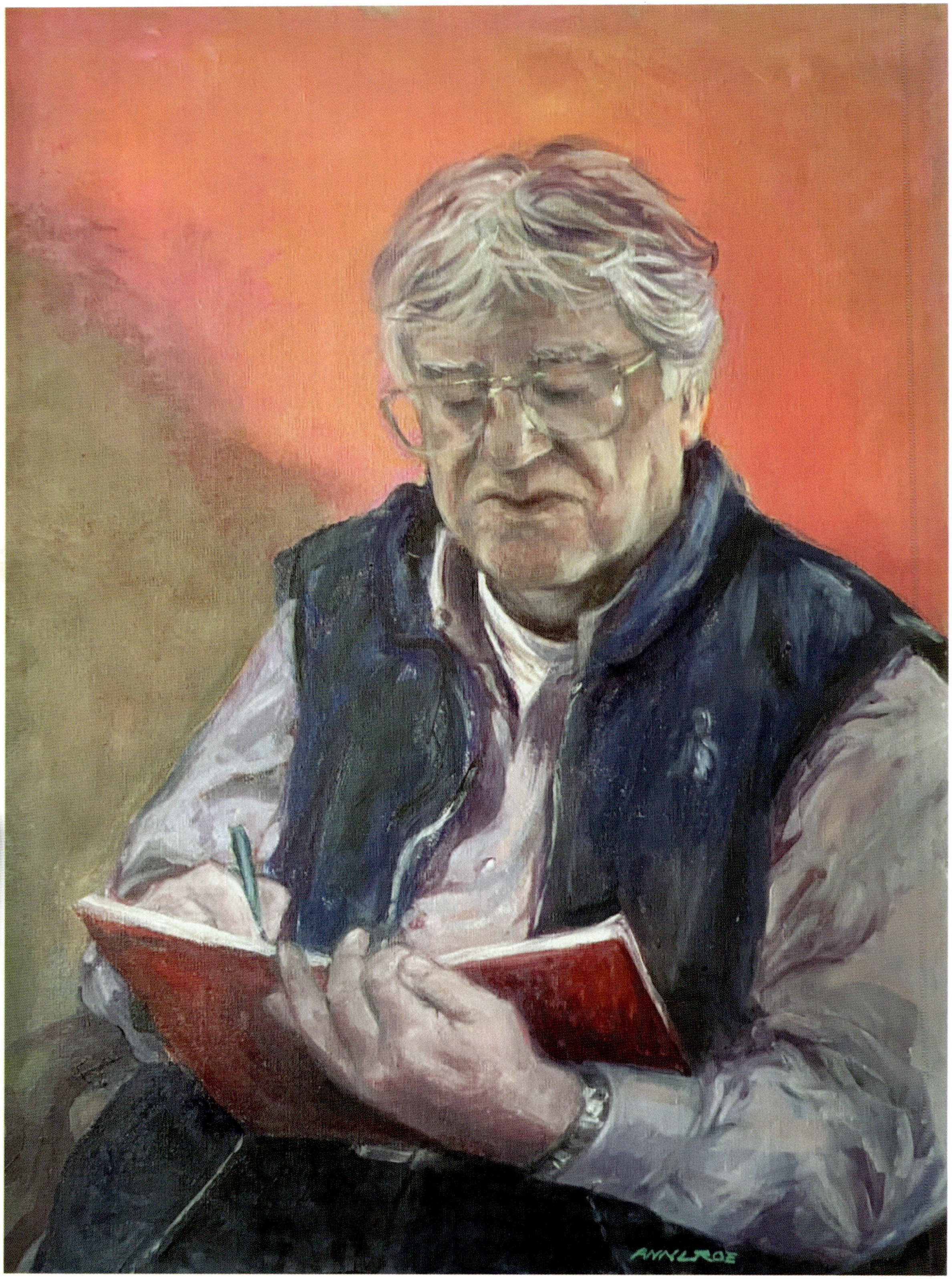

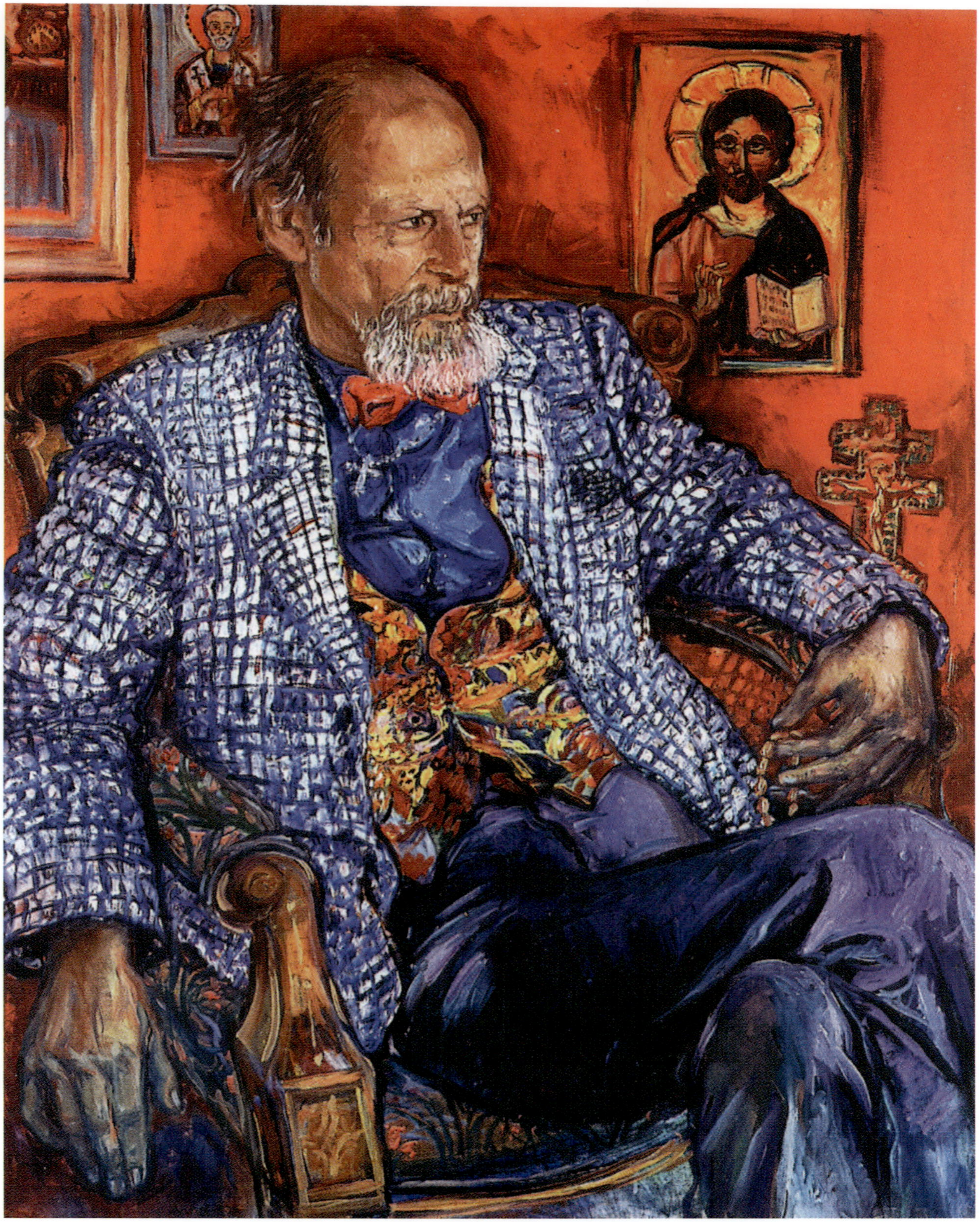

Nico Bliss. We met Nico on one of our trips to Russia. The city of Yaroslavl is twinned with Exeter which was our link with Russia. I took, with Alan, a group of Colyton Grammar School young artists to Yaroslavl along with an exhibition of their work which was displayed at a school for artistic children. Later we held a reciprocal exhibition of the Russian children's work at CGS, which proved very successful.

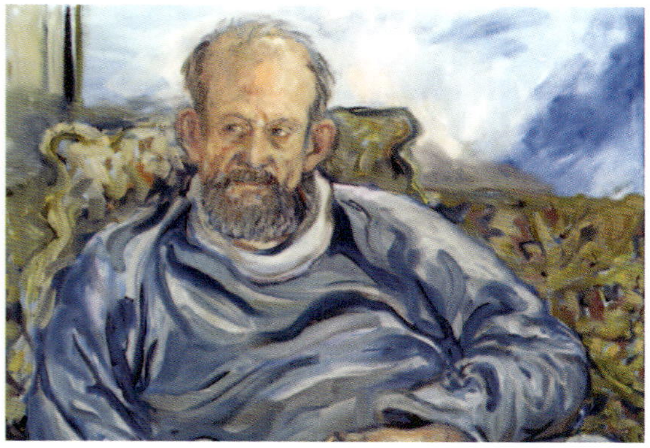

Nico came on one of our trips to Russia via the twinning association. He became a friend of ours and was a willing sitter for me. One of my portraits of him won a prestigious prize when exhibited in Exeter. Nico was formerly a Priest in the Church of England but later changing to the Russian church. In later years he married a Russian lady. The deep red background and icon in the painting are descriptive of Nico's Russian religious links.

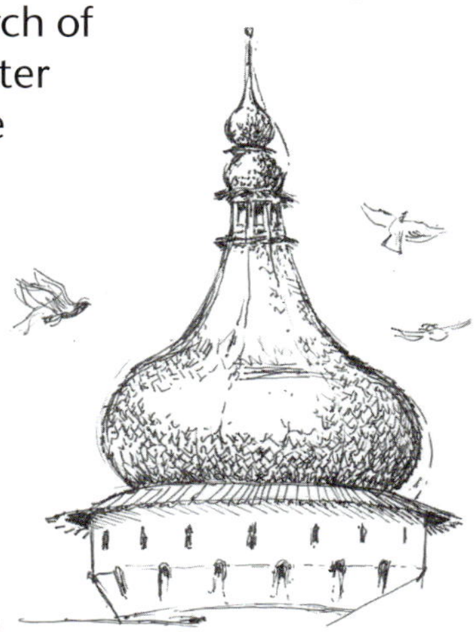

DAVID GUNN JOHNSON, affectionately known locally as 'The Revving Vicar' was a very enterprising clergyman who happily agreed to pose for his portrait. He came buzzing up our drive and on to our lawn on his giant Harley-Davidson motorcycle for his sitting.

David could be seen roaring around Colyton on his motorcycle with his colourful wife riding pillion. Clearly he was not the only Man of the Church riding a motorbike, as I saw a Christmas card he sent out one year showing David with a group of fellow ecclesiasts also on their bikes.

He sat very well while I painted him. Both his daughters also sat for a class in the Grammar School and were very willing to dress up for the occasion. I was also looking forward to painting David's wife's portrait but somehow life took over and it never happened, although I know she would have been good fun to paint as she has always loved dressing up, and is an excellent actress.

The background of my painting shows one of the beautiful stained glass windows in our church here in Colyton with David in his ecclesiastical robes and with a bible in his hands. It is a large painting as I felt it needed to be. I used this painting for promotional cards that I had printed and which I used as a Christmas card one year.

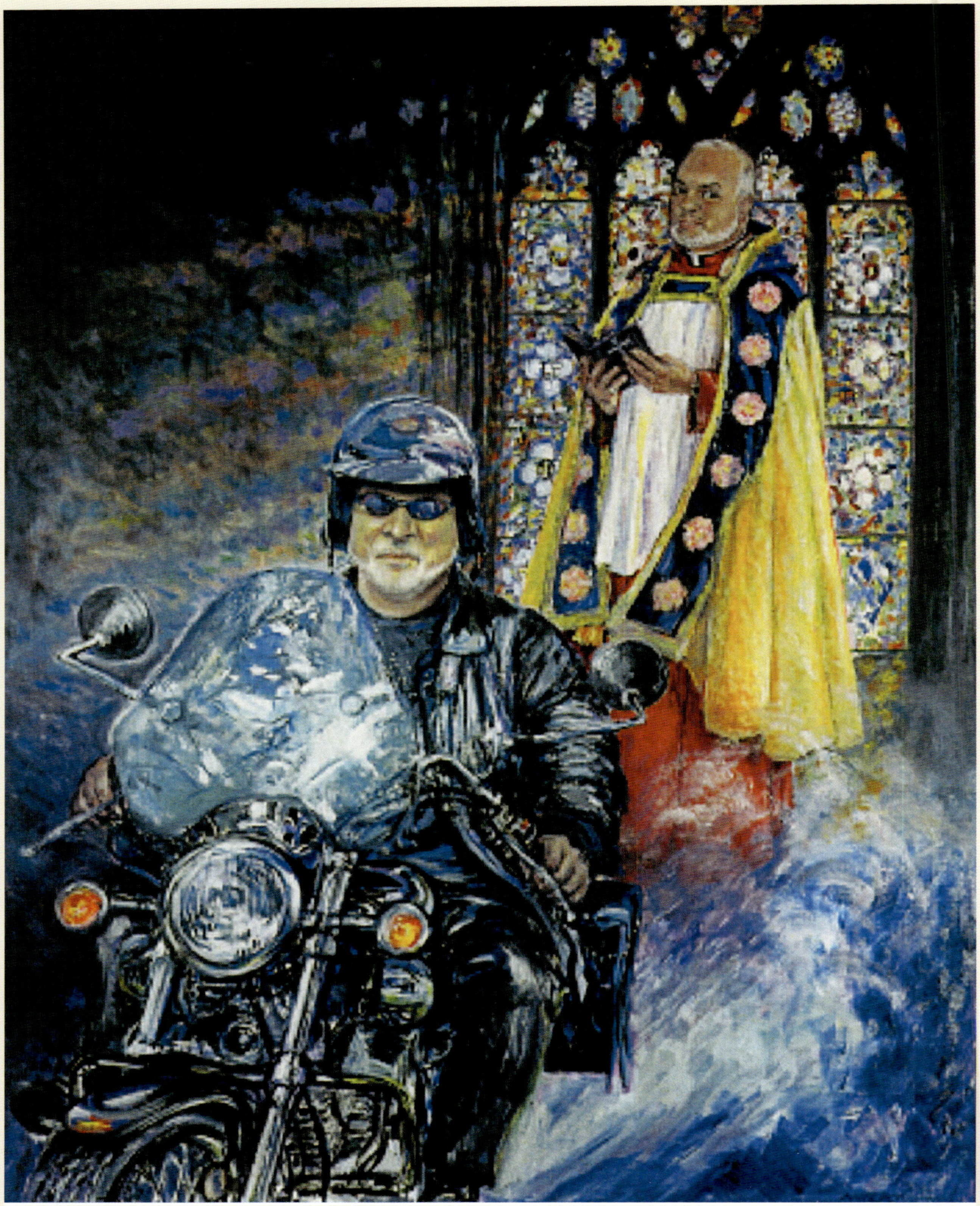

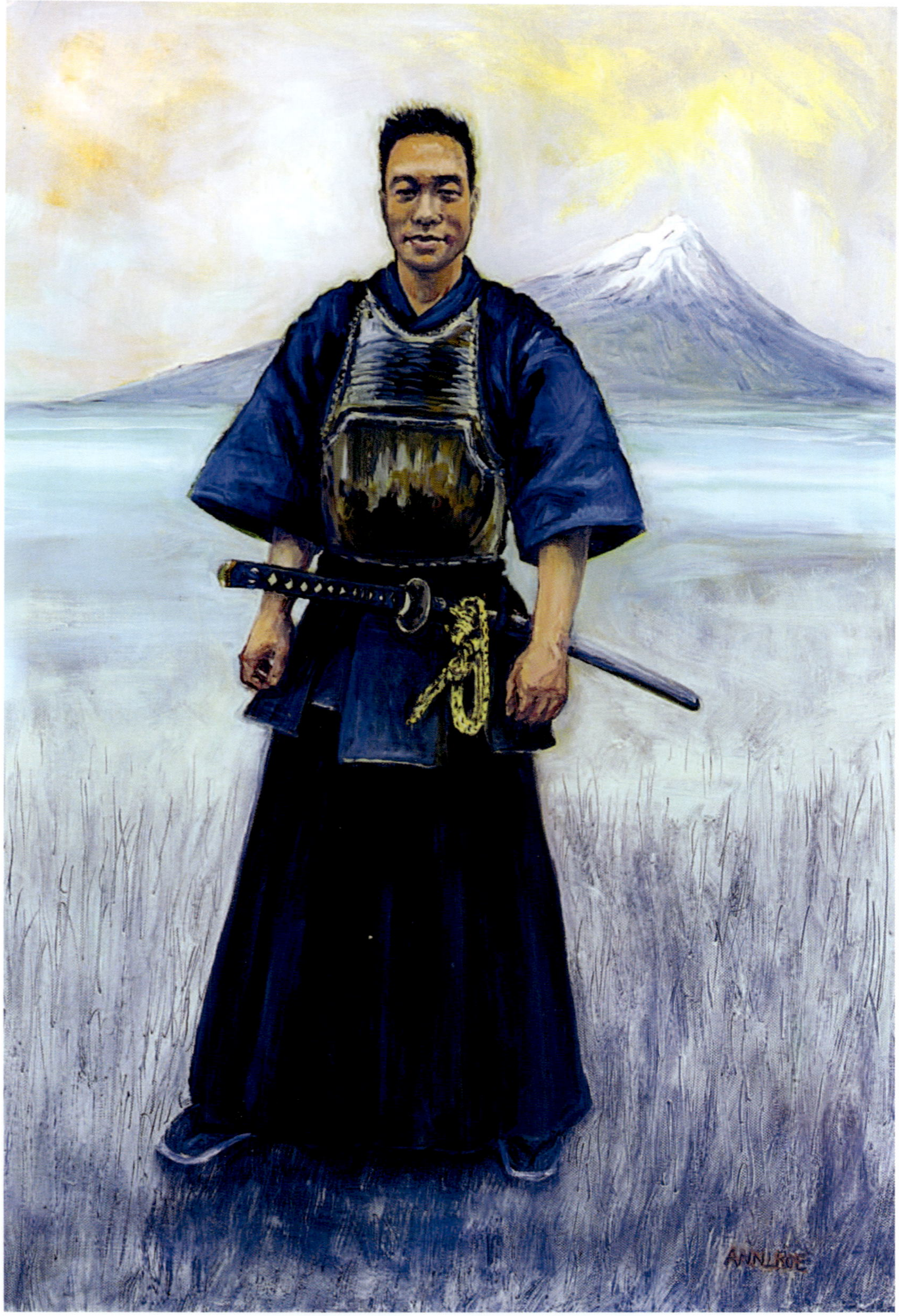

RYAN HYASHI. Ryan is an amazing, scary magician, who uses Samurai swords in his act and wears wonderful Japanese outfits. He is also a charming Japanese-Canadian, and thus speaks perfect English. I made some sketches of him while he posed at one of Blackpool's Magic Conventions.

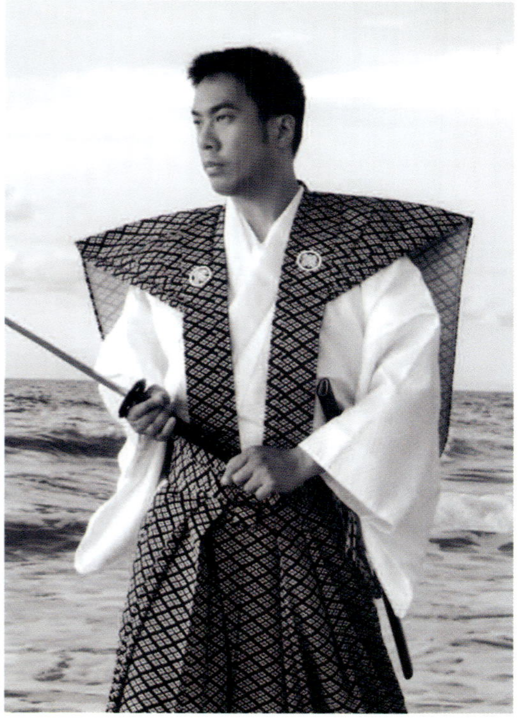

For his initial portrait he went back to his hotel to change into something more dramatic and colourful. Ryan works all around the world and does not often come to Britain, but I hope to meet up again with him one of these days when he returns to the UK.

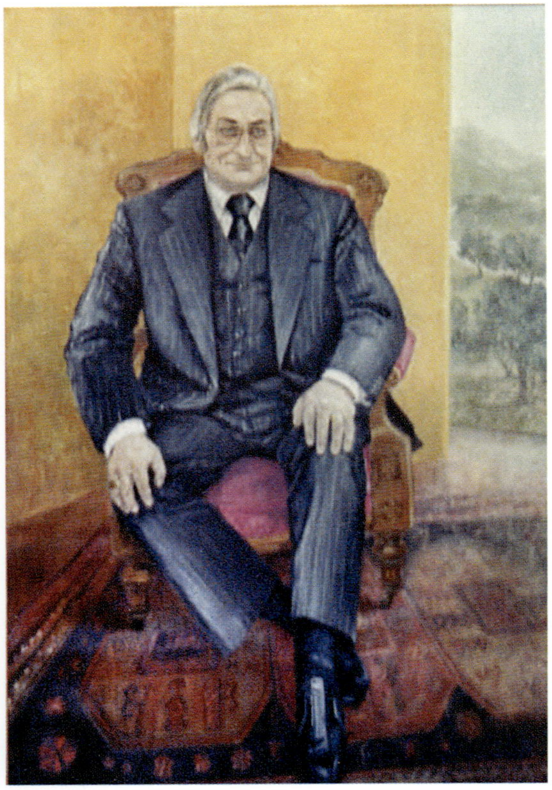

Peter.

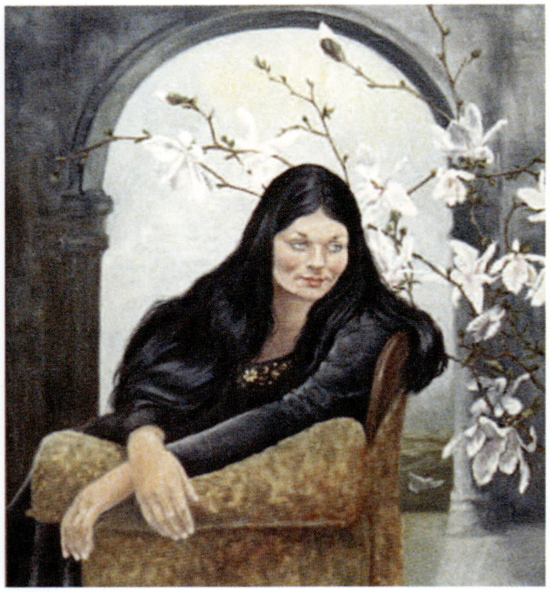

Peter's 'Lady' - among the magnolias.

THE MYSTERIOUS PETER. It was a cold winter's night when Alan and I set off in our car filled with Alan's magic props for the show he was to perform at the Webbington Hotel, south of Bristol in the Mendip Hills. Lorna Luff (Liza Minnelli's sister and daughter of Judy Garland) was the star of the evening, an extraordinarily good singer, just like Judy Garland. I watched her rehearsing and running through her pieces and was determined to see her final performance which was in the second half of the show, with Alan in the first half performing his magic.

But unknown to all of us, snow was silently falling, coming down thick and fast and by the end of Lorna's performance the audience, plus everyone in the hotel, were totally snowed in. Celebrity comedian Frankie Howerd, who lived close by, apparently was the only one able to make it home.

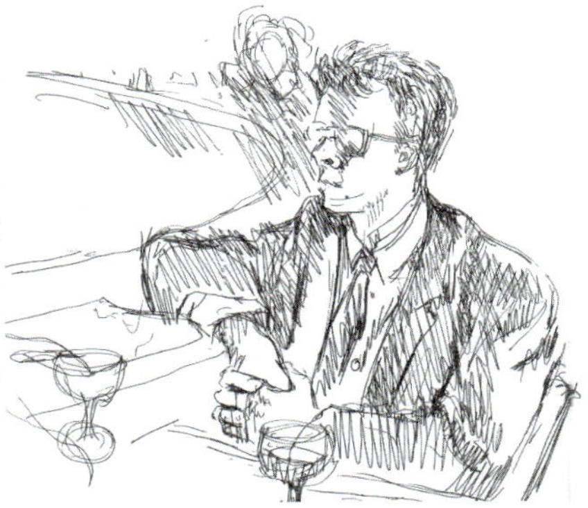

So, as always when I have time on my hands, I started to sketch people in the bar and among the people there was Peter and his friend Cyril. The drawings were much admired and from this fortuitous meeting, we set up a future portrait session in Devon for Peter. Later, when this snowy event was but a memory, Cyril and Peter came down to Devon and stayed at the beautiful Combe House Hotel in Gittisham for what turned out to be a memorable weekend.

Peter wanted a large and imposing portrait, life-size, which required the use of a step ladder for me to reach the highest points of the canvas. He wore a Saville Row suit and a diamond ring and his chair was placed on a Persian carpet. Cyril was sent out to buy champagne and brandy at frequent intervals during the sitting. We had several weekends like this, and I later completed portraits of two of Peter's children plus his then girlfriend, who I asked to pose leaning over the end of a chaise longue.

Something of an enigma and seemingly wealthy enough to indulge his slightest whim Peter had, one morning while at his home, the mad idea of flying to Paris for lunch. Being Peter he managed to find a pilot, plus a plane, and achieved at breakneck speed the unbelievable. He was certainly a person you could never forget, but when he finally came in a van to pick up his paintings a doctor had told him he needed to stop drinking. He was very quiet and utterly different without the alcohol and no longer the outrageous but charming character he once was. When he picked up the paintings and all were safely put in his van, he disappeared over the hills and far away. We never saw him again, but we will never forget him!

Above: I've never been able to resist making impromptu sketches of individuals and groups, especially when they are unaware of my presence. My sketchbooks are full of such drawings and, in the case of our enforced winter's night at the hotel, it led to a fascinating encounter.

SIMON BRADLEY. We have known Simon since he was 11 years old and he is now a firm member of our family. He was a keen magic enthusiast and when at Colyton Grammar School was constantly catching Alan at any spare moment to discuss magic tricks. Simon was a welcome presence in my Art Department. He was obviously a talented boy and, with a friend, worked on an animation film, with a stop motion camera held in my department. He became one of the youngest members of The Magic Circle with his thesis on magic. He continues to perform magic and produces excellent lino-prints and paintings which he successfully sells from his home in Cornwall and at local artistic events and exhibitions.

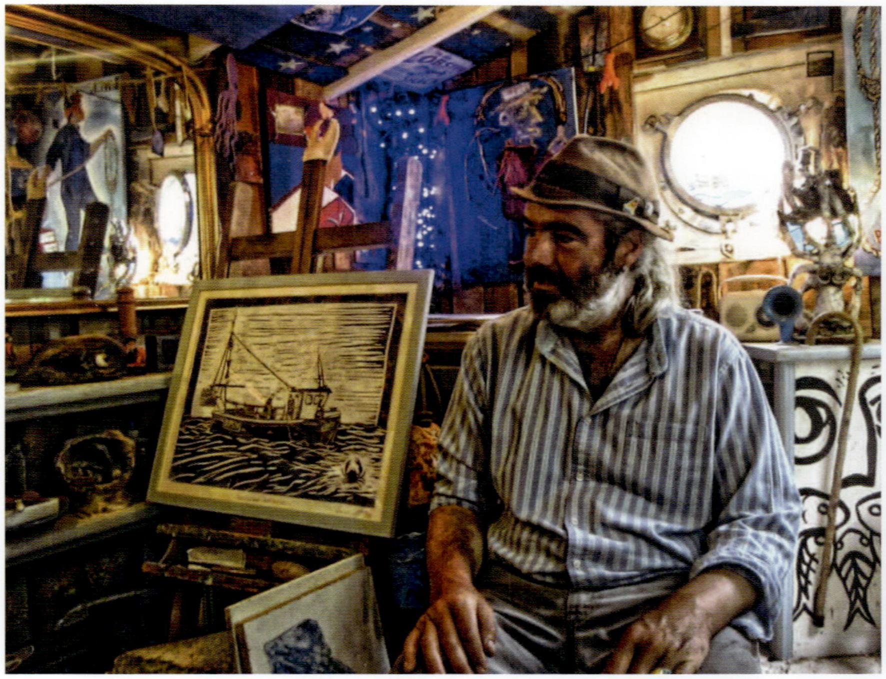

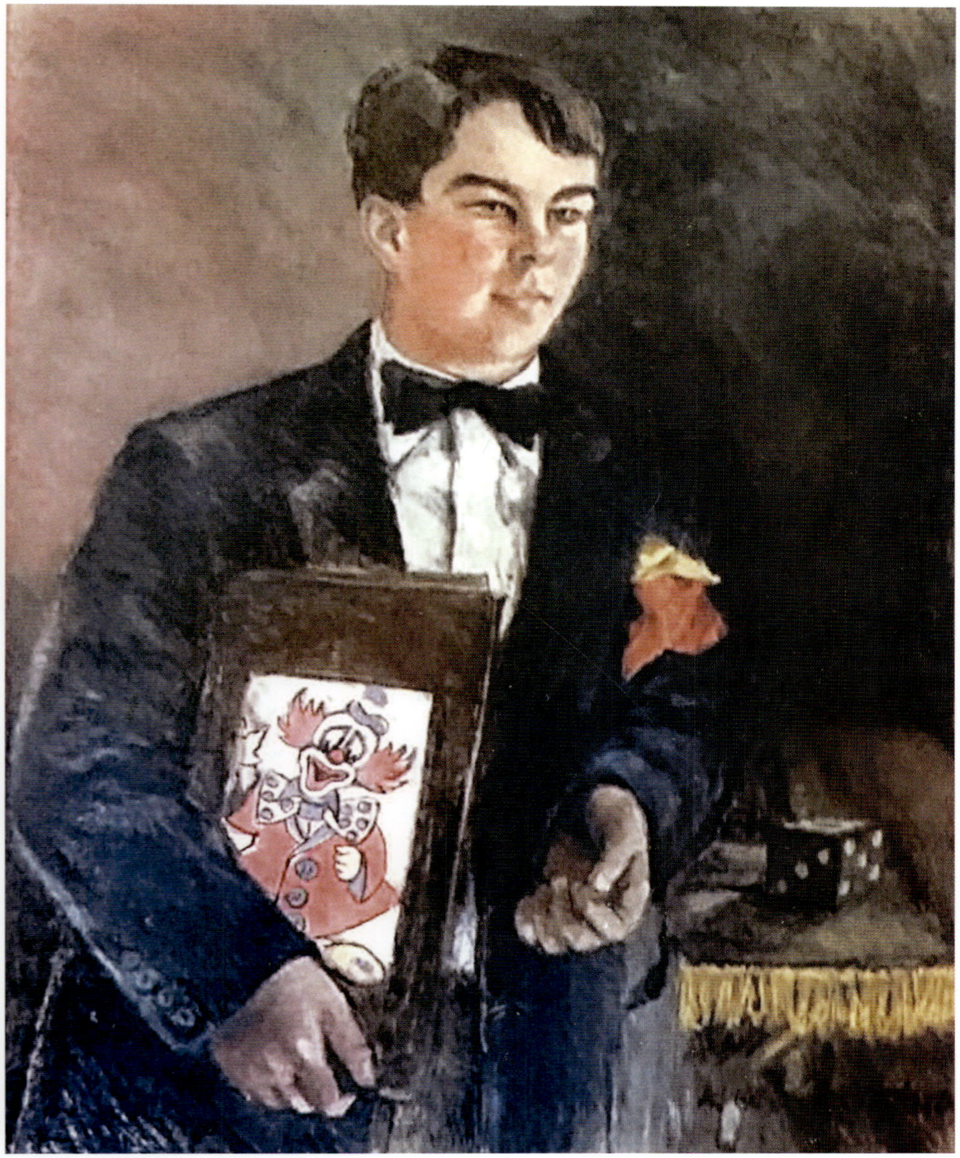

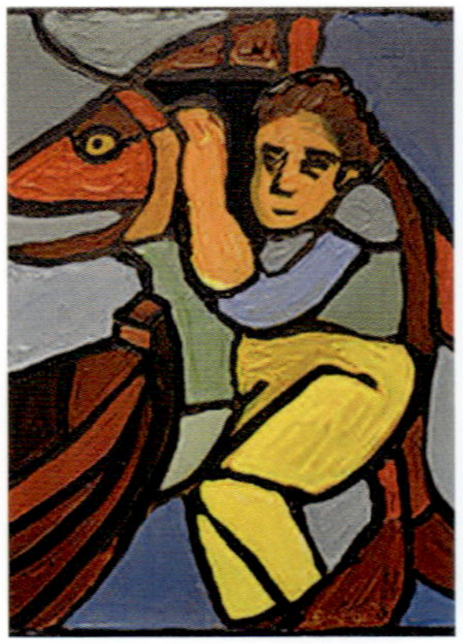

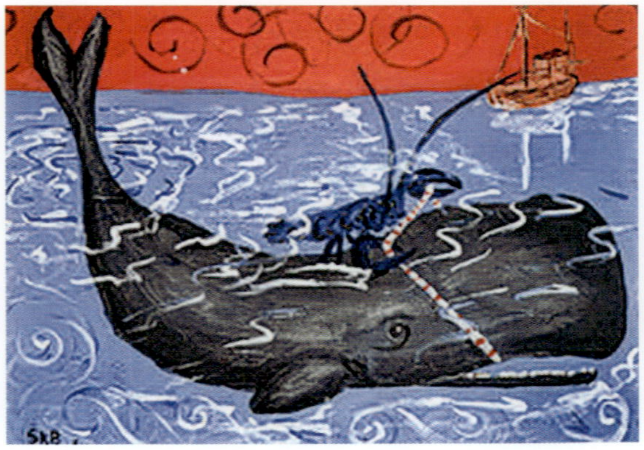

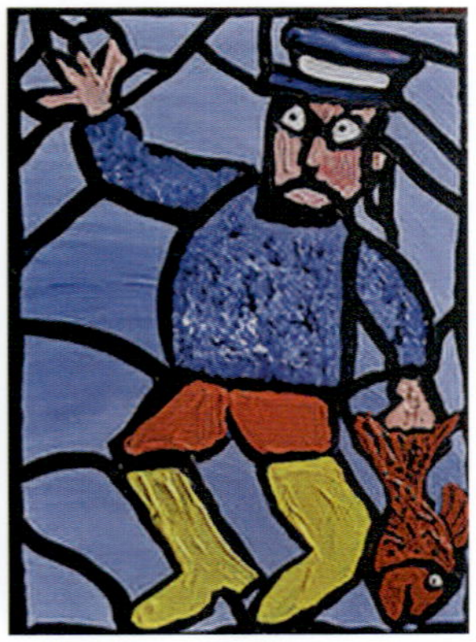

Above: My early portrait of Simon when he was starting out on his career in magic. He now refers to me as his Godmother. I like this kind accolade.
Above left: Simon in his truly magical studio at Cadgwith in Cornwall.
Left: examples of Simon's artwork.

Lydia Corbett (Sylvette David). Over several years while exhibiting in the Delamore Arts annual exhibitions on Dartmoor, I had met and spoken to this little French lady who wore plaits. I finally asked if she would be willing to sit for me, but she felt she was too old or words to that effect. Then Alan Cotton arranged for Lydia to be interviewed by her daughter Isabel Coulton at a Q&A session at the Kennaway House Gallery in Sidmouth which Alan and I attended. Following this Lydia asked me to paint her portrait.

Lydia's life had been transformed by meeting Pablo Picasso who asked her to sit for him. She was only sixteen years old and had her hair in a pony tail (a style said to have been seen and adopted by Brigette Bardot). For some time Lydia became Picasso's muse from which date he created several iconic portraits and sculptures.

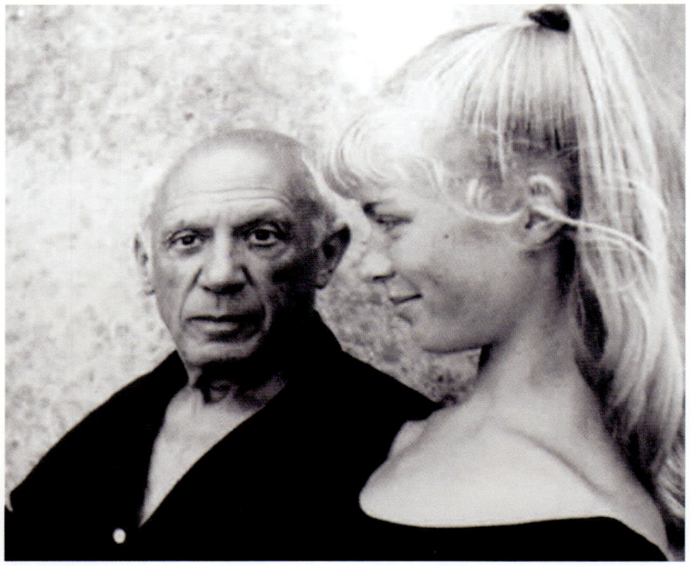

We spent some time with Lydia when we visited her home, filled with her own paintings and sculptures. Picasso's influence was everywhere in much of the work she had made. After sketching her and taking photos, we returned home to complete the painting. Lydia's artwork is the subject of numerous books and many exhibitions.

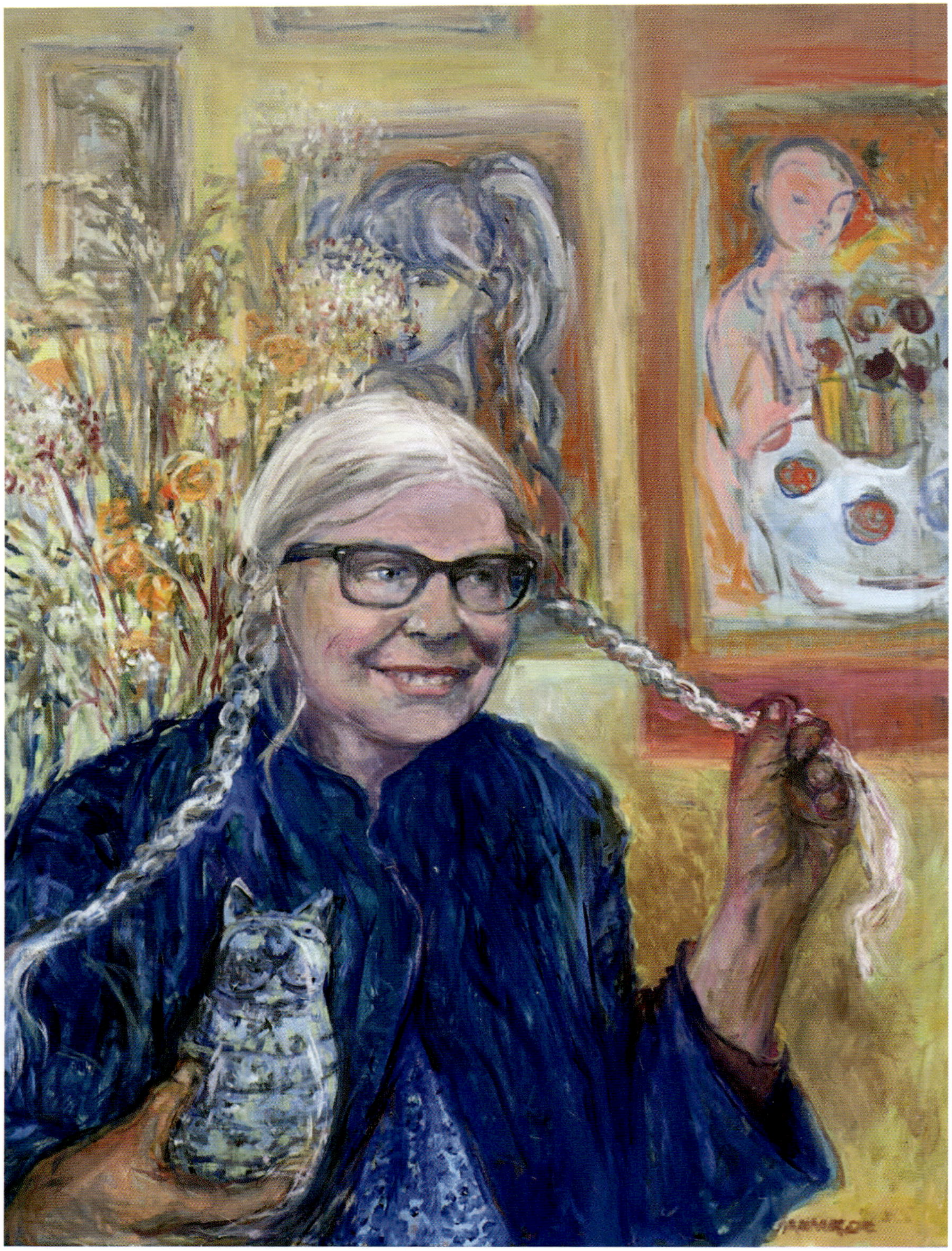

Left: The teenage Sylvette David (Lydia) with Picasso.

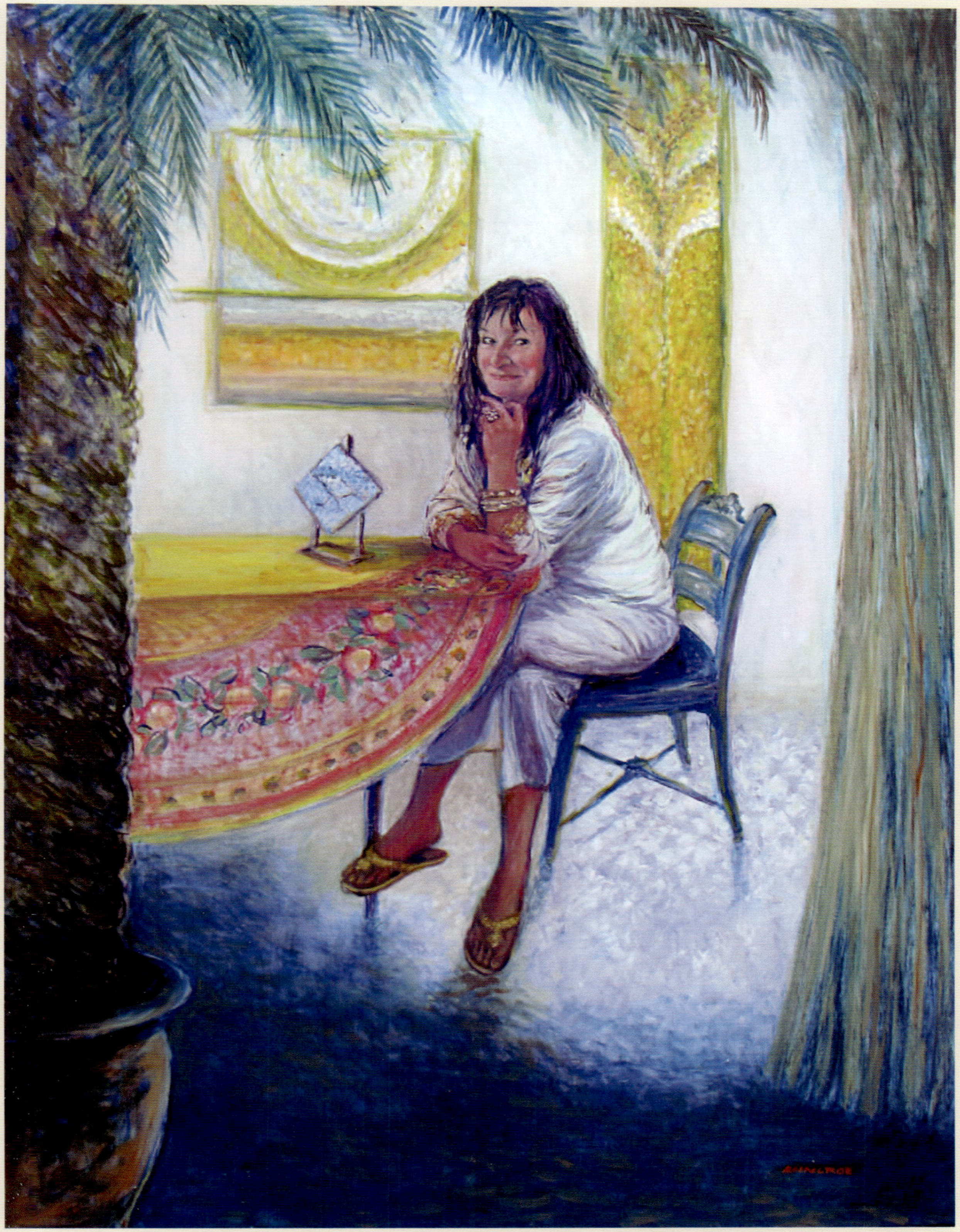

ELAINE M. GOODWIN. Elaine's wonderful glitteringly beautiful mosaics have always fascinated me. While I was teaching, she came to my Art Department and ran some excellent workshops for my A-Level students. One girl, as part of her exam work, used the skills she'd learned to produce a mosaic for a mirror frame which was quite beautiful.

Elaine has made her home in places as far apart as India and North Africa. She had a house in Morocco for many years, and when I painted her portrait, I put something of a Moroccan influence into the composition. When she lived in Exeter, I visited her beautiful home; a feast for the eyes, full of her mosaics. She now lives in Burgundy where she owns a huge house, transforming part of it into a studio and gallery and holding regular exhibitions.

Elaine is a special artist with a world-wide reputation. She uses small ceramic pieces (purchased from a generations-old family firm in Italy), through which her finished work brings dynamic light and colour to any space.

Elaine has written books on mosaics, helpful to those who want to learn about this lesser-known form of art. She regularly exhibits her work throughout Europe and beyond and has held an excellent exhibition at the Royal Albert Memorial Museum in Exeter and another at the Chelsea Art Club.

Elaine is full of *joie de vivre* and I wish I could see her more often!

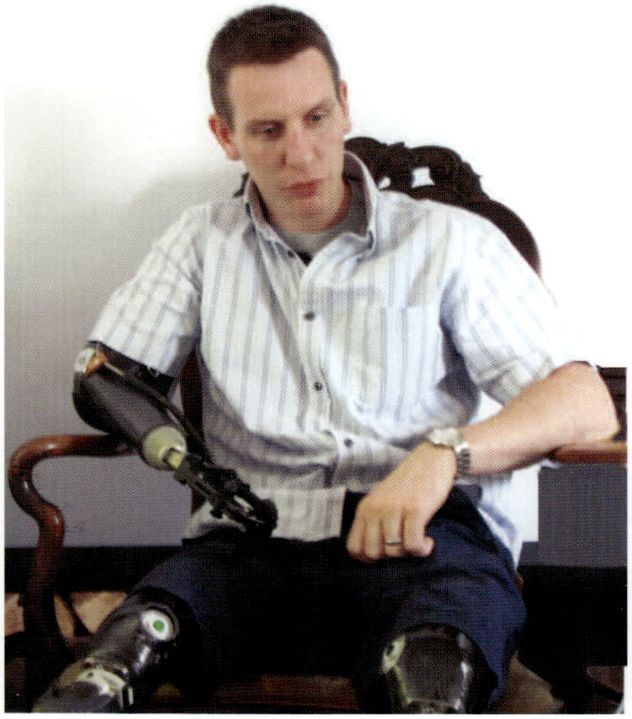

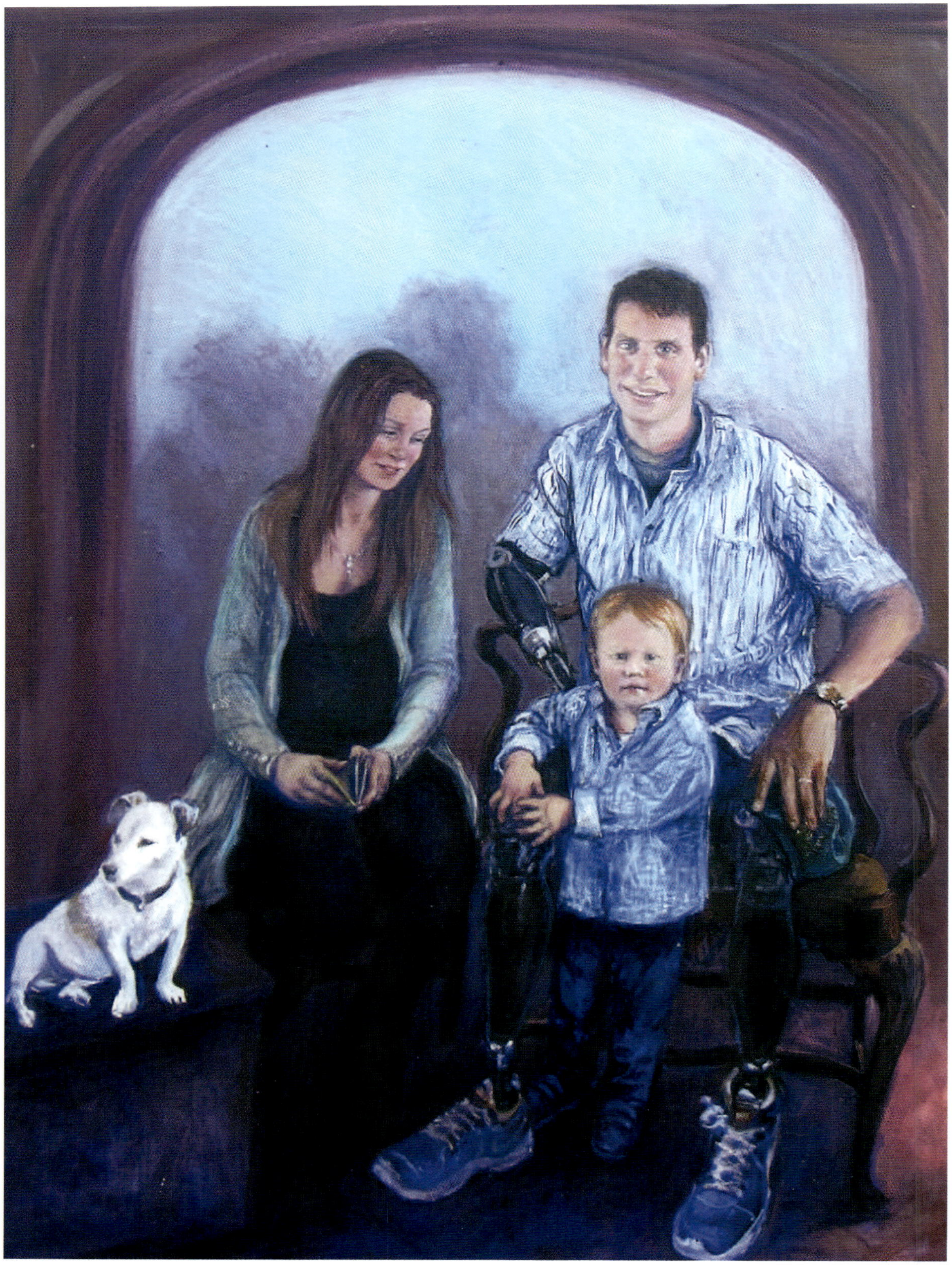

CAPTAIN JON WHITE came and sat for me sometime after returning from Afghanistan where he had lost three limbs. He and his wife had just built a house, an endeavour which was televised. Their home included many unusual adaptations which enabled Jon to live comfortably. The portrait included their dog and their son. Jon's wife at the time of painting this portrait was expecting a little daughter.

Jon very kindly opened a South West Academy of Arts exhibition at the Castle in Exeter where this portrait was displayed. I later met a friend of his at the Royal Academy Summer Exhibition in London who had also suffered injuries in Afghanistan. Jon never complained about his situation, but has been a courageous young man getting on with life in every way that he can.

It was a privilege to have known Jon, a great role model for us all.

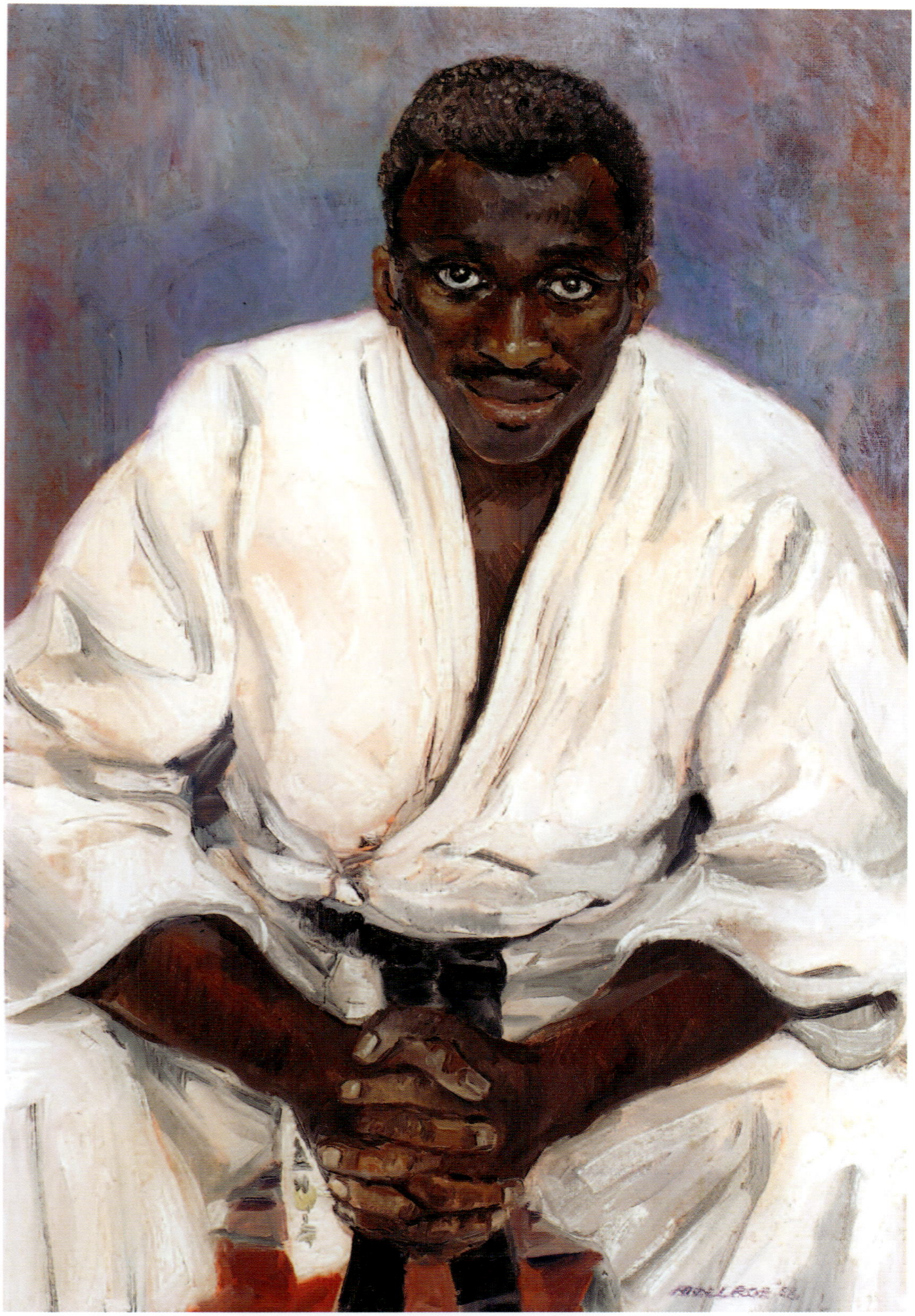

We arranged for this young man, a Judo Martial Arts Black Belt, to come and sit for me one day. It was such a long time ago, that I sadly do not remember his name. He was studying Judo with Amry our son. I recall he was a very good sitter and later I put his portrait into a South West Academy exhibition in Exeter.

THE GIBSON FAMILY. On returning to Britain from Hong Kong at the changeover in 1977 from British to Chinese rule, the Gibson family moved into our former home, Oroolong House, and filled it with laughter, family and friends (and two tortoises). It was just what the old house had been like when we lived there. This delightful family were happy for me to paint portraits of many of them and some of these paintings hang on their walls today.

Right: Morgan with her twins.

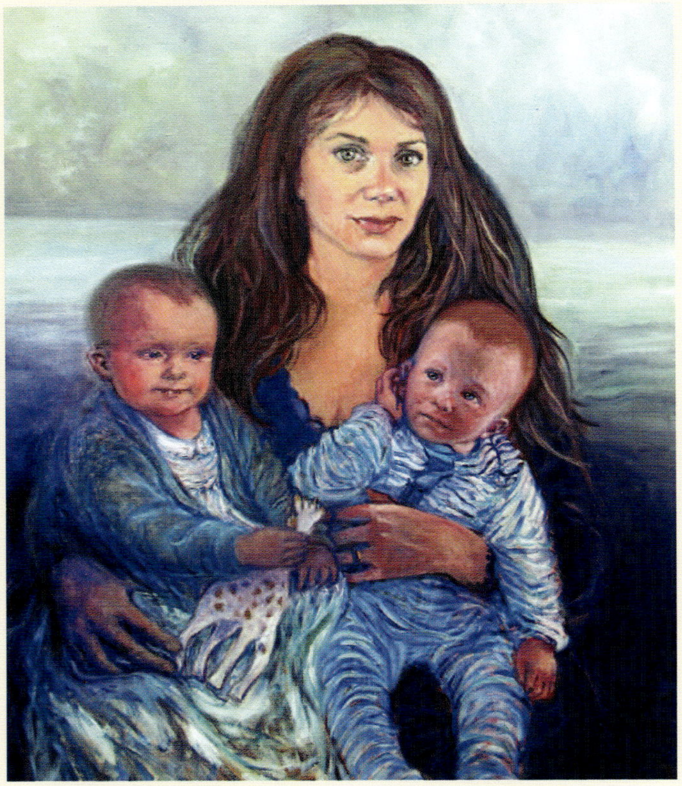

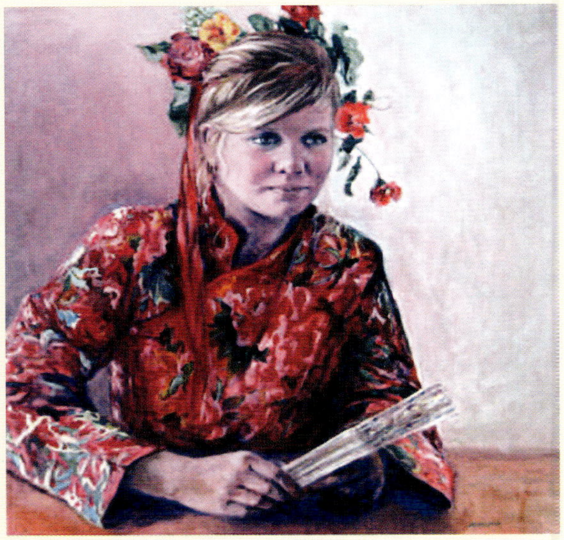

Above: Rosie Gibson.

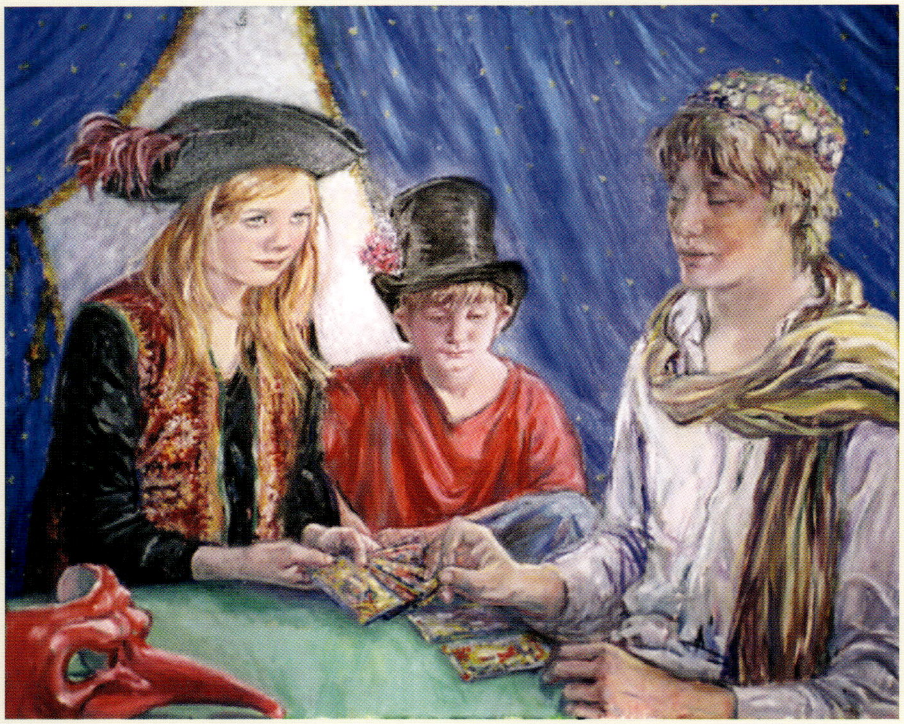

Left: Rosie, Felix and Fraser, three of the Gibson children.

Right: Felix, who was born in Hong Kong, in the Year of the Cockerel.

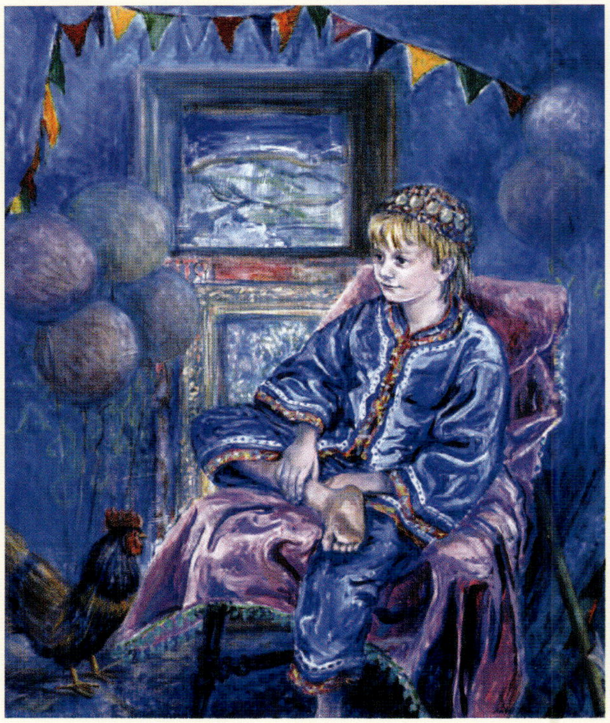

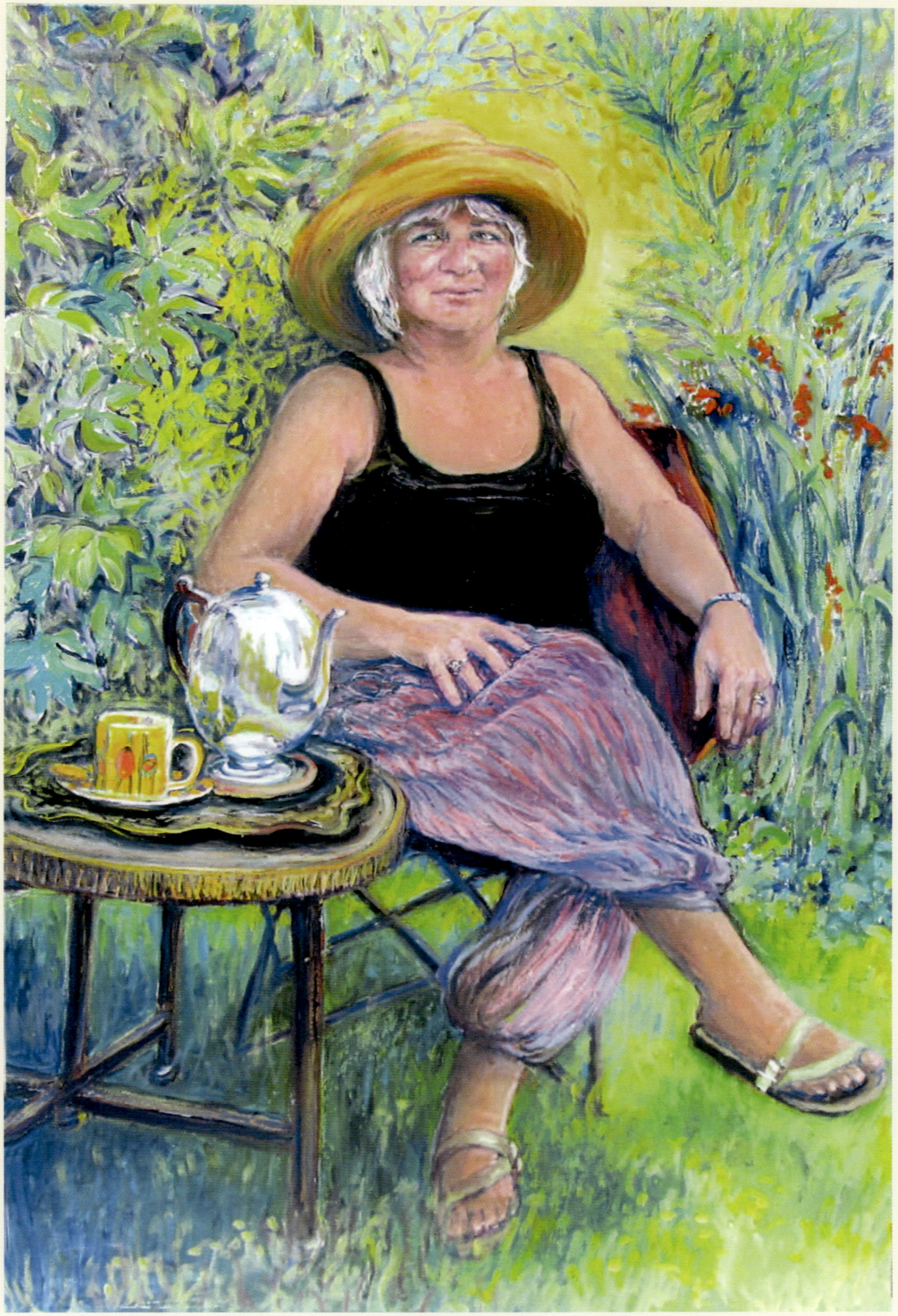

Sandy Gibson. We had built our new home, Rupack House, in what had been part of the garden of Oroolong, so travelling for sittings was no major problem! Sandy Gibson still comes up here for a coffee very regularly, so we more recently planned a sitting in the garden with our coffee pot placed on an old fold-up Indian table, this being a nod towards her life travelling all around the world.

Planning a painting is always a major consideration for the painter of portraits. Sometimes it can simply be a close up of a person, but often devising the background carefully can provide additional connections to the sitter's life and character, just as with my morning with Sandy, painting in the summer garden when the sun shone.

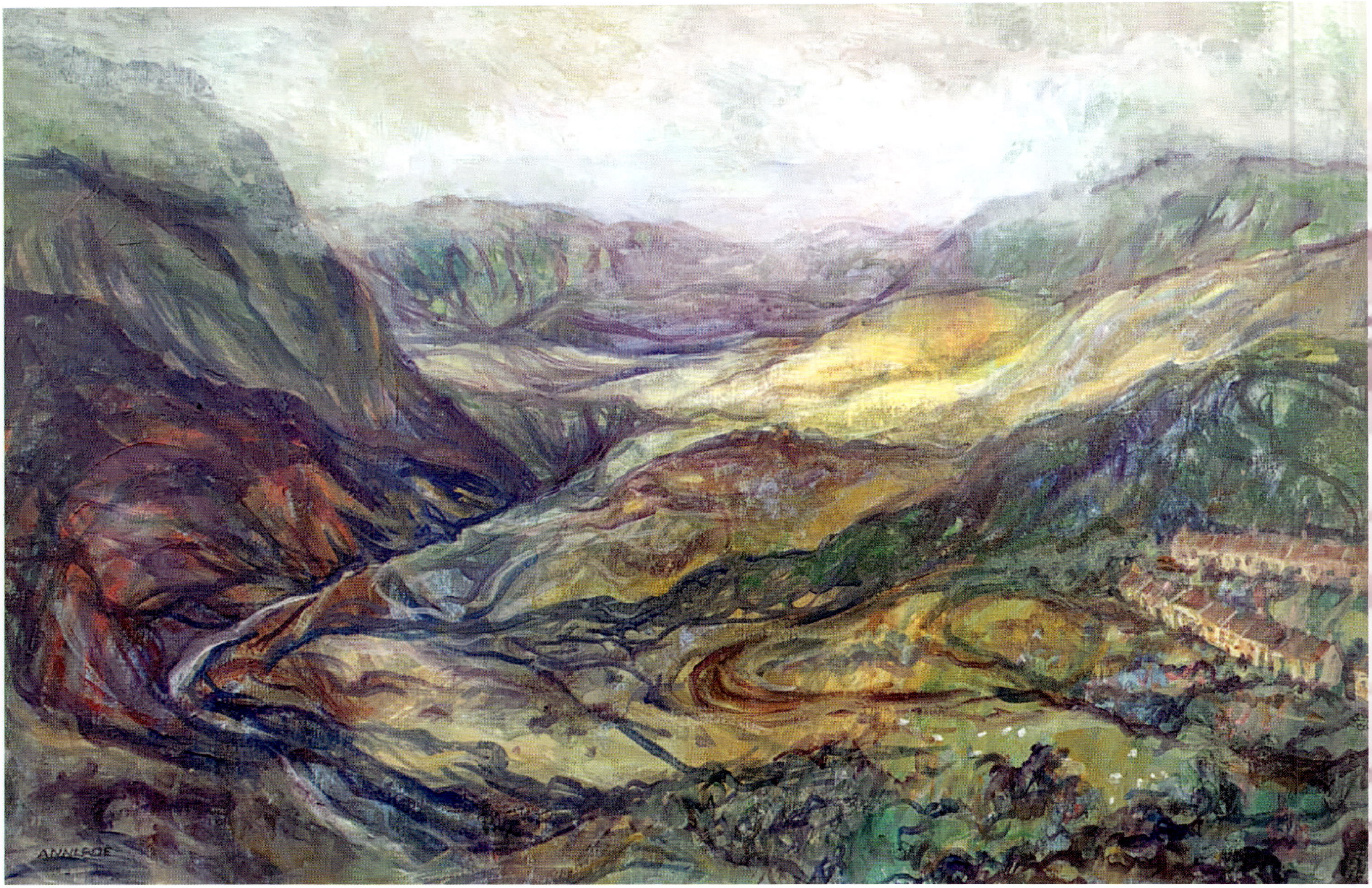

Landscapes and Still Lifes

"It relaxes my mind to paint flowers. I do not bring to it the same tension of spirit as when I am in front of a model..."

Pierre-Auguste Renoir

The 'tension' Pierre-Auguste Renoir describes when painting the human form is inevitably felt by the portrait artist and I'm no exception. The obvious dilemma, 'does one paint the sitter as they see themselves, or as you see them' is an issue one faces on each occasion, though this is not always the case and getting to know the character, temperament and expectations of the individual before one starts can help avoid disappointment on both sides. Not everyone necessarily agrees with my interpretation of them on canvas but that is the portrait artist's lot.

Though not all today's artists concur, I was of a generation in which the basis of all painting was the ability to draw. While some of my fellow students found the application to the study of sketching more difficult than others, to me it has always been pleasurable, indeed something of an obsession as my sketchbooks bear witness. I seldom travelled without pencil and paper and enjoyed observing people and briefly capturing them, often unaware of my presence.

I derived the same pleasure from sketching and painting landscapes and still lifes. With no sitter to satisfy and no time constraints, the artist is at liberty not only to chose their subject but also to interpret the scene as they wish, with complete freedom of expression. I love this and always have.

Following our retirement from teaching at Colyton Grammar School, Alan and I found an interesting painting course holiday in Tuscany which we thought sounded exciting. Little did we know that this would start the beginning of a friendship with husband-and-wife team Derek and Di Drew who organised some amazing painting holiday venues where I was taken on as tutor to those who had joined the course. We first met Derek and Di in a delightful Tuscan village called Peralta. The village had been recreated from a crumbling wreck by the sculptor Fiore de Enriquez who turned it into a magical, artistic venue. It's still thriving today and is a lasting legacy to Fiore whose life and work is touched on earlier in this book.

A number of paintings, sketches and photographs are included here to illustrate our European adventures along with other examples of my landscapes and still lifes.

Opposite: Mountain cottages in the Rhondda Valley.

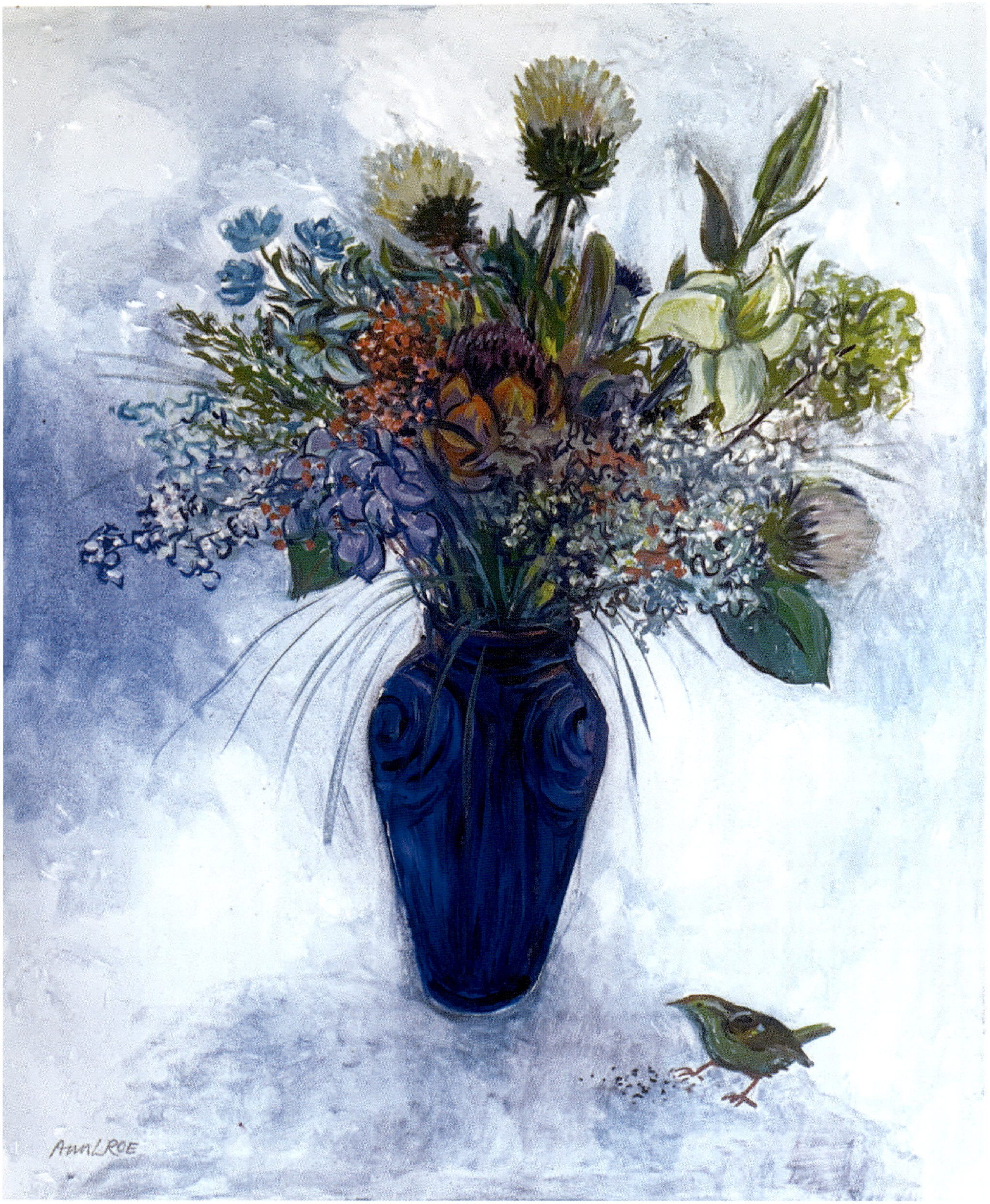
AnnLROE

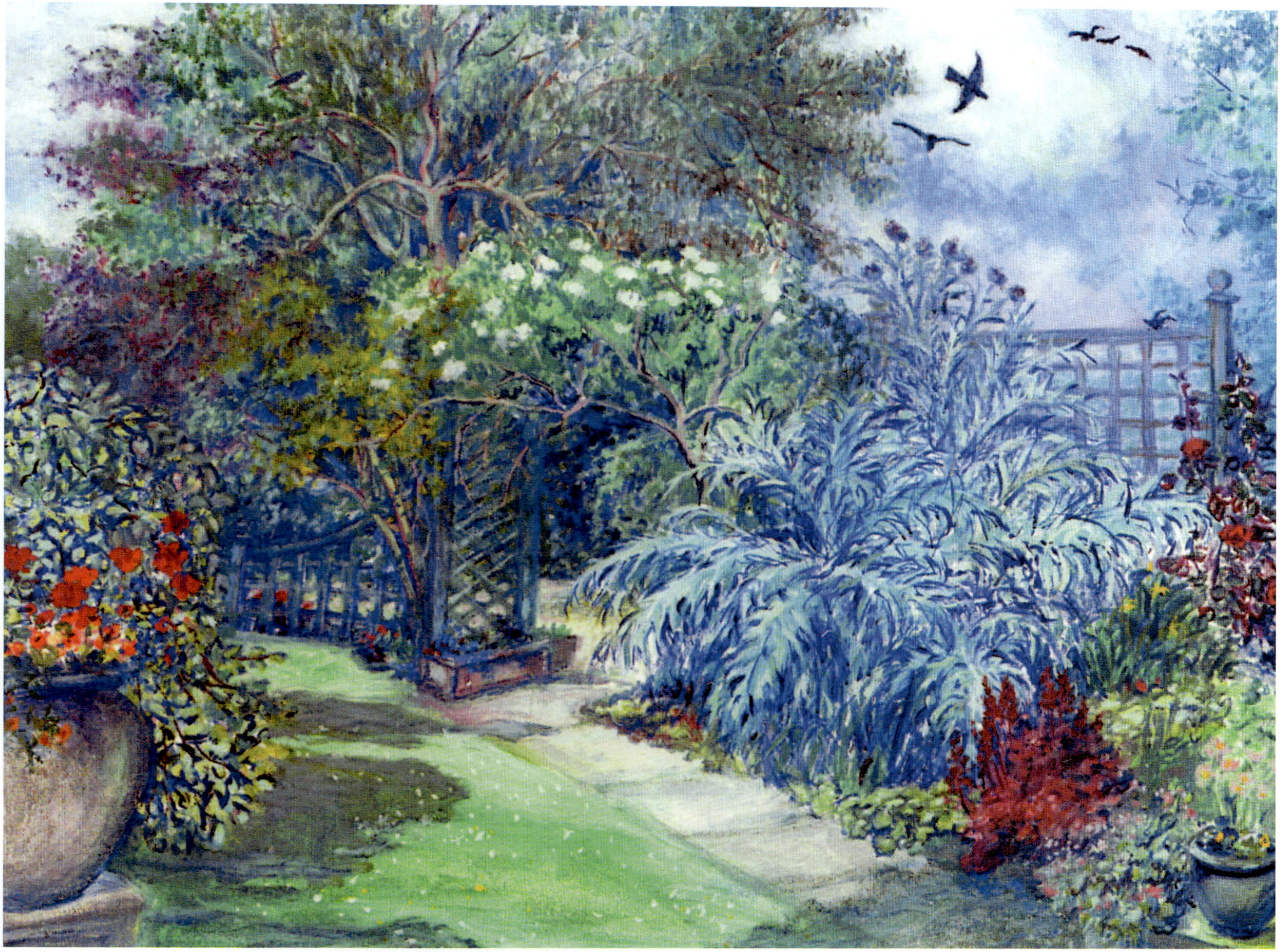

The garden at Rupack House.

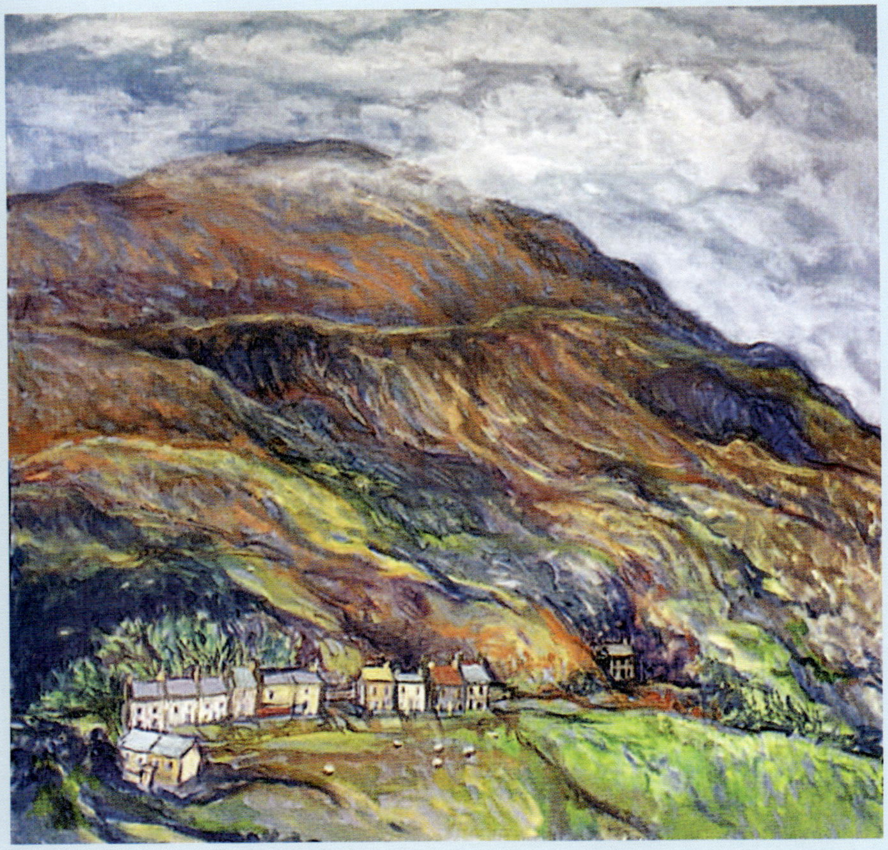

Mountain cottages in the spectacular Rhondda Valley, once almost exclusively a place of mining communities, this was my husband Alan's ancestral home.

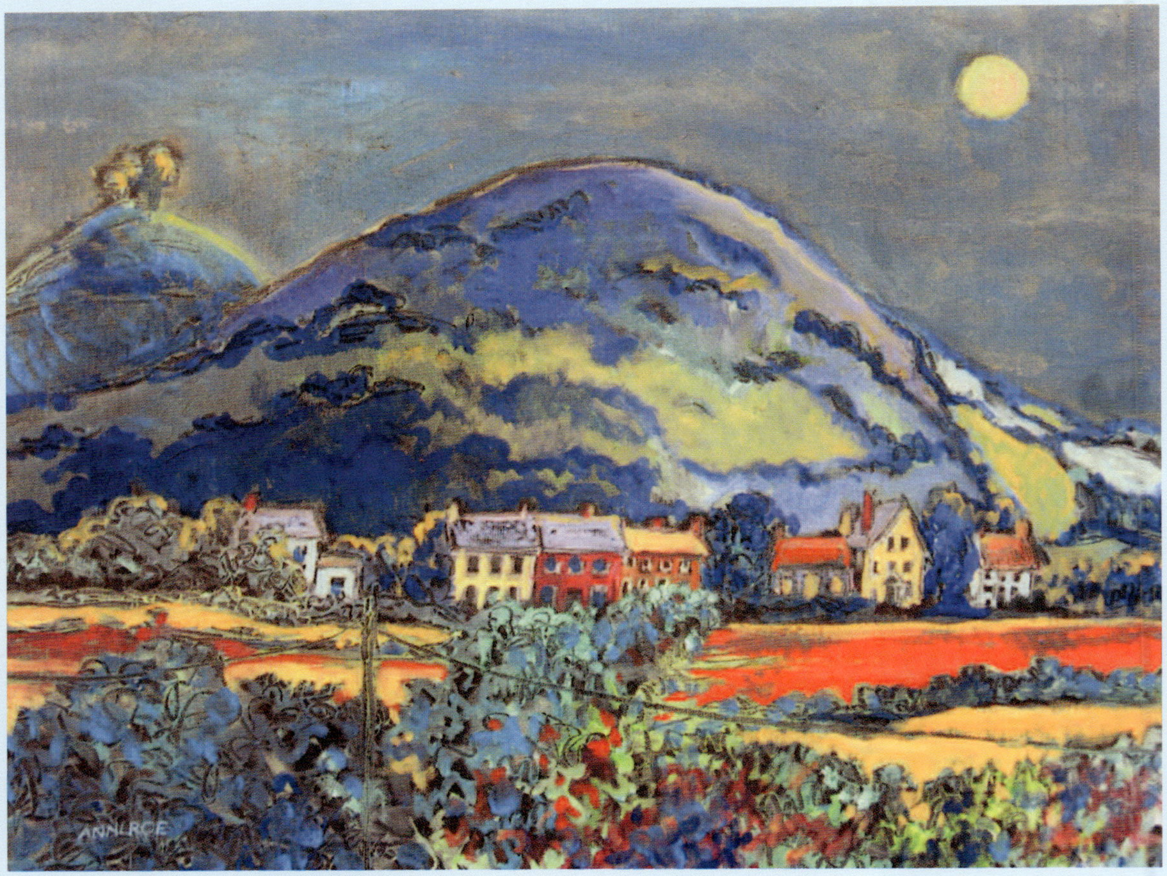

The old road to Bridport. I painted this scene at the side of the main road. Today the view is obscured by the growth of the trees and bushes in the foreground.

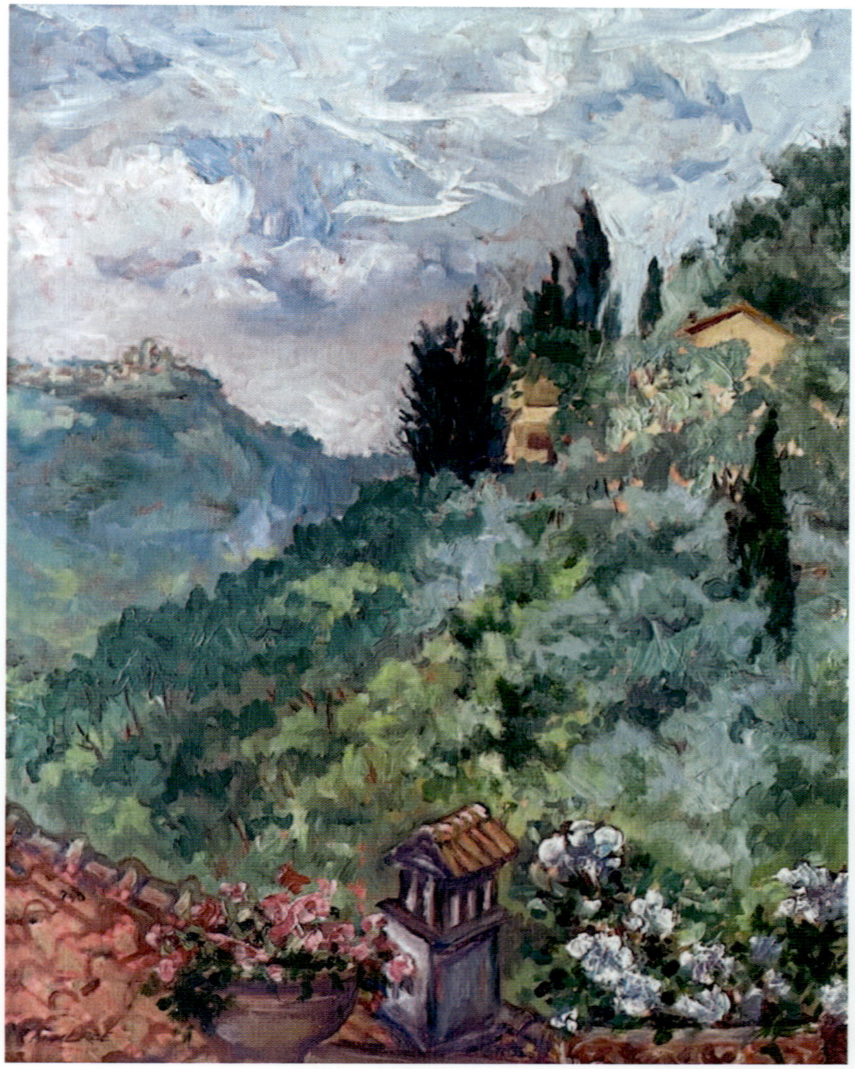

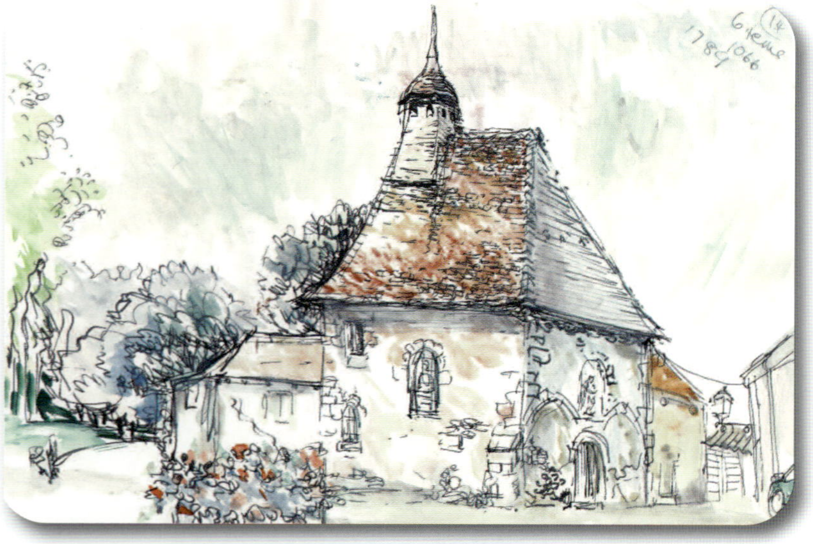

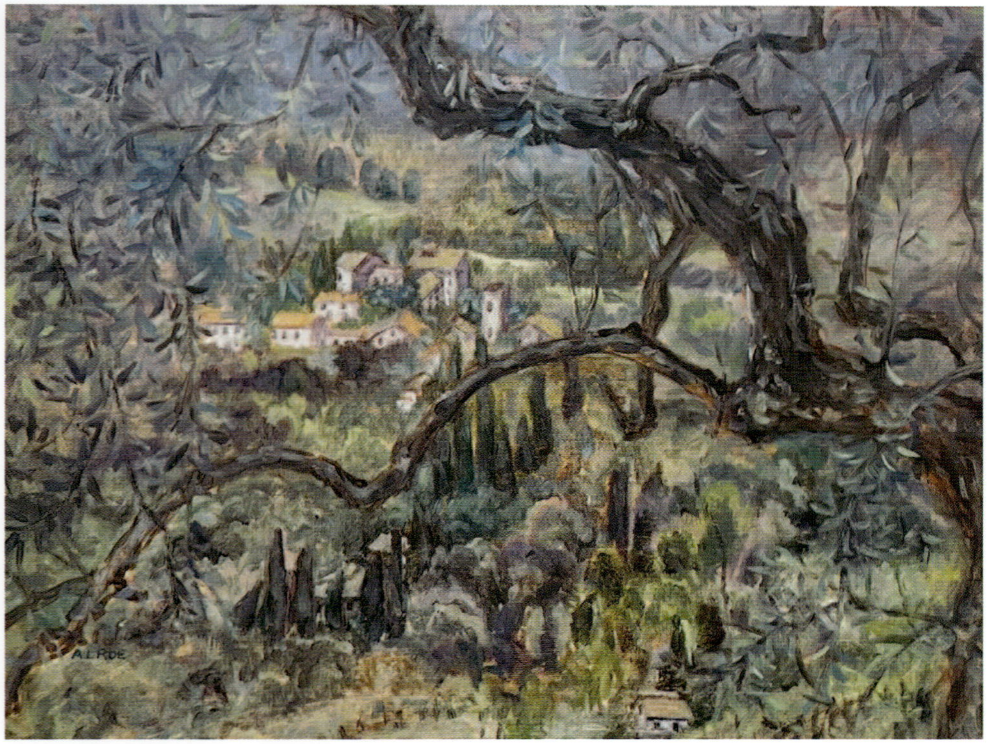

Above: The view from Peralta, Tuscany.

Above right: From one of our visits to France, a water-colour sketch of the Church of Notre Dame de Voeu in Normandy.

Right: Olive trees on a Tuscan hillside.

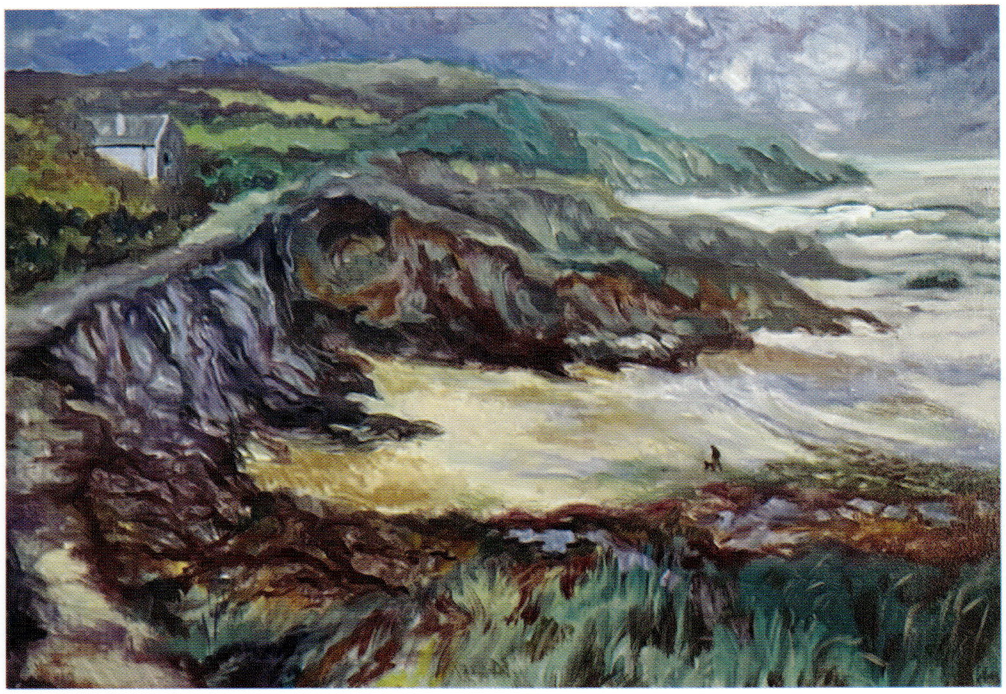

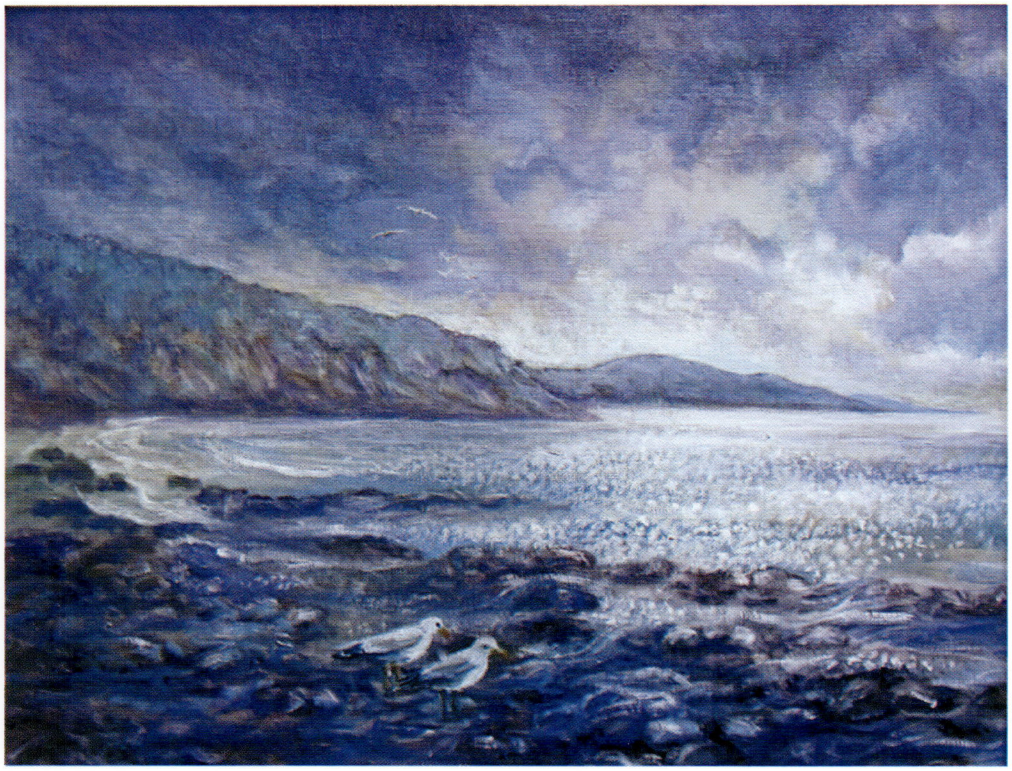

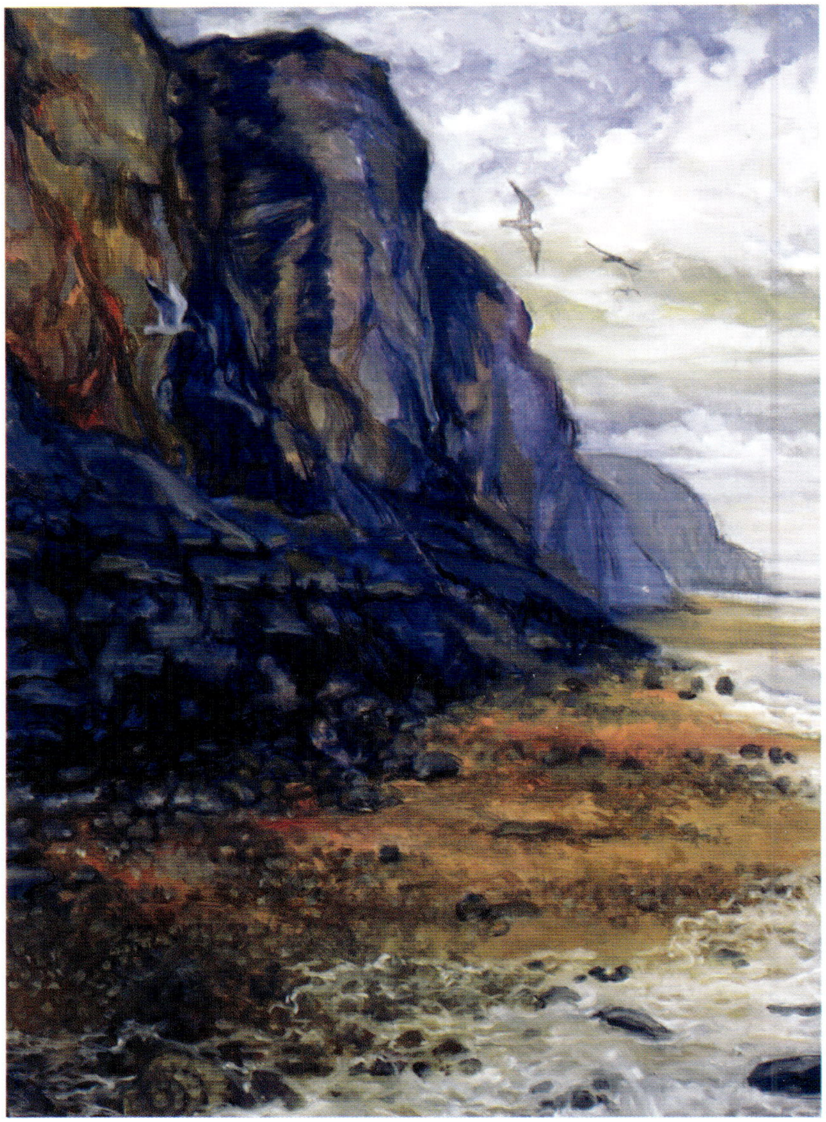

Above left: Alan walking the dog on a beach in South Wales.

Above: East Devon cliffs and seashore.

Left: Lyme Regis. Two gulls on the seashore.

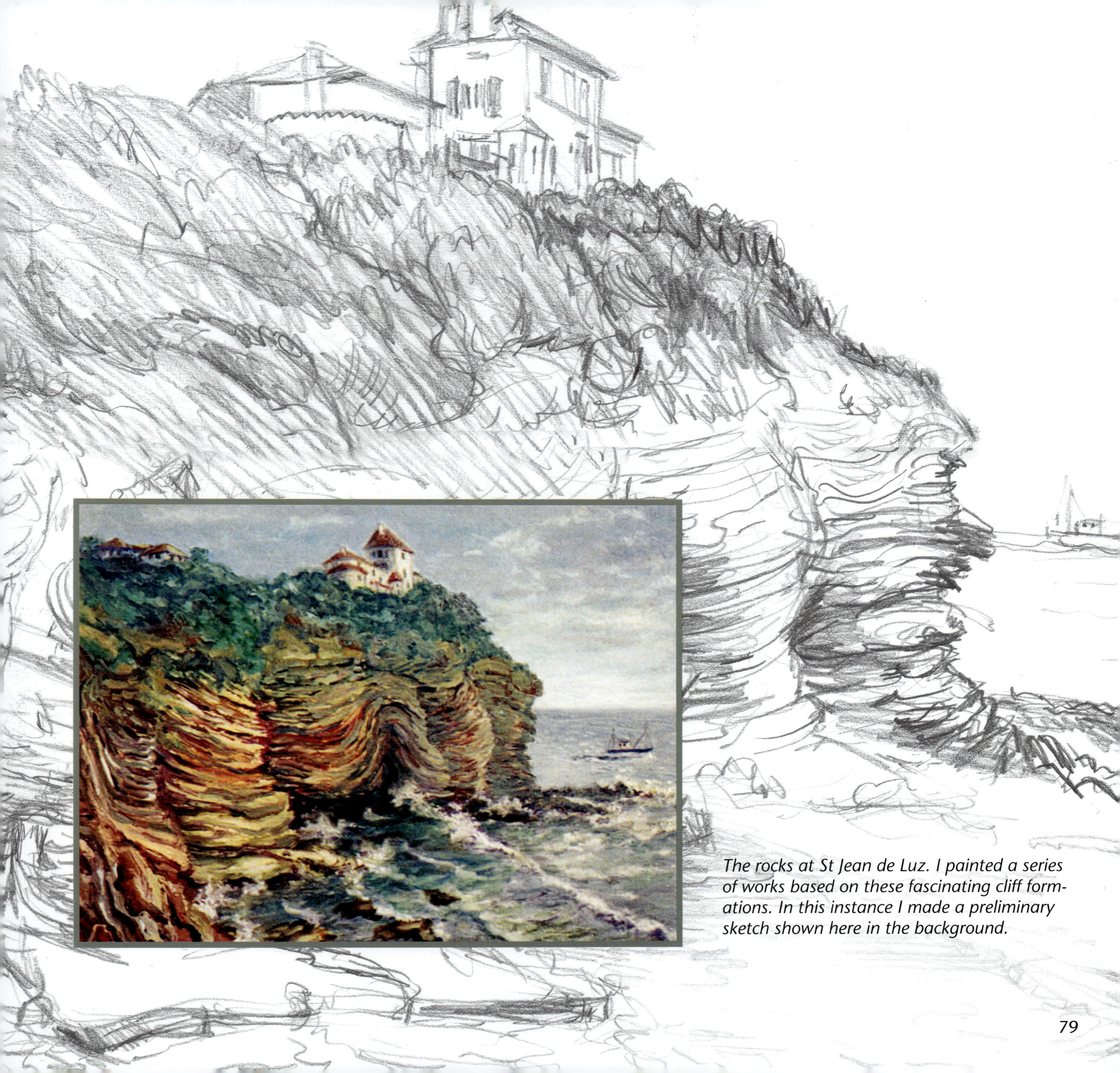

The rocks at St Jean de Luz. I painted a series of works based on these fascinating cliff formations. In this instance I made a preliminary sketch shown here in the background.

I have always loved painting landscapes and flower compositions. These two topics I prefer to paint straight off with no initial sketching. In one of my flower painting I simply kept adding more flowers from the different seasons which I liked.

The wonderful Dutch painters of yesteryear had the same idea, so that seasonal differences were completely blurred into insignificance. The delightful colours and shapes of the flowers, taken from different times in the year's calendar, resulted in joyous paintings.

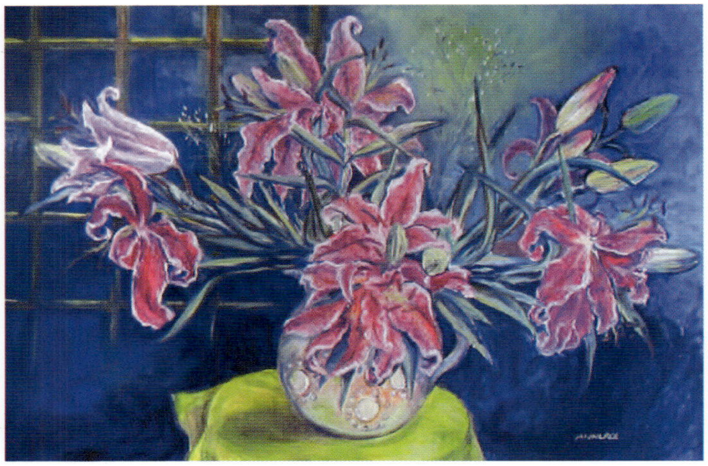

Above: Still Life

Right: Ferns, Flowers and Fruit.

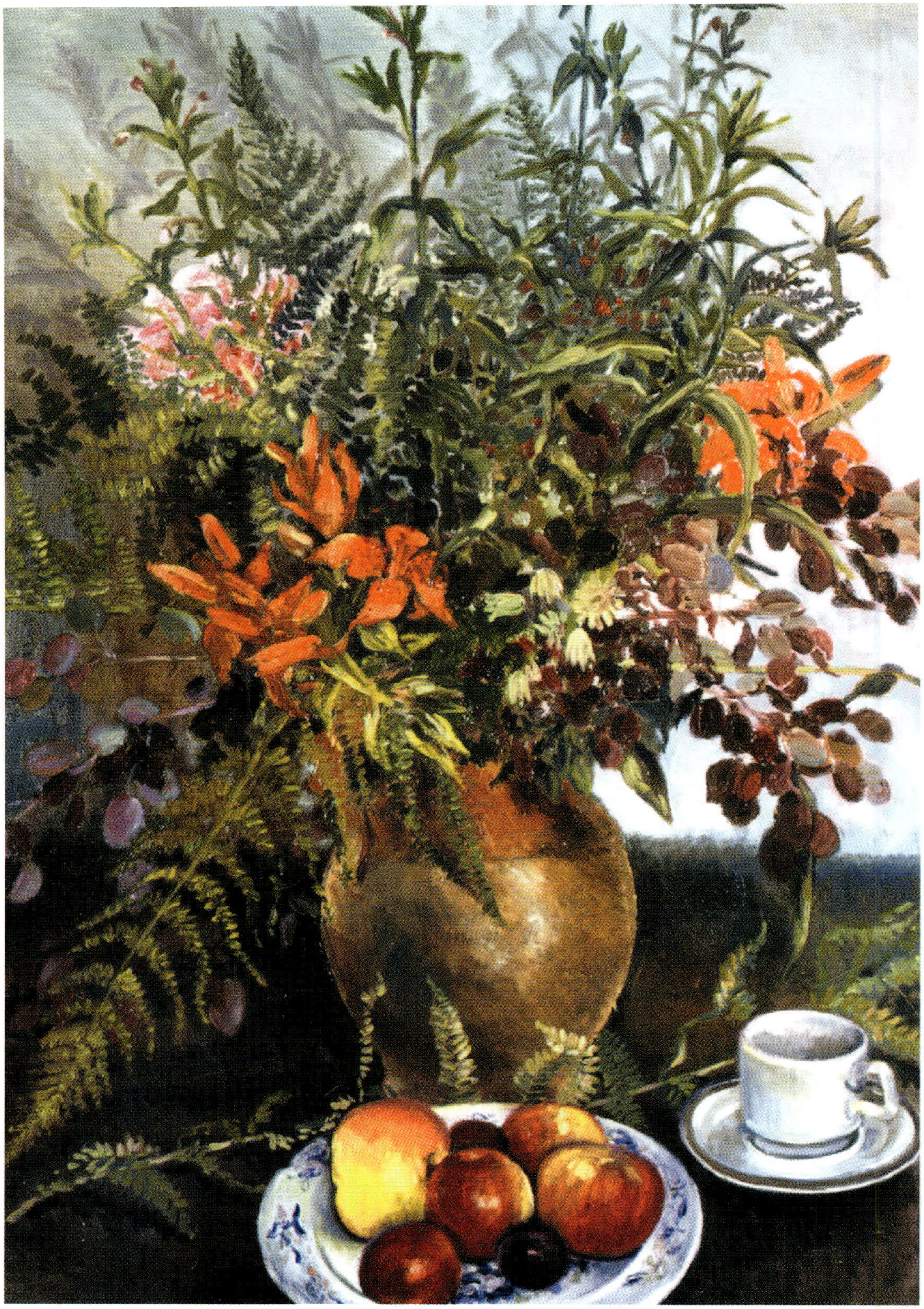

Opposite page: 'The Falling Apple', a painting now owned by Derek and Di Drew (see page 85).

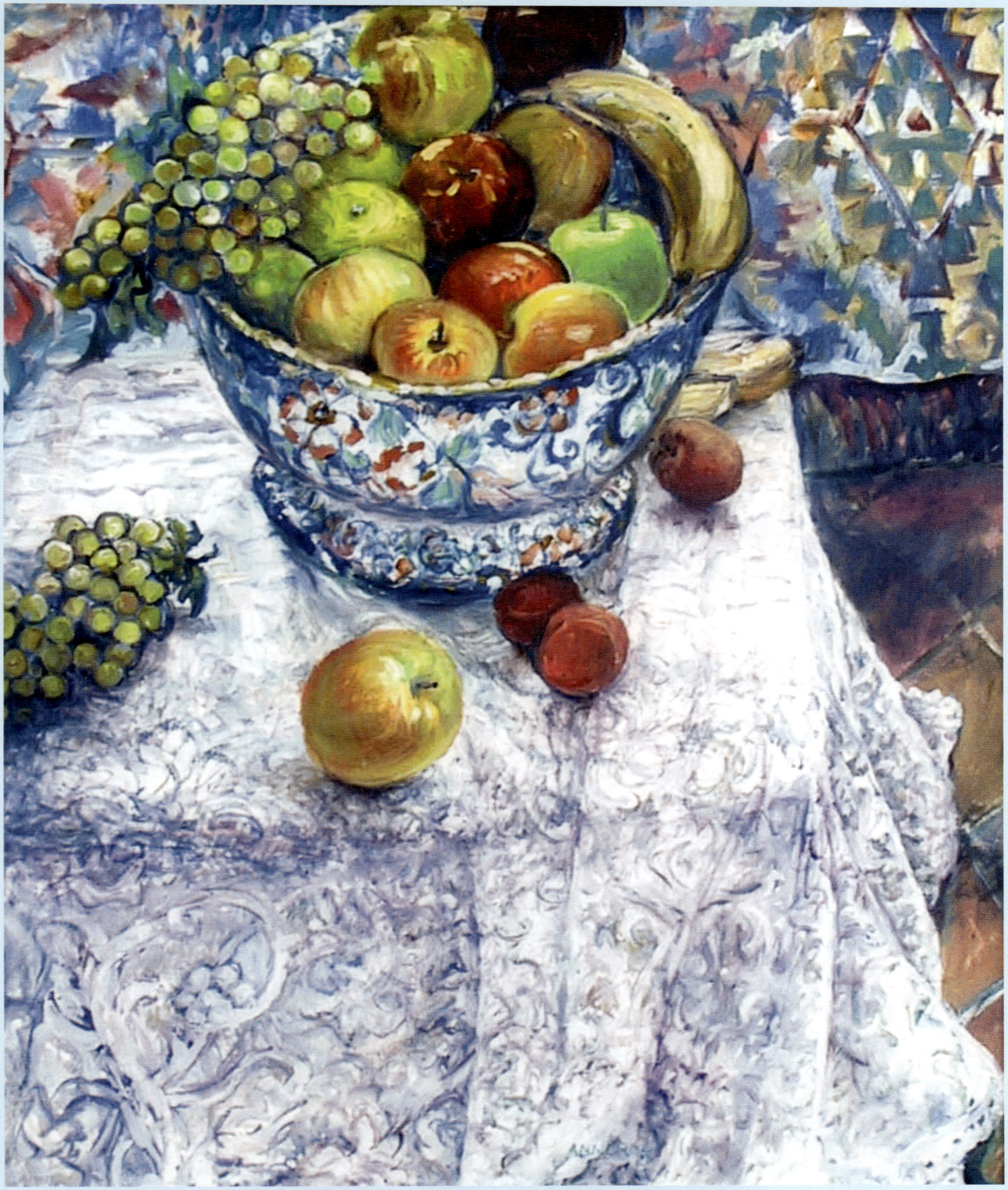

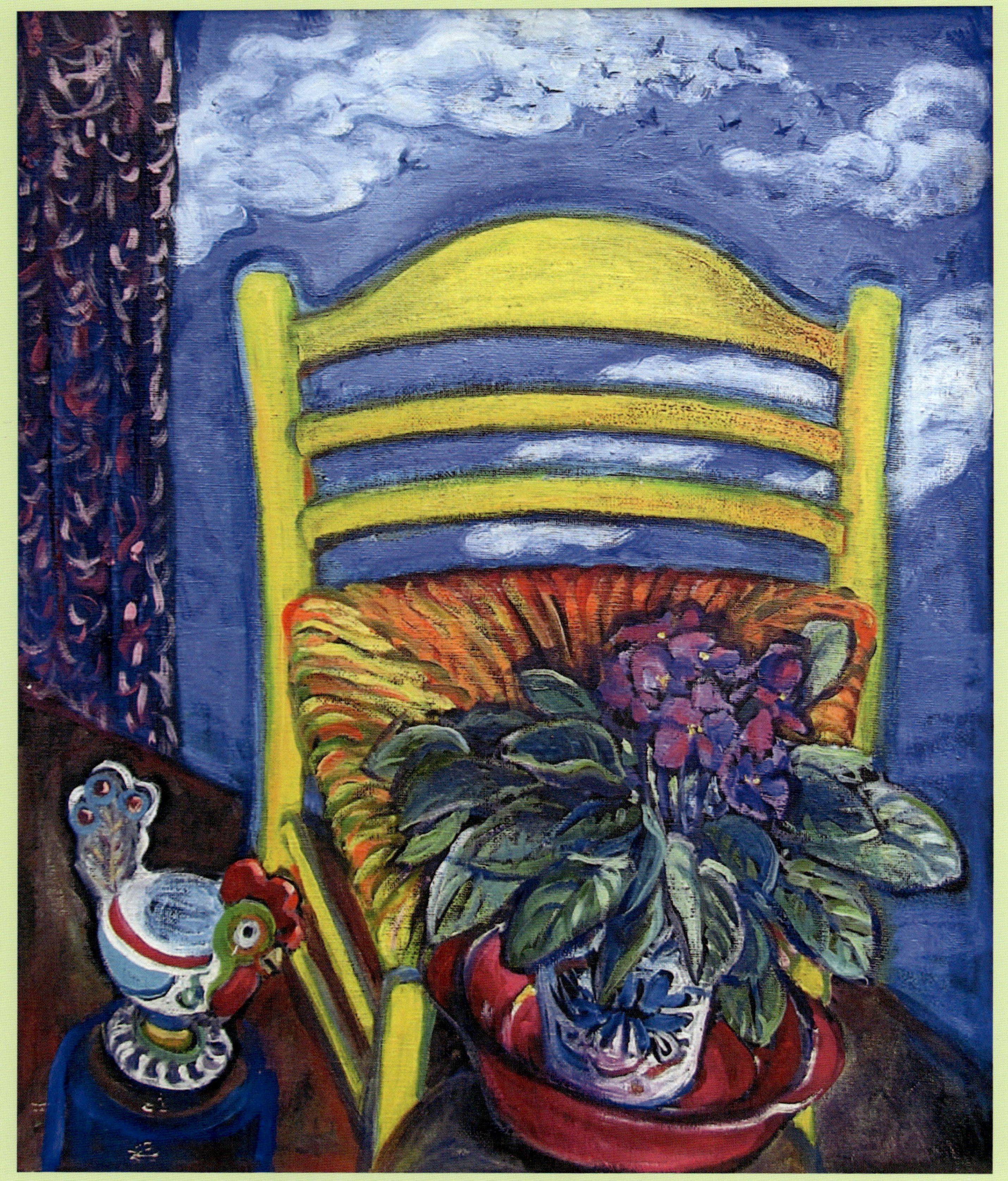

An idea taken from a David Hockney painting 'Vincent's Chair and Pipe'.

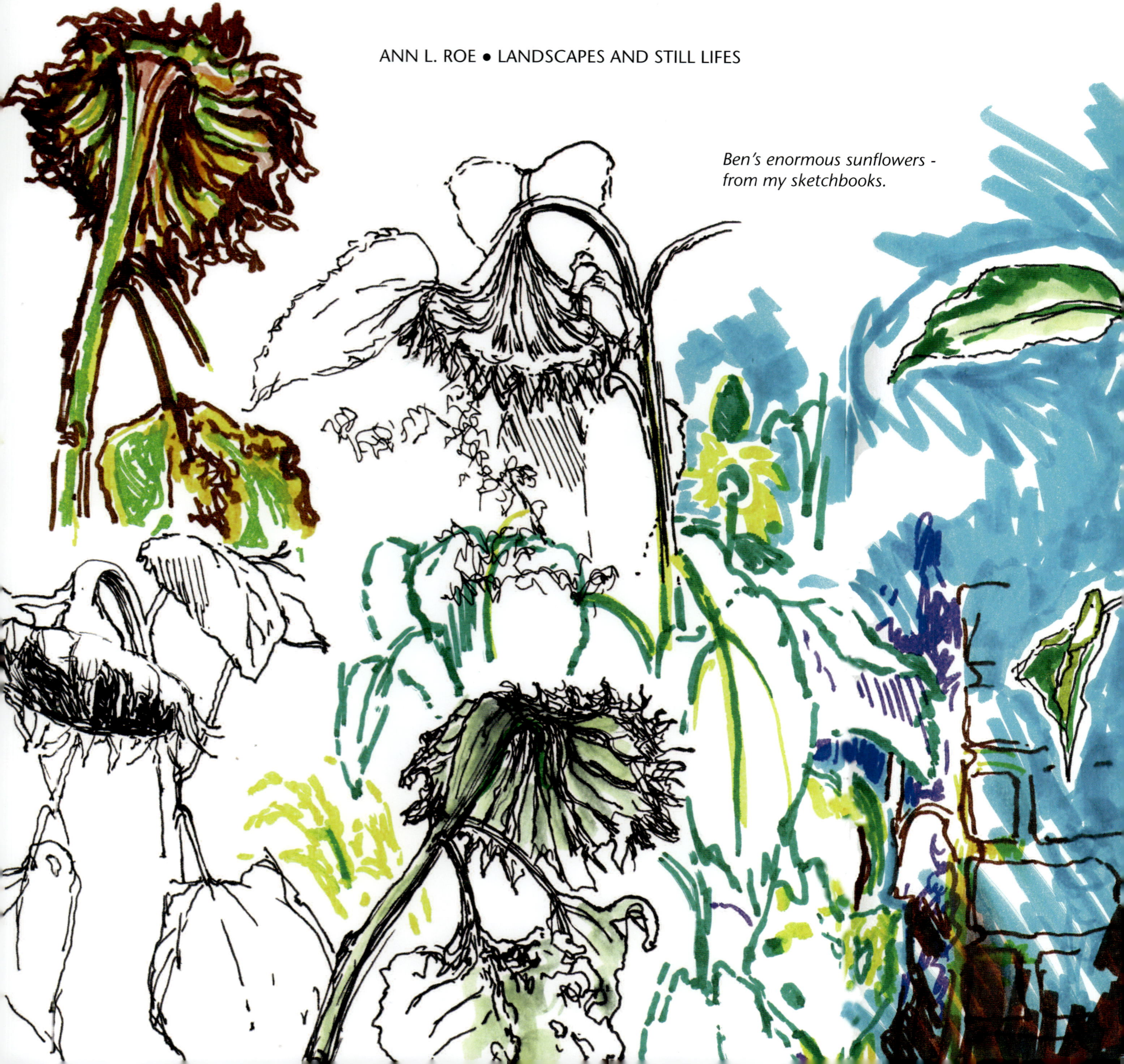

Ben's enormous sunflowers - from my sketchbooks.

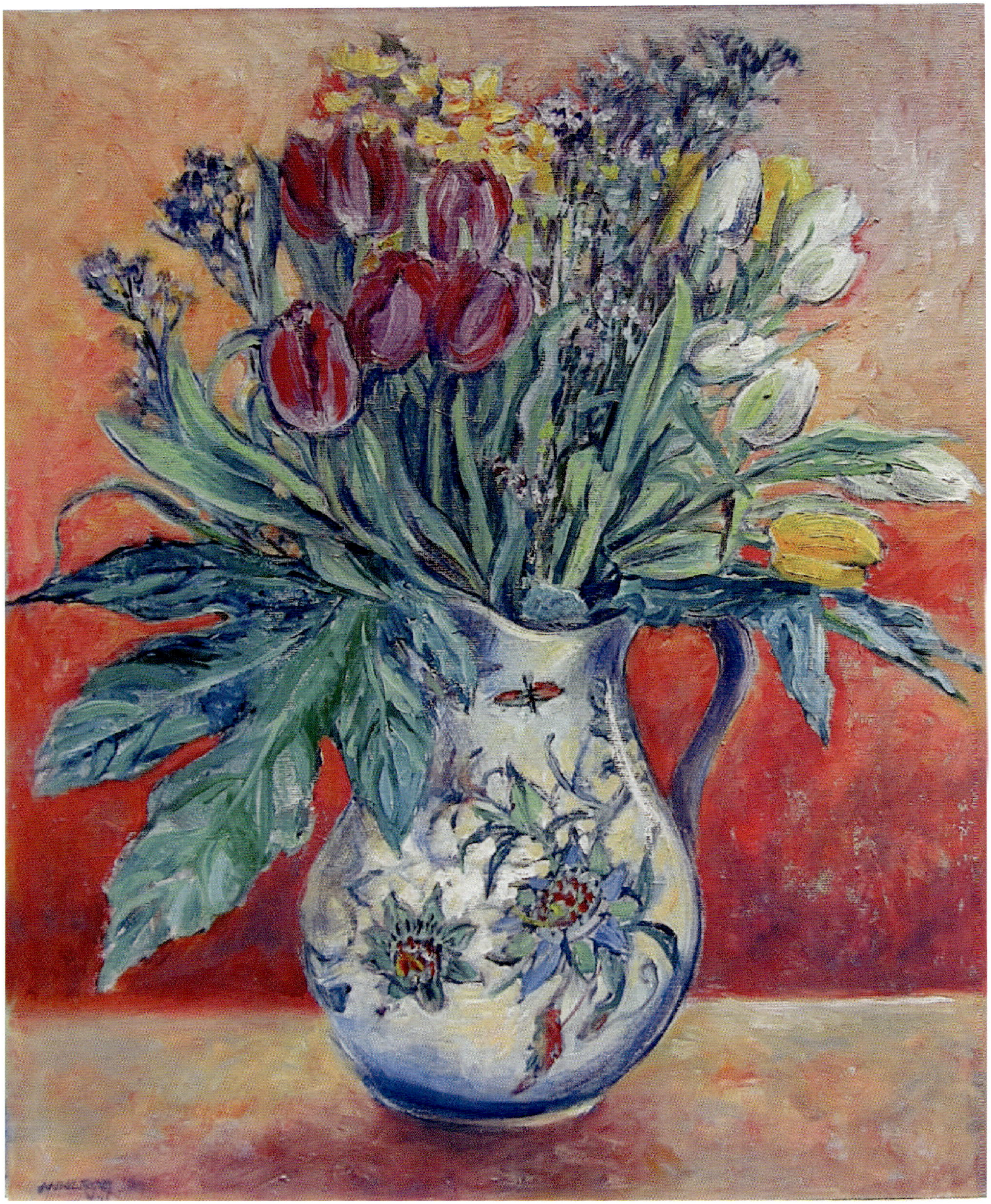

Tulips in a Portmeirion vase.

My first experience of France, aged sixteen, when staying with the Pintaud family in Ciboure, close to St Jean de Luz, not only set the seal on my career as an artist, it also instilled a life-long love of European travel. The opportunities provided by our two year's at the Foire de Caen, Alan's membership of The Magic Circle (described in the final part of this book), and my tutoring role at Derek and Di Drew's studio in Tuscany following my retirement from teaching, were wonderful, fulfilling and exciting times.

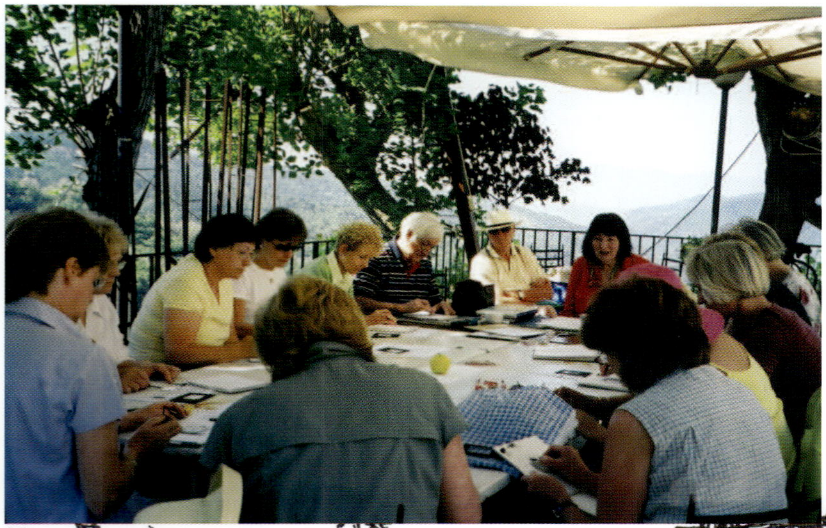

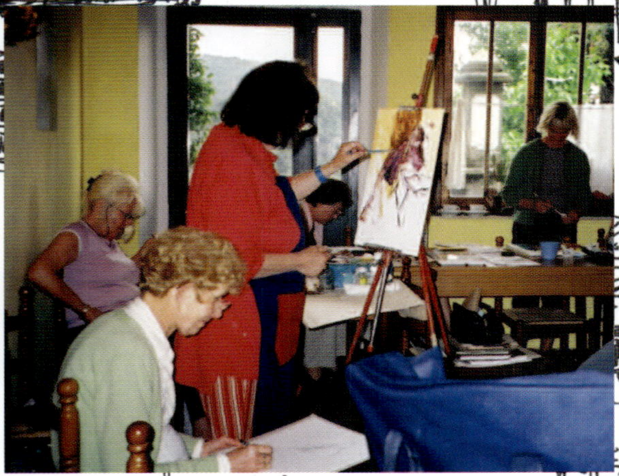

Right: Peralta, Tuscany, tutoring a class outdoors with Alan second from my right in the striped shirt. Below: Indoors on a wet, misty day in 2004.

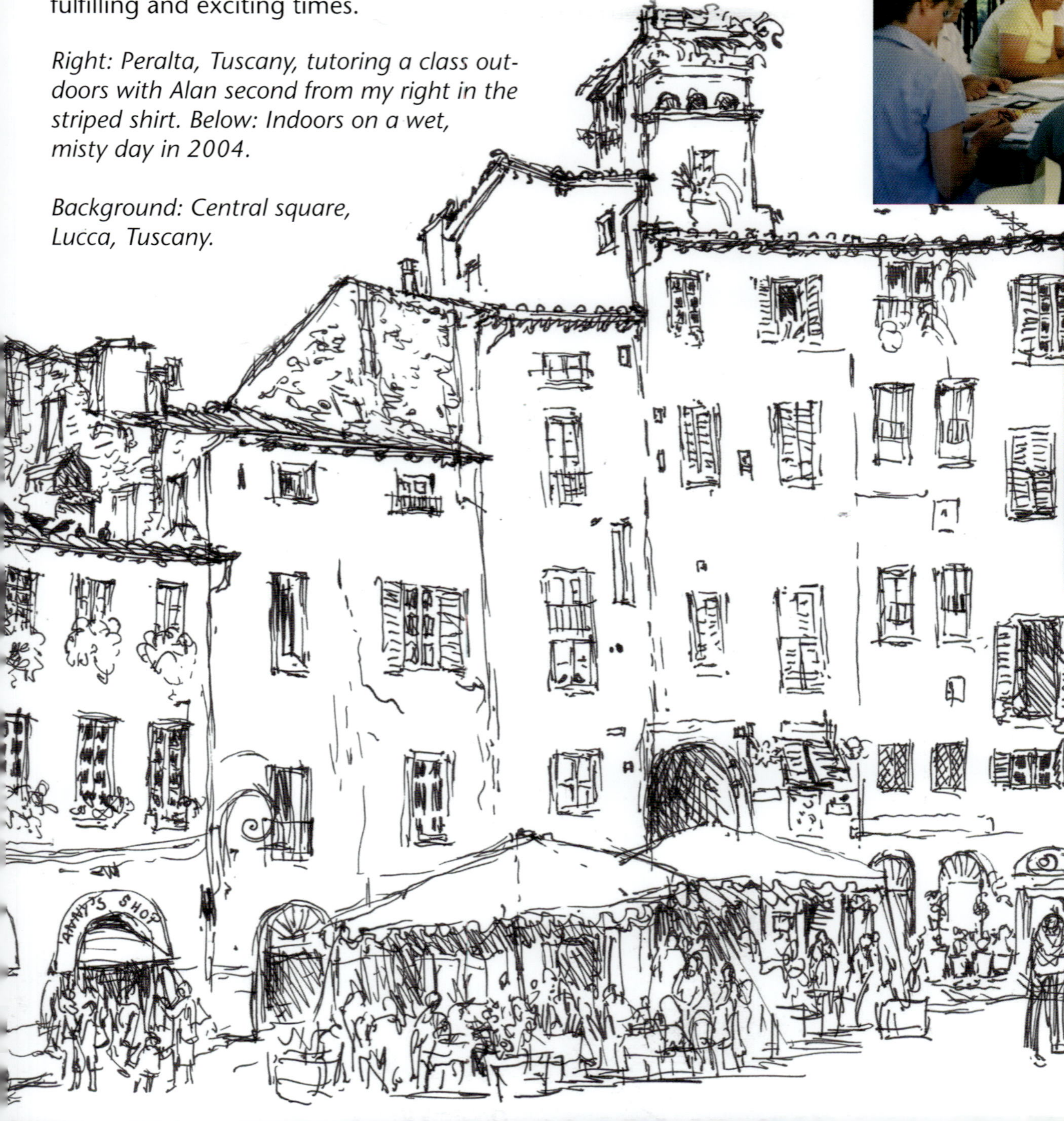

Background: Central square, Lucca, Tuscany.

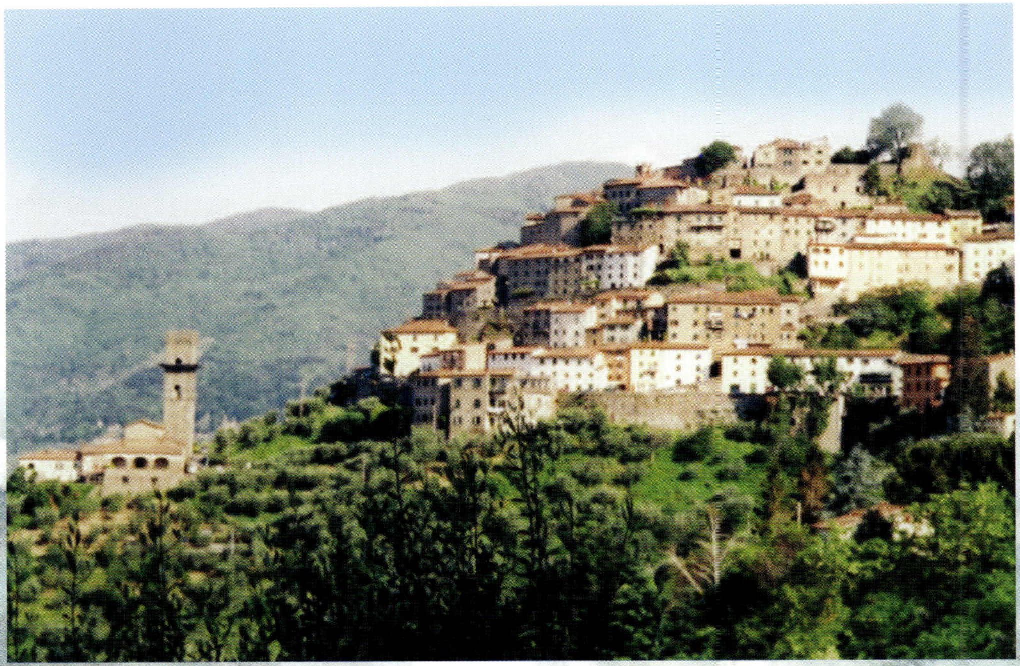

The spectacular Tuscan village of Vellano.

Below: A sketchbook watercolour of the breathtaking Tuscan landscape.

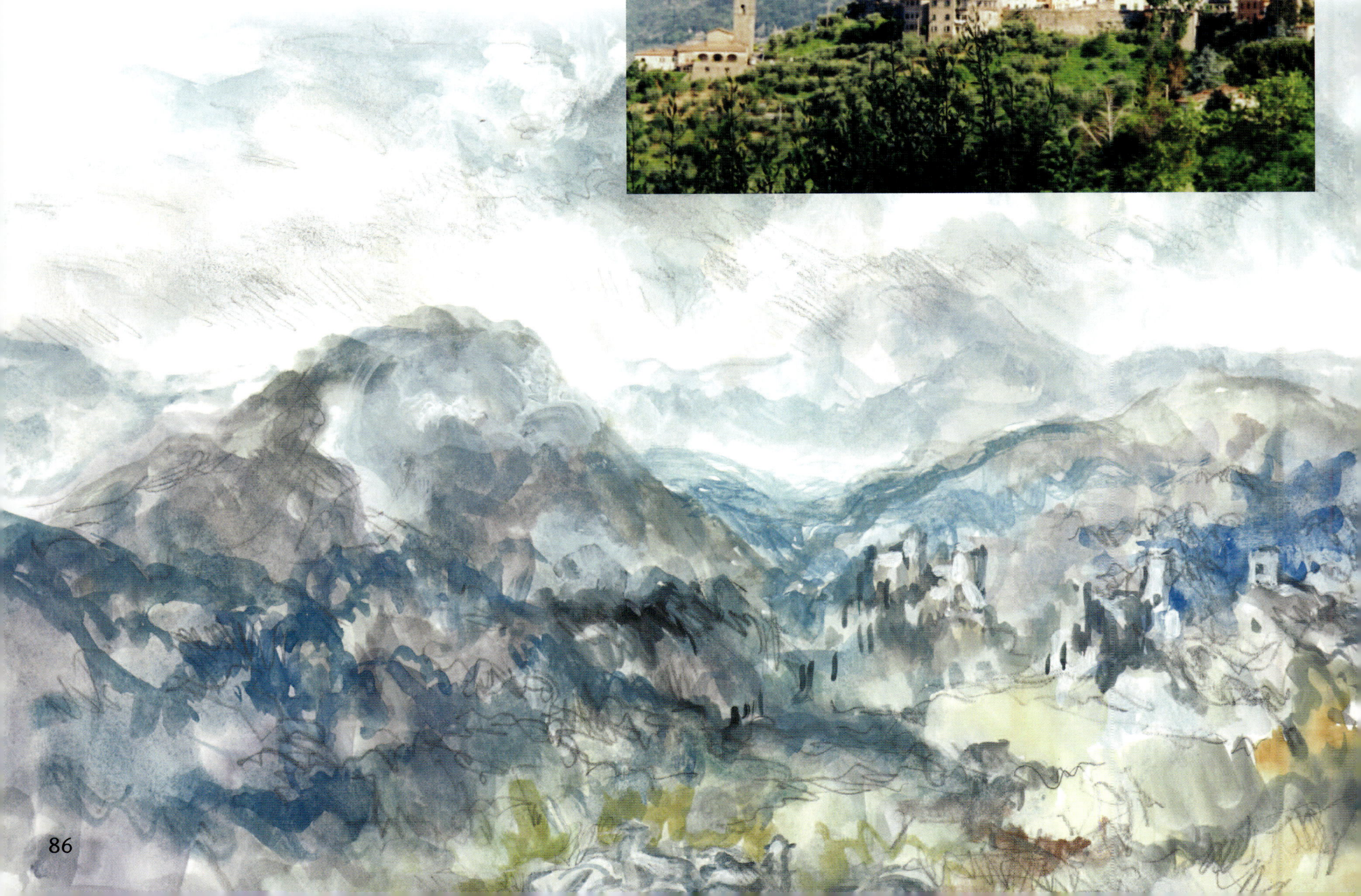

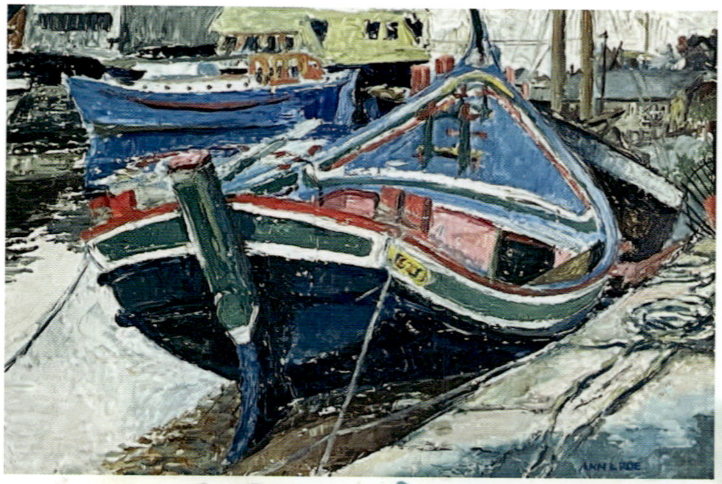

Left: A colourful Portuguese fishing boat.

Below: The stupendous Rocamadour, France.

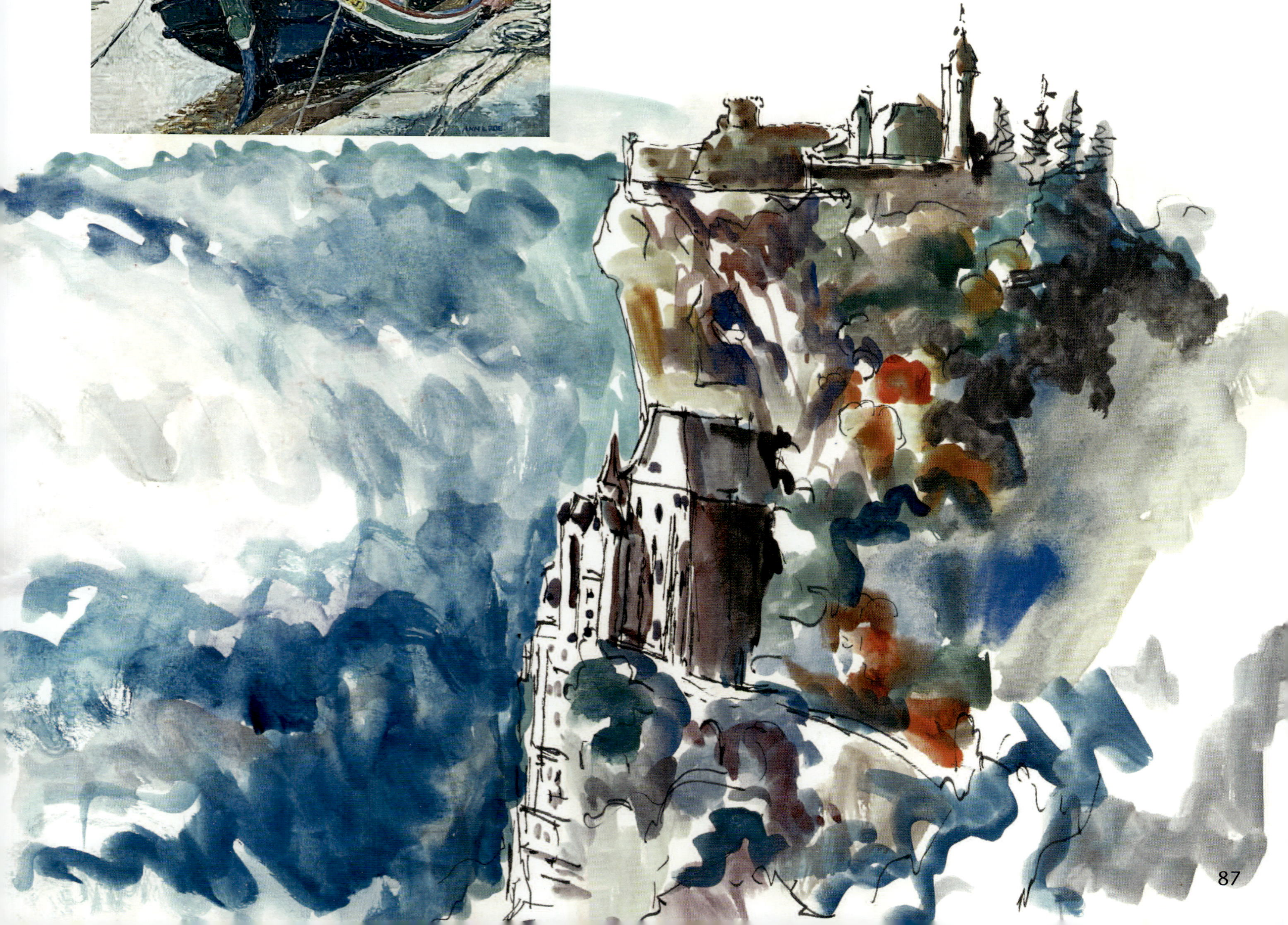

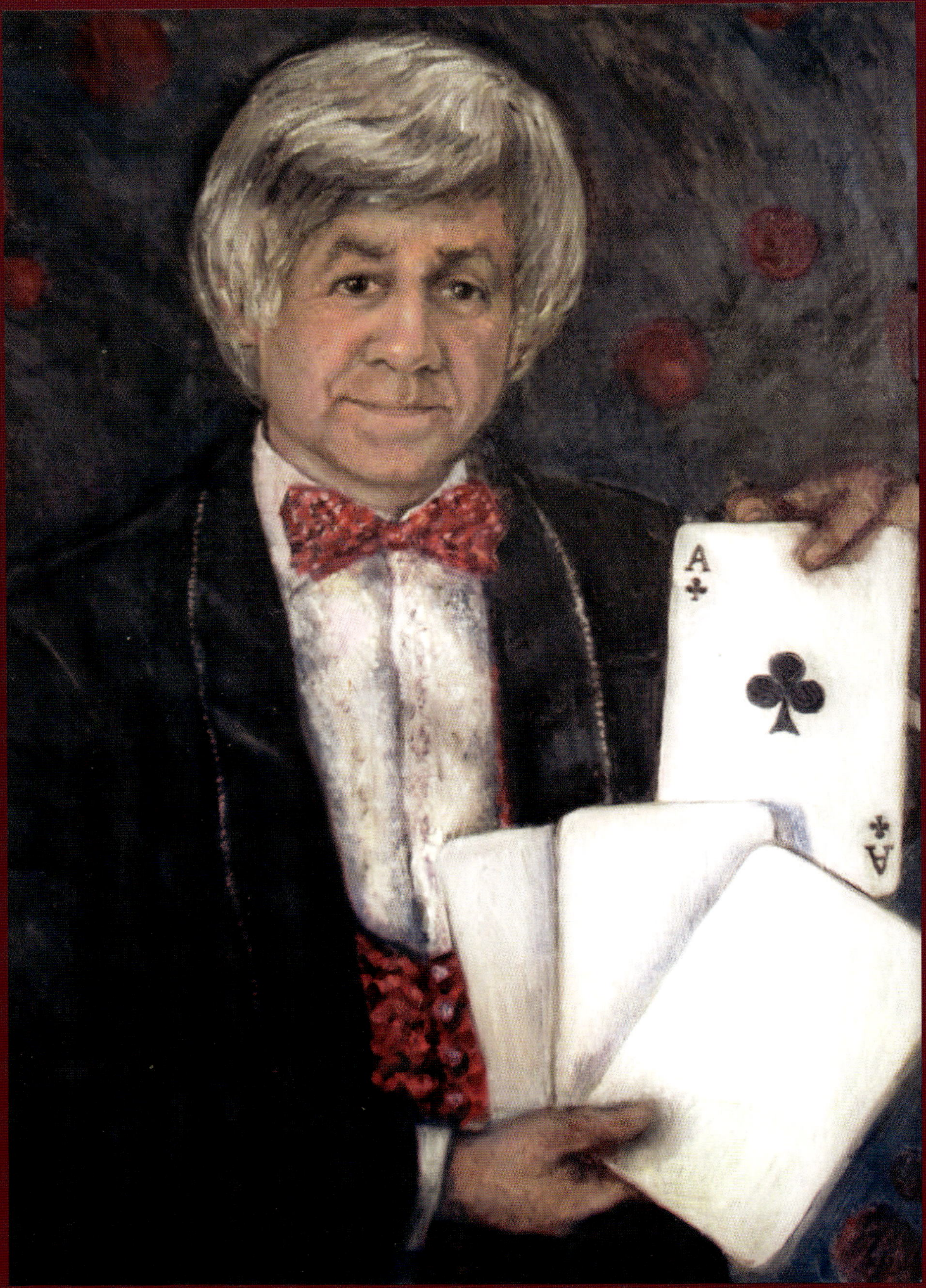
A
A

A Touch of Magic

When I look back on my life as a wife and mother, an artist and teacher, there's certainly been a touch of magic about how it has all worked out. I hope the words and pictures in this book reflect this sense of good fortune in the many hundreds of people I have painted and sketched and the opportunities that my art had opened up by way of the friends I have made and the places I have visited.

There's another and rather more down-to-earth reason for the naming this chapter and that is simply that so much of my life with my husband, Alan, has been entwined with his mastery and love of performing magic. This too has opened up a wonderful world of travel, meeting fascinating people and making life-long friendships.

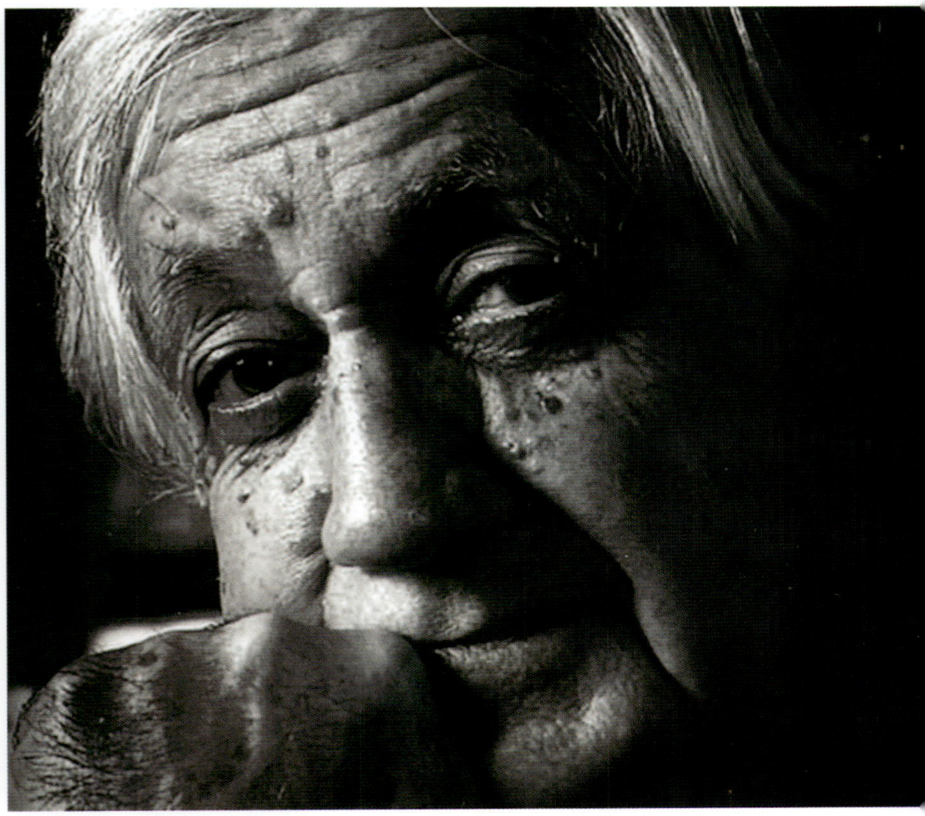

The portrait of my lovely Welsh husband was painted some years ago. Most opportunities I had to paint or sketch Alan were when he was asleep somewhere (as with other family members there are many times when they have no time to sit for me). Life can often be so busy! I have more than three paintings of Alan, but this photo of him, taken by my son-in-law Chris and which appeared alongside Alan's obituary in the *Magic Circle Magazine* and on the Order of Service at his funeral in 2024 is, I think, one of the very best.

The write up about him in the Circle's magazine was by Simon Bradley in which he wrote 'Some magicians are clever and others charismatic: Alan was a combination of both'. Alan had once signed a book for Simon and inscribed it 'Magically may you always be there for me', and he always was!

Opposite: My portrait of Alan, magician extraordinaire!

Alan's interests were broad and on a visit to Nice, along with his cousin Ann and her husband Roy Saer, he spied a sculpture by Niki de St Phalle outside the Hotel Negresco in Rue des Anglaise. It was of a trumpeter and this, along with an unexpected sighting of a Russian Church down a narrow back street, inspired Alan to produce an extraordinary and colourful painting which included two of his magic props – ducks. He used this painting for a Christmas card one year calling the painting 'Midnight in Moscow with Peaking Ducks'. Alan died in 2024 and, throughout his life, it was obvious to all who knew him that Alan's family was of utmost importance; including those from Wales and England, and Adrian in Santa Fé where he lives with his son and his wife's son. Plus our innumerable friends, and various pets!

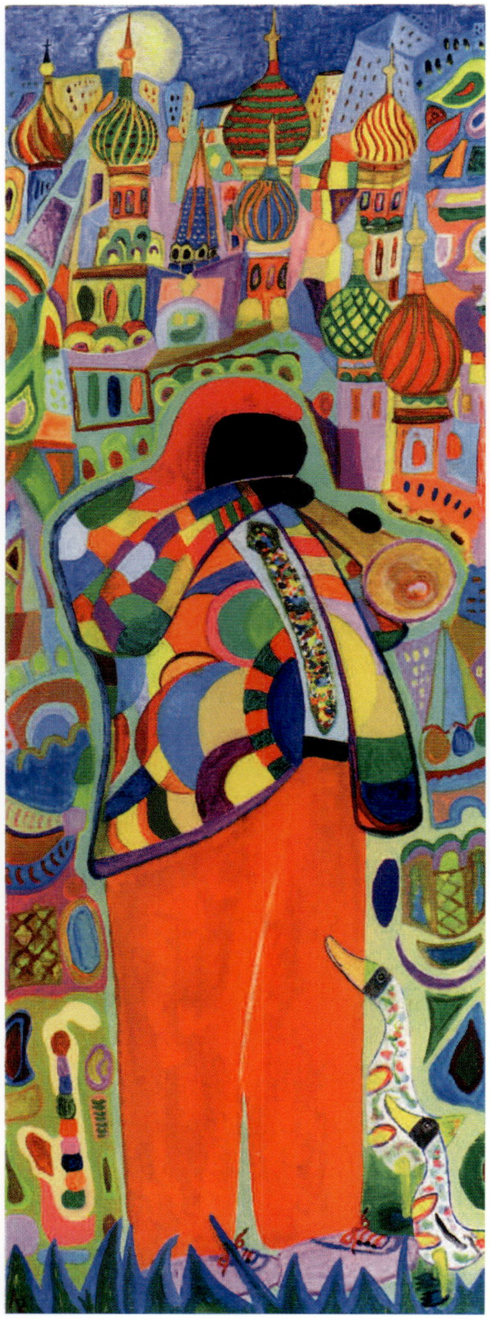

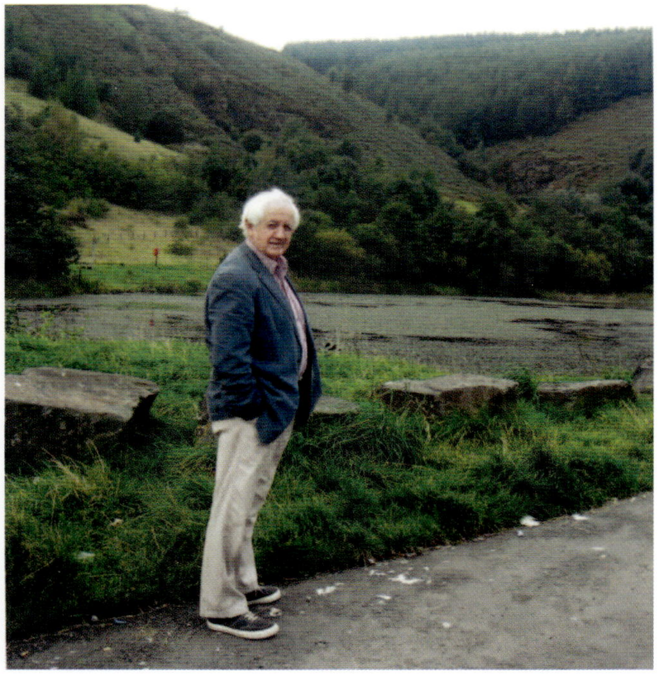

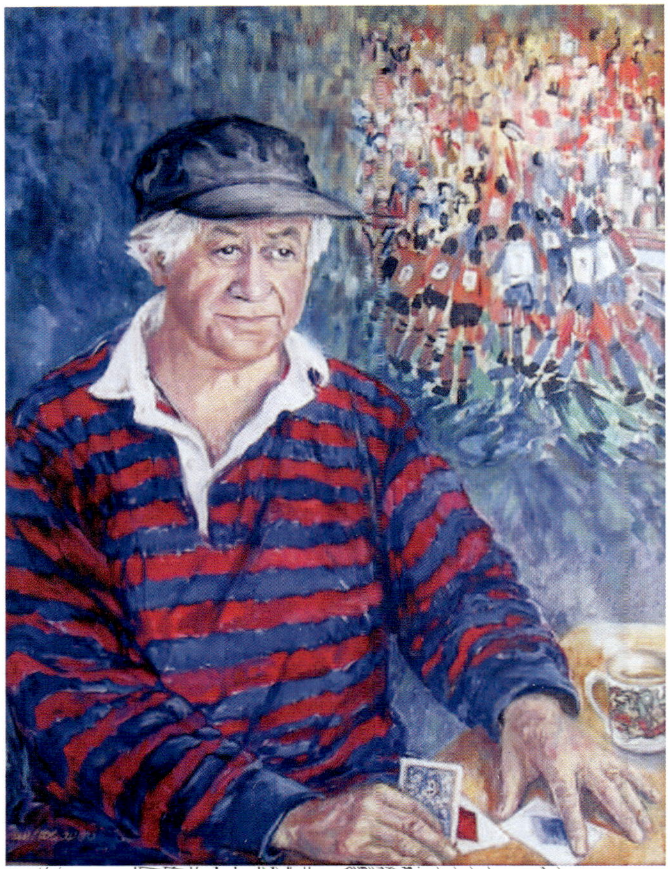

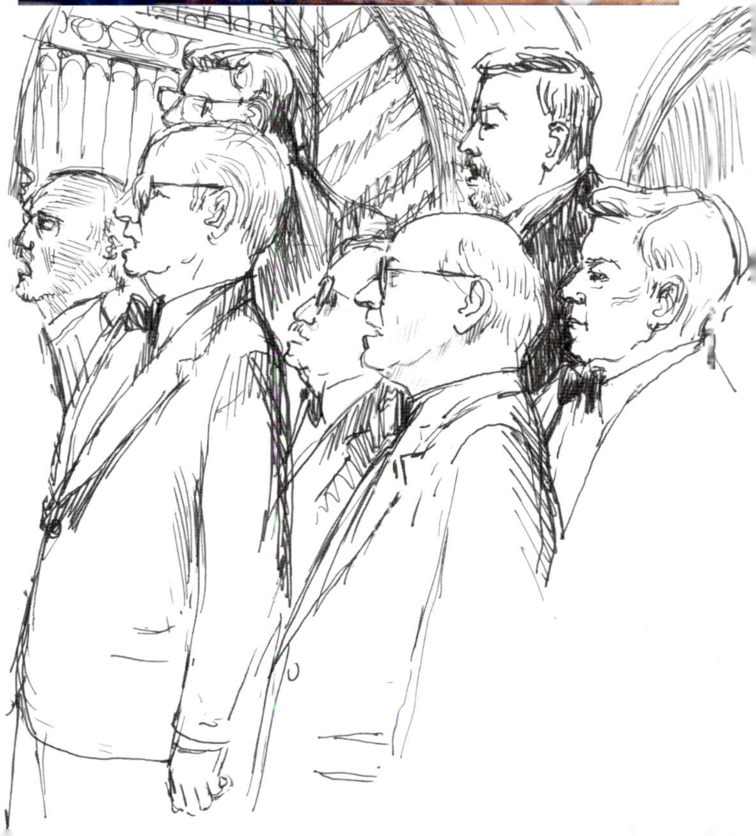

Left: 'Midnight in Moscow with Peaking Ducks'.

Above: Alan in the land of his birth, South Wales, in an area of former mining activity where we used to walk our dogs.

Top: My portrait of Alan playing cards while dreaming of the Welsh rugby team.

Right: My sketch of a Welsh choir. Alan took every opportunity to join in a singsong.

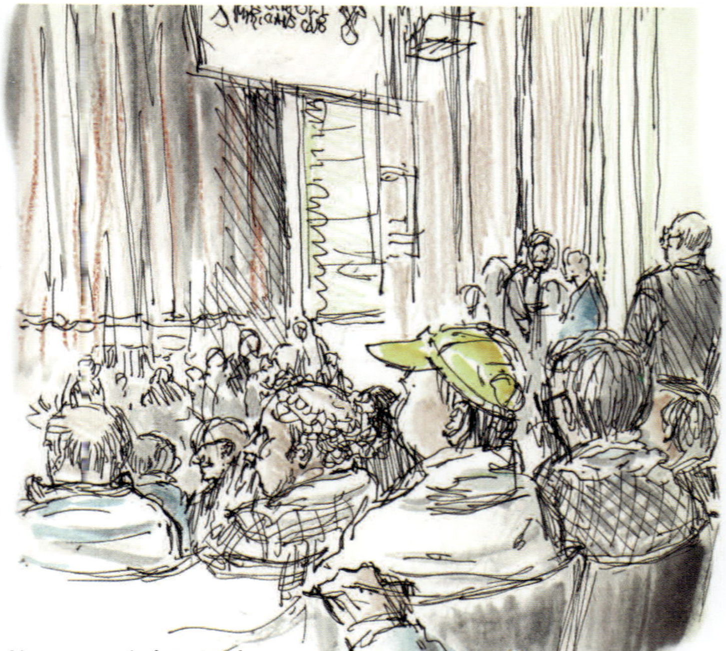

Korean night at the Opera House Blackpool in February 2003 with brillaint young magicians performing.

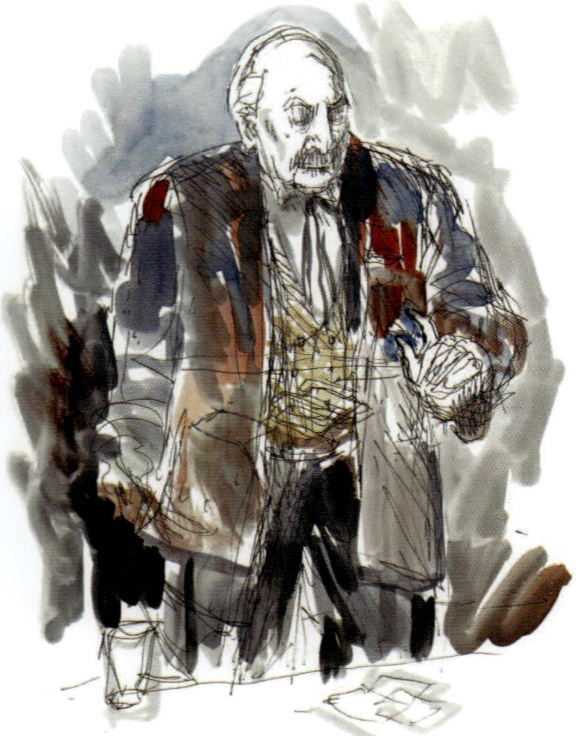

René Levant performed marvels with playing cards – and with only one hand.

The magician Belinda Sinclair.

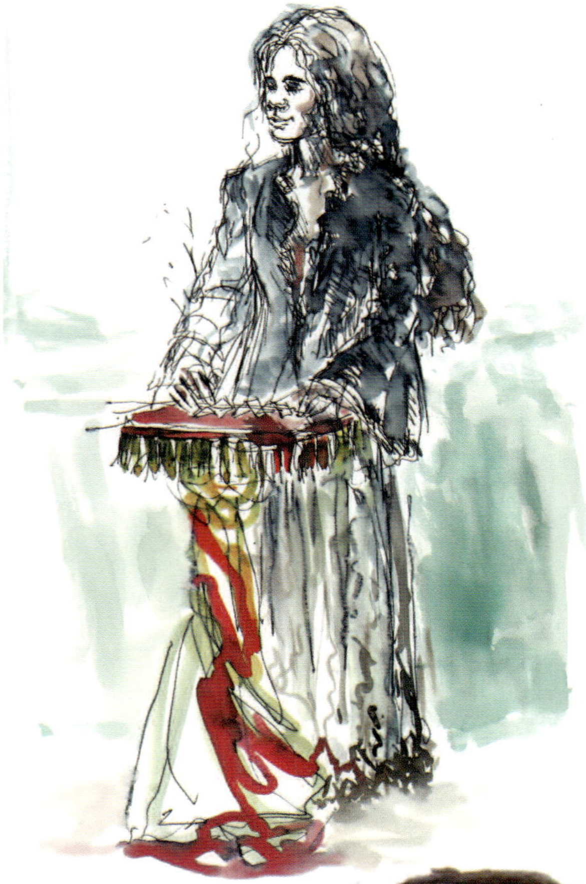

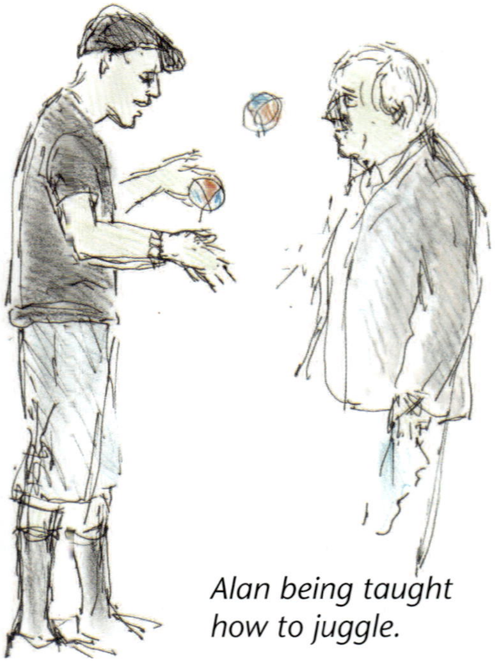

Alan being taught how to juggle.

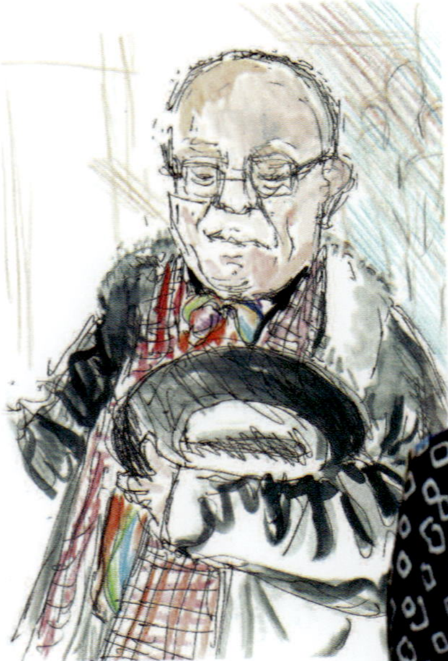

Ali Bongo.

Sketching Derren Brown in our hotel at a Magic Circle event in London in July 2005.

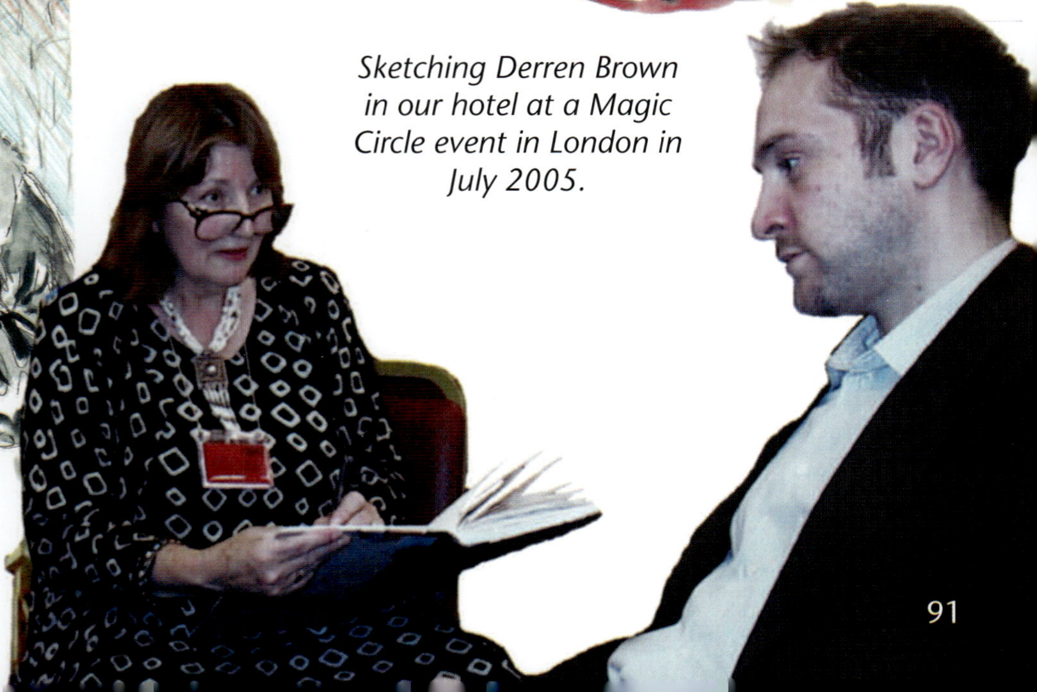

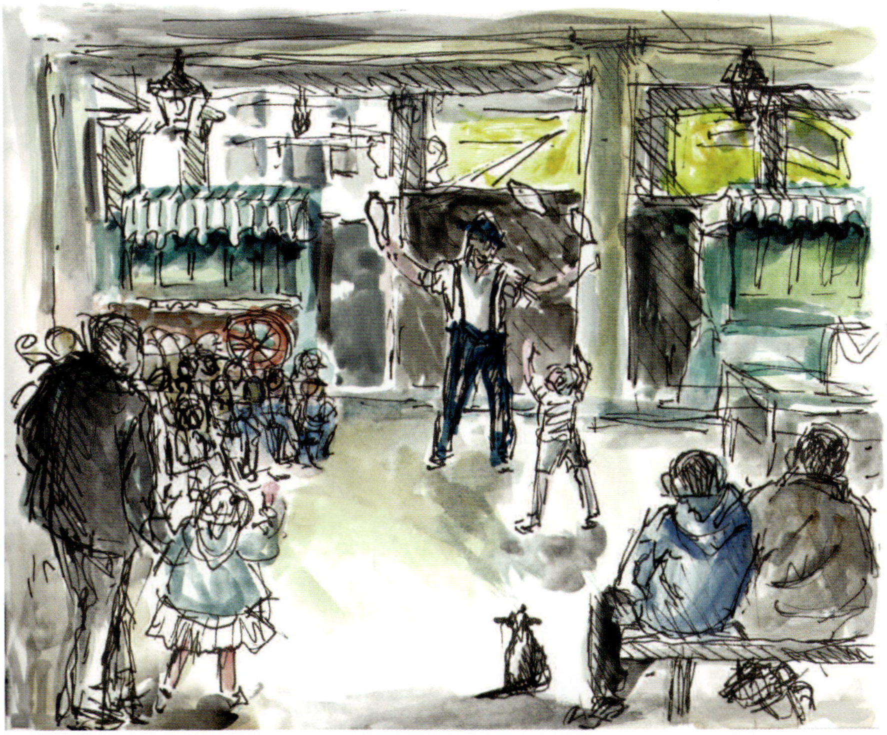

A busker in Covent Garden.

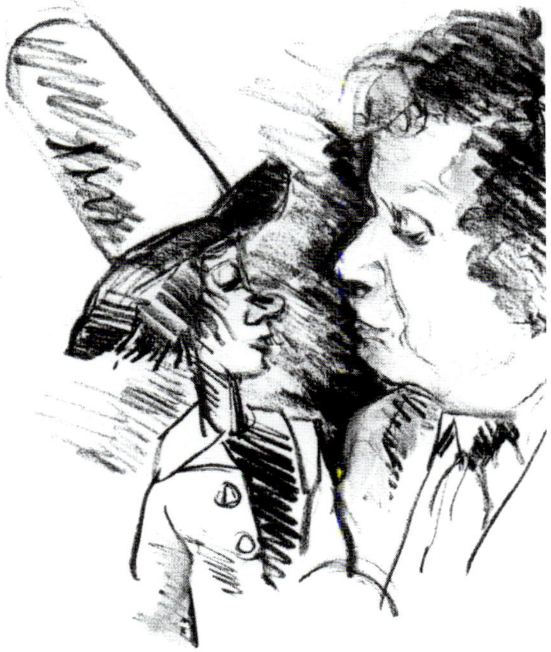

Ken Dodd with one of his famous Diddymen.

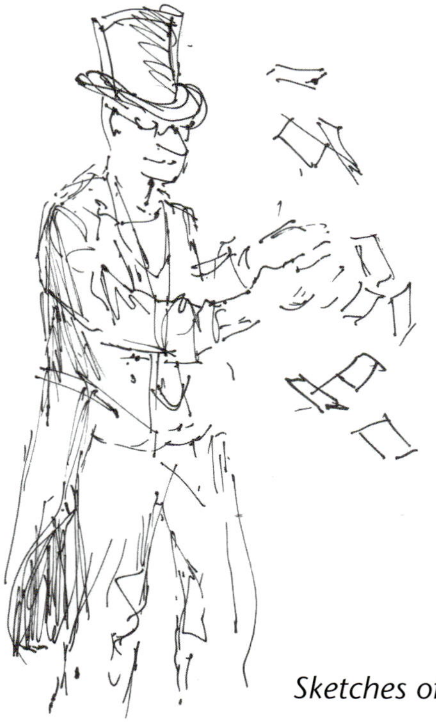

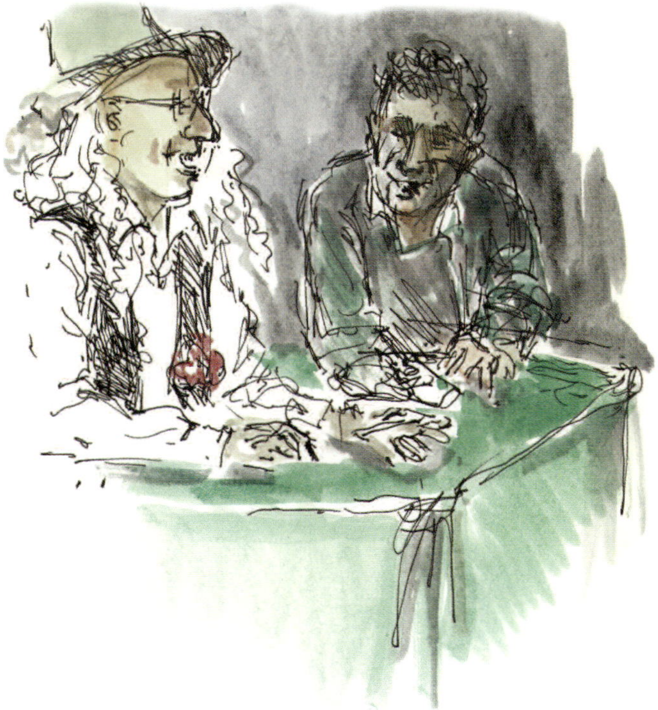

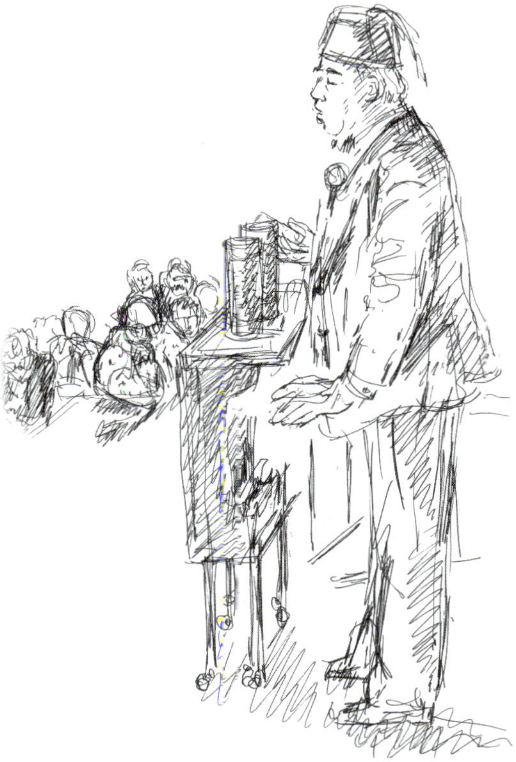

Sketches of various acts at Blackpool

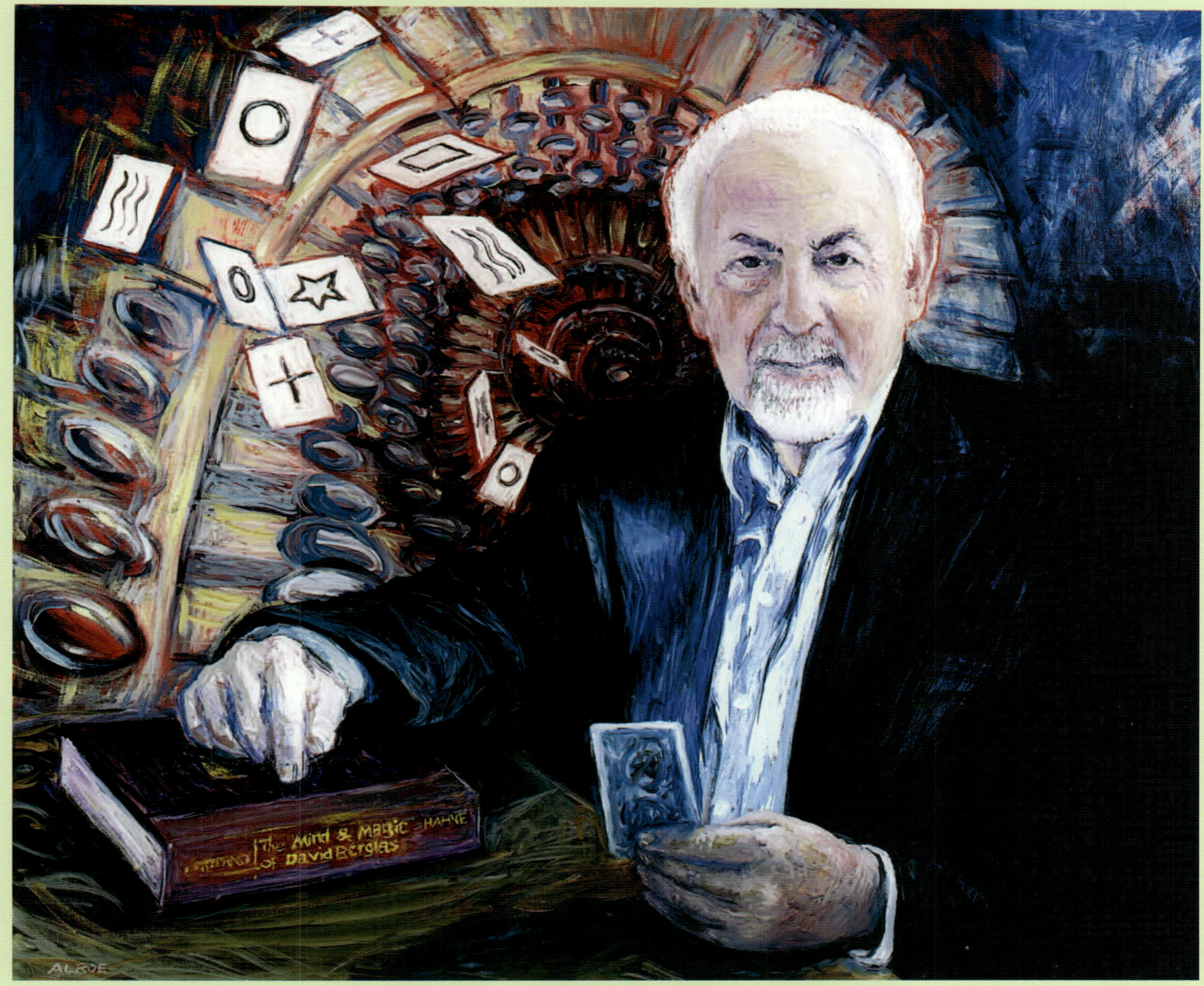

DAVID BERGLAS. A brilliant magician, David was a President of The Magic Circle and (while I am writing this) his son has recently also become President of The London Magic Circle – a very prestigious position. I met David in Rimini at a Magic Convention and we discussed a portrait. I did some sketches and visited him in his North London home, completing the portrait in my studio in Devon. In my painting he is holding his book *The Mind and Magic of David Berglas* while in the background is the winding staircase in The Magic Circle in London.

We met David's son at the sensational Grand Hotel in Rimini where we spent a few days. The hotel had hosted many famous people over the years. Through its glamourous marble hallways and Italianate rooms stars of stage and screen and many royal personages have passed; dancing to live music on warm summer evenings under the stars. In this idyllic Mediterranean setting, after eating a sumptuous meal, Alan and I revelled in the one and only wedding anniversary that we ever celebrated. What a memory!

Ali Bongo. As my husband, Alan, was a member of The Magic Circle we have enjoyed many visit to their events over the years. One colourful character who was always present was Ali Bongo (William Oliver Wallace). After seeing him wearing a flamboyant Italian silk shirt I asked him to sit for me. He agreed and he travelled down to Devon for a few days for the portrait sittings. His car was full of an amazing number of exotic props and we had fun choosing those he would like included in the picture.

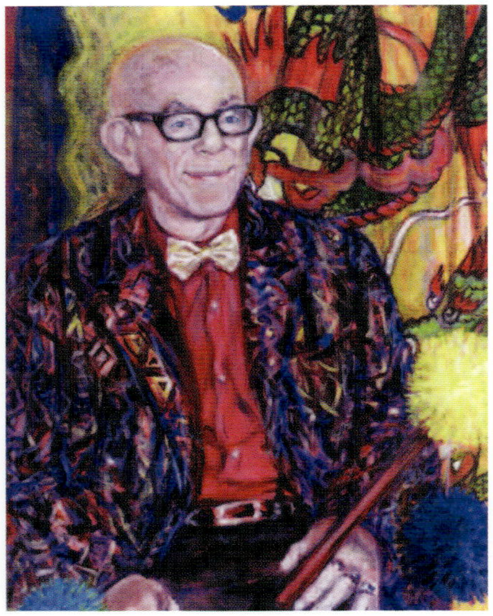

The result was two portraits, with one chosen by him for his Christmas card, which he sent to his magical friends all round the world. The painting also appeared on the cover of several magazines, reaching a worldwide magic fraternity. The original painting was purchased and now hangs in The Magic Circle's headquarters in London, while a print is displayed at the Magic Castle in the USA. While on its way there the painting was placed on top of the courier's van when the driver stopped for petrol. Forgetting it was there the package flew off onto the highway but amazingly it was later recovered undamaged.

Ali Bongo sadly died in 2003. At his funeral his trademark Turkish-style shoes were placed on top of his wicker casket. These are the shoes in the background of the portrait opposite. Ali's little happy song, recorded by him, was played at his funeral; it was a moving tribute to a very clever and influential magician, who was always willing to help and encourage others.

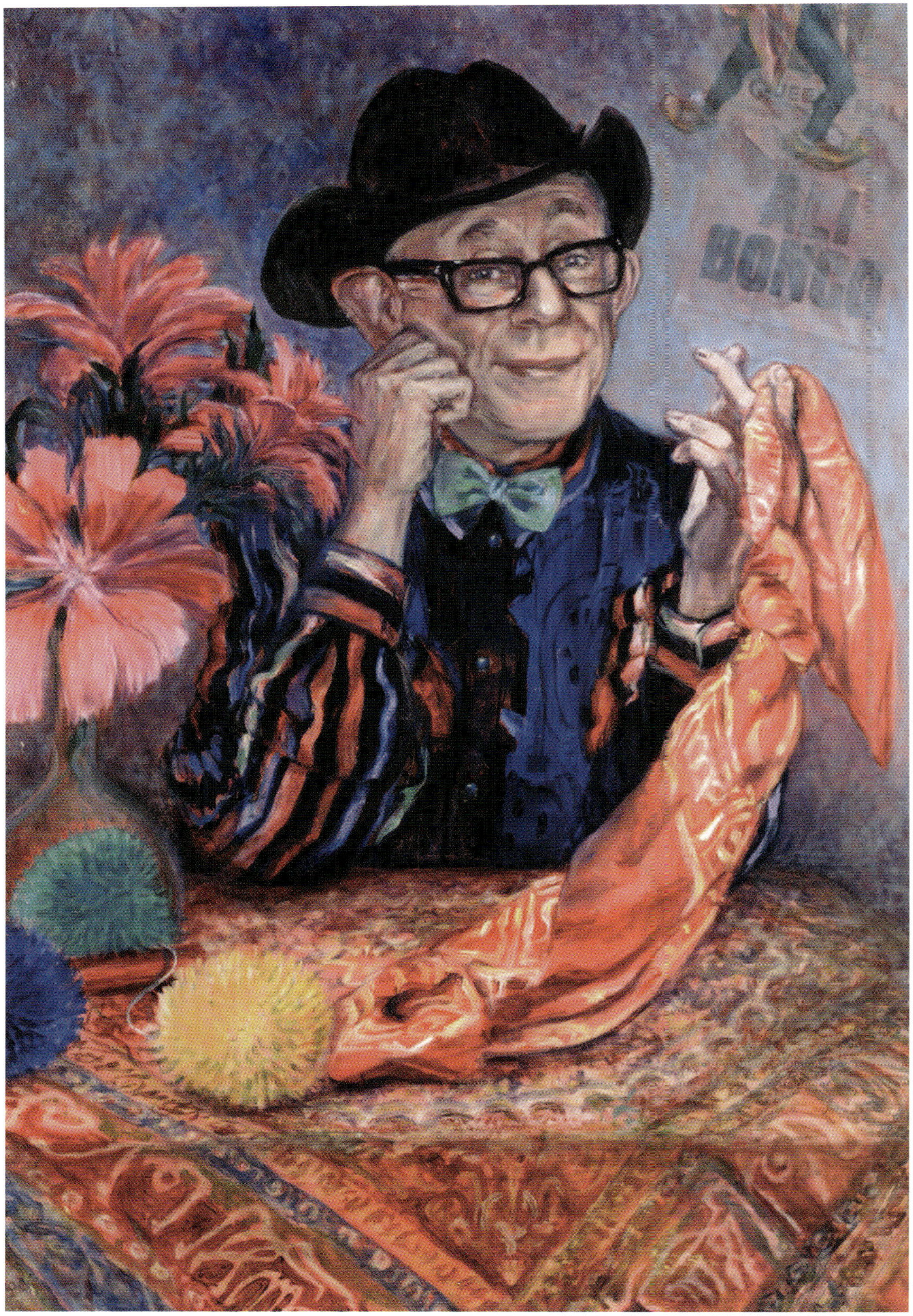

My sketchbooks aside, which contain hundreds of works completed over almost eight decades, the majority of finished works included in this book are portraits of family, friends and others who have been approached to have their likenesses reproduced in paint. Now and again, however, I have painted people just for fun, inspired by events and chance happenings, a random handful of which are reproduced here.

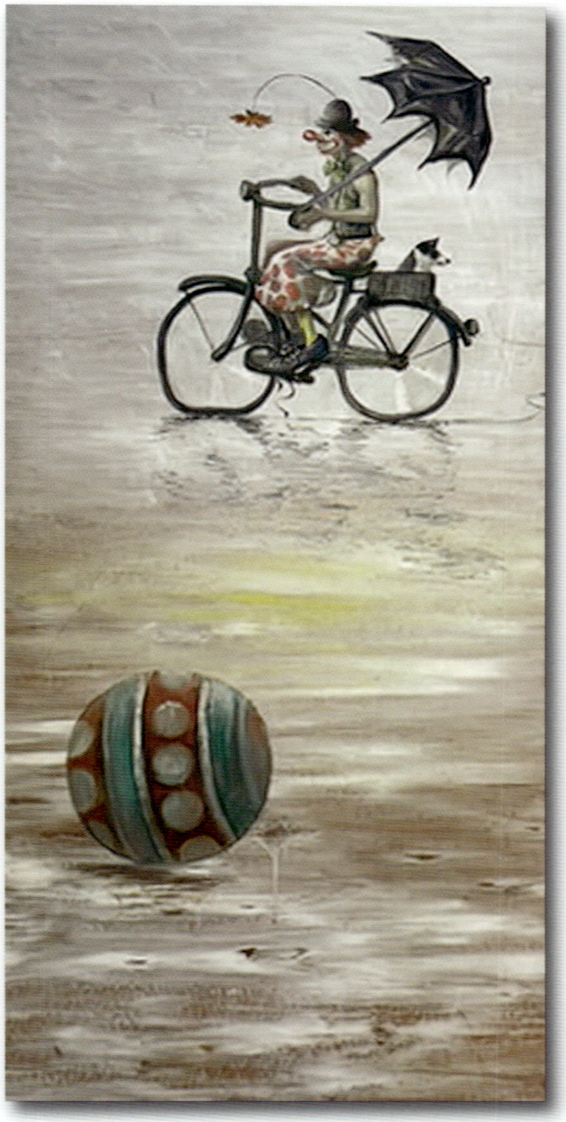

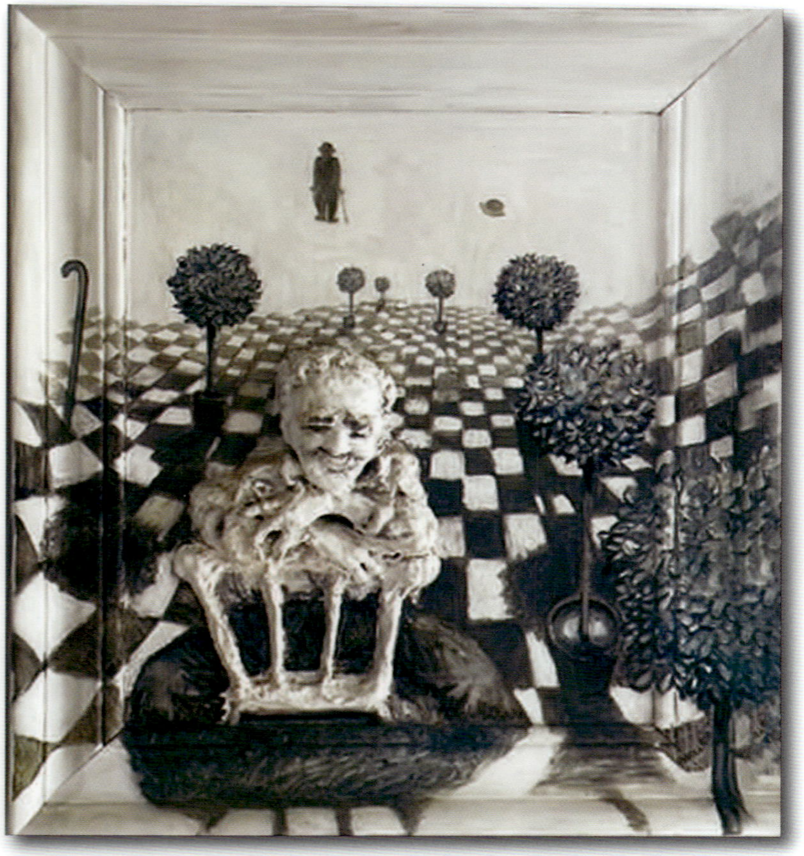

My imagining of Charlie Chaplin and Arturo Brachetti fall into this magical imaginative category of work. My 3D artwork of Charlie Chaplin shows him in the foreground as a film producer and in the background as the image of the little lost soul of a man alongside his floating bowler hat and walking stick, as seen in his early silent films.

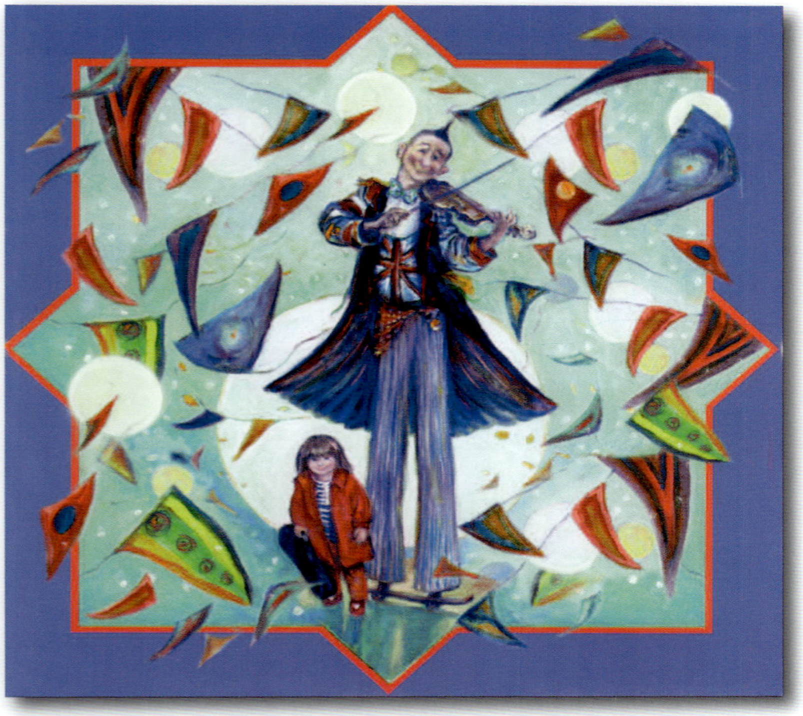

Arturo Brachetti was a character of amazing talent who performed as a quick change artist. He filled West End theatres alone night after night with his act. Later he came and gave a talk to the London Magic Circle, where I was able to talk to him. My painting of him is a creative image but based on his colourful persona.

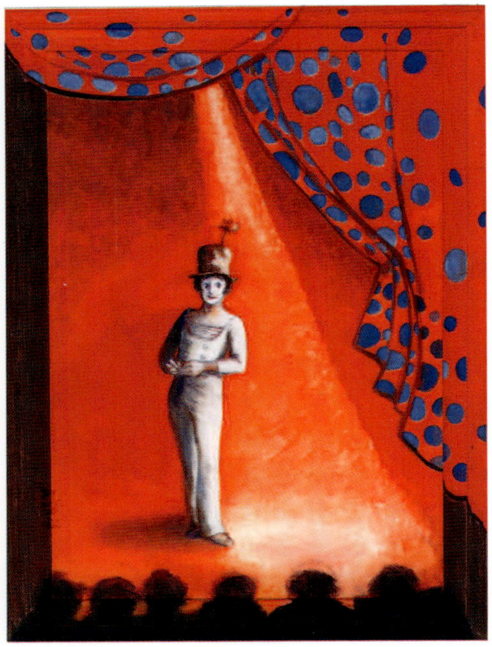

The mime artist Marcel Marceau as his alter ego 'Blip' the clown. The inspiration for this painting was a live performance in Amsterdam to which I had taken my A level students I was stuck on how to paint the frame, so we took the painting to Paris and slipped into his theatre where Marcel was working with some of his students. When he was free, we introduced ourselves and showed him the painting. Marcel suggested gilding around the frame so on our return to England I completed the painting. He later wrote to me asking if he could buy the painting, but we had already decided to keep it. We sat chatting with him for a while and he borrowed Xanthe's sketchbook and made a delightful drawing for her – he was a charming man.

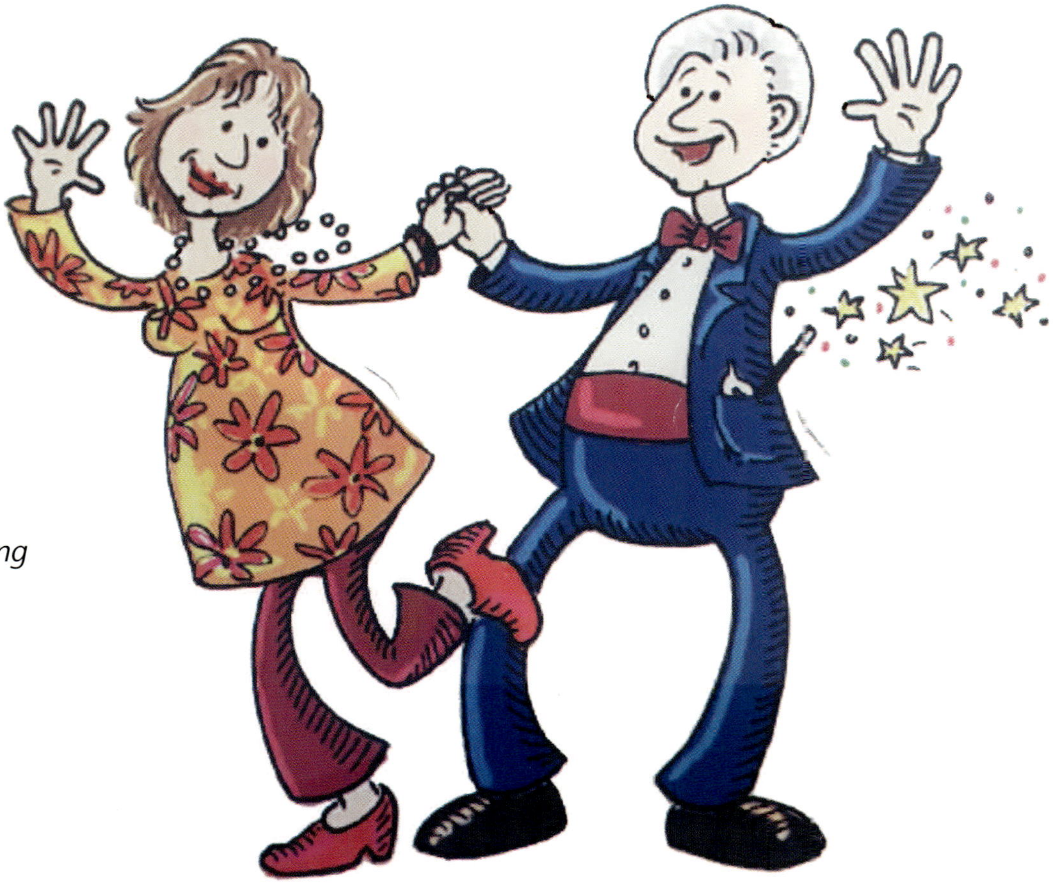

Lolo's illustration of me and Alan in party mood, enjoying ourselves. Just as I hope you have enjoyed this book.

"... for as long as forever is."

From the poem *Twenty Four Years* by Dylan Thomas